Groucho Marx
and Other Short Stories
and Tall Tales

Groucho Marx

and Other Short Stories and Tall Tales

SELECTED WRITINGS OF GROUCHO MARX

AN UPDATED AND EXPANDED EDITION

Edited by Robert S. Bader

APPLAUSE
THEATRE & CINEMA BOOKS

AN IMPRINT OF HAL LEONARD CORPORATION

Applause Theatre & Cinema Books
An Imprint of Hal Leonard Corporation
7777 West Bluemound Road
Milwaukee, WI 53213

Trade Book Division Editorial Offices
33 Plymouth St., Montclair, NJ 07042

Updated and expanded edition published by Applause Theatre & Cinema Books in 2011

Original edition published in 1993 by Faber and Faber

Printed in the United States of America

Book design by Mark Lerner

The Library of Congress has cataloged the Faber and Faber edition as follows:

Marx, Groucho, 1890–1977.
Groucho Marx and other short stories and tall tales: selected writings of Groucho Marx/edited by Robert S. Bader
          p.   cm.
Includes bibliographical references.
I.   Bader, Robert S. II. Title
 PN 2287.M53A25   1993
 814'.52–dc20   93–15821
                                        CIP

ISBN 978-1-55783-791-2

www.applausebooks.com

CONTENTS

I. THE GUS SUN ALSO RISES

II. HOMICIDE ON THE RANGE

III. FORWARD MARX

IV. JAMISON, TAKE A LETTER

V. MARX REMARKS

VI. THE SCHWEINEREI

FOREWORD

Robert Bader should get a medal. Make that two medals.

The first for giving us *Groucho Marx and Other Short Stories and Tall Tales* eighteen years ago.

Reviews and comments on the original book gave the impression that all people writing about it had conspired to use the phrase "A must for the Groucho fan." (Sometimes I ponder the question, "What sort of person would *not* be a Groucho fan?")

The second medal is for the good news that—should you have missed it before—Bader has not only brought back this wonderful material in this new volume but embellished it with nineteen—yes, nineteen—new pieces from The Master. I dare you to read any page without laughing out loud.

There's one new piece in this book that is, as they say, well worth the price of admission. And then some. It's a speech delivered by Groucho in 1952 at the University of Oregon titled "Humor from Silent Screen to TV." I found it necessary to divide reading it into two sessions to avoid laugh fatigue. It's almost like coming across an unknown Marx Brothers movie, so abundant are the humor and the wit and the pleasure.

Groucho valued writers above actors and told me that his fondest dream was to be remembered for his writing above all else. (He also told others, of course.)

Julius Marx was a born writer. I have treasured letters he wrote to me that could be used in a writing course at Yale as models of perfect wording, fresh images, deft turn of phrase, high intelligence, and a well-read, educated man's vocabulary. In short, a lively and delightful original style, all of it bathed in incomparable wit. All from that self-schooled man Woody Allen has called the most greatly gifted of comedians.

One of his epistolary traits was the startling, non-sequitur P.S. Here's a prime example. In a letter giving me wise career advice, he closed in the following Groucho manner. Thank God I read all the way to the end.

Yours until hell freezes over,

Groucho

P.S.: Did you ever notice that Peter O'Toole has a double phallic name?

Mark Twain wrote a hilarious humor piece with a title that would apply easily to Bader's Groucho anthology. It was called, "A Cure for the Blues."

By sheer chance as I write this, an article in today's *New York Times* warns of a coming paper shortage. Play it safe and, for birthdays, get extra copies of this book now.

Dick Cavett

THE SERIOUSNESS OF BEING HUMOROUS

Every comedian at some time or other desires to play Hamlet. Every humorous columnist has, in the bottom of his trunk, a tragic play that some day he hopes to see produced. Just as very few comedians play Hamlet, so very few of these plays are produced. Perhaps it is for the best. However, the point that I am trying to bring out is that all humorists are serious people at heart. The fact that they have to be continually funny makes them so. They also realize that humor is regarded in a light vein, that for a thing to be really worthwhile it must have depth and a certain amount of vitality. Basically their humor contains these qualities and knowing it they endeavor to bring it out in serious material. Generally they fail, for they only know the field of comedy. The path of the drama, the tragic, is new to them and they stumble and fall over strange objects. The same is true of the comedian who ventures into Hamlet.

Well, I'm glad the above is over. You know, I'm a comedian and I always did want to write something serious, like the rest of the humorists. I guess, after reading it, you will believe what I said about humorists being failures when it comes to the writing of serious material.

Thinking up jokes is by no means an easy task. I'm sorry I ever started. I was playing in vaudeville at the time and one night I put a gag of my own in the set extemporaneously. It went over big, but spoiled the scene and Chico almost killed me. However, my vanity was pleased and as I thought of more I added them to the act. Soon I started to contribute "wise cracks" to humorous weeklies and the leading columnists. It was then that my brothers and I thought that we could arrange our own act. I was using mostly all of my own material and of course Harpo didn't need any lines and the main work of Chico and Zeppo was what is technically known as the "business." That was how it started.

Writing humor is mostly the result of habit. After you do it for a while you just can't get away from it and you feel ill at ease when you are not doing it, although you may hate it. After writing humor for a time good jokes begin to occur to you. Then, there is what is known as the "wise crack" on current topics. This is obtained by following the newspapers and twisting a current event. This work makes a humorist a wide awake fellow. Nothing is going on without his knowing about it.

As soon as a person becomes known as a comedian he becomes a slave to his own humor. Everybody believes that he must be funny at all times, and he tries to live up to their expectations. As for myself, I am always trying to think of new and better jokes. There is not a performance that goes by without my adding at least one new crack.

I have received several good offers to conduct a humor column, but so far have refused them all. I realize how difficult it is to be funny and I believe that the place for me to be funny is on the stage. There I do not have new material for every performance and my voice and mannerisms add to the comedy. Conducting a column I would not have these and I would have to be funny in cold type, and far too often to suit me. Yes, sir, this business of being funny is far too serious. Undertaking is much the more cheerful job of the two. And I do hear that humorists never die of old age—the strain is too much for them.

Groucho Marx
St. Louis Post-Dispatch
November 13, 1927

INTRODUCTION

In a show-business career that spanned over seventy years, Groucho Marx successfully conquered every entertainment medium, becoming a star of the vaudeville stage, Broadway, motion pictures, radio and television. But, as the author of seven books, a play, two film screenplays and over one hundred magazine articles and essays, Groucho quietly conquered another medium, one in which he was as proud to work as any of the others. His writing is often overlooked in studies of his career, perhaps due to the quantity and variety of his other work.

Throughout his literary career, Groucho was dogged by two constant criticisms. The first, that he was funnier in films than he was in his writings, was a complaint about which Groucho could do nothing. It made no more sense than the same complaint made in reverse about Robert Benchley's movies. Should Groucho have stopped writing or should Benchley have stopped making films because they were each better at something else?

The second criticism is the incorrect and unfair assumption by many critics and even by his biographer that Groucho used a ghost writer. Most Hollywood celebrities who wrote books had professional writers do the actual work. The fact that Groucho publicly stated on many occasions that he abhorred ghost writers is clouded by his relationship with Arthur Sheekman. Friends for many years, Groucho and Sheekman had an unusual literary relationship. They worked in collaboration and each offered the other editorial help. For a brief time in the early 1940s, Groucho fronted for Sheekman, who was having trouble selling his work. By thus lending his name to another writer's work, Groucho subjected all of his literary endeavors to suspicion from critics who simply refused to believe that an entertainer could write.

An elementary school dropout, Groucho more than compensated for his lack of formal education by voracious reading. He socialized and corresponded with great writers and most of his closest friends were not entertainers but writers, both great and otherwise. Commenting on Groucho's self-education, Dick Cavett told of a conversation with Groucho in which the English novelist Iris Murdoch's name came up. Groucho said he had read all her books and hoped to meet her when he was next in London. Cavett didn't admit that he'd read none of her books and only knew her name. Later he characterized his lack of knowledge as a sure sign of someone who has been to college. A 1991 HBO documentary about Groucho concluded that he "sought the companionship of writers because in his deepest heart he wanted to be acclaimed as a writer, not a performer."

In the years just before the Marx Brothers became Broadway stars, Franklin P. Adams was the dean of New York's newspaper columnists. By today's standards his influence is difficult to understand. Playwright (and sometime Marx Brothers writer) Morrie Ryskind recalled, "if [Adams] recommended a book, people bought the book. If he recommended a show, you went to see the show." It was as simple as that. FPA's *New York World* column "The Conning Tower" was *the* place for a young writer's work to appear. In fact, submissions from the likes of James Thurber, Dorothy Parker, E. B. White, George S. Kaufman and Marc Connelly marked some of their earliest published work. Years later, Groucho reflected on FPA's eminence: "In those days we all tried to get a piece into his column. When I finally got a little piece in it, just a little one, not more than an inch, I thought I was Shakespeare."

When the Marx Brothers became an overnight sensation on Broadway in 1924, Groucho noted some subtle differences in his life: "Now it wasn't so hard to get into FPA's column," he wrote in *The Groucho Phile* in 1976. He provided this example of a typical contribution:

May Day Carol
by Julius H. Marx
(author of Nashes to Nashes and Stutz to Stutz)
My wife takes the breast of the chicken;
"The leg is for junior," she sings,
But listen: I feel just like Eugene O'Neill—
All God's chicken has nothing but wings.

Not exactly Shakespeare, but Groucho's pride was certainly justified. Highly coveted FPA space was being devoted to his writing. Something of a poet himself, Adams was especially fond of Groucho's verse. "May Day Carol" wasn't Groucho's only poetic submission of the period:

What 25¢ Buys in the Bay State

For twenty-five cents in old Boston Town
One can purchase baked beans that are done nice and brown.

Or a New England dinner that's beautifully boiled,
Or five copies of the *New York Morning World*.

—Julius H. Marx

Other less influential columnists also printed contributions from Groucho. These usually took the form of either short dialogue sketches or humorous observations on current events.

Says Julius H. Marx:—
Radio will never hurt the musical girl shows No John will ever sock up five and a half dollars to look at a neutrodyne machine through a pair of opera glasses.

The following spring he would become one of the earliest contributors to a new magazine devoted to, in the words of its founder and editor Harold Ross, "gaiety, wit, and satire." The magazine was the *New Yorker*. Another early contributor, James Thurber, wrote in 1959 that "when the *New Yorker* was six weeks old in April 1925, it printed the first of four short casuals that year, signed Julius H. Marx. In 1929 there were three more pieces in the magazine, this time signed Groucho Marx. I think Harold Ross insisted that Groucho come out from behind his real name and admit, you might say, who he wasn't." The casuals were basically the same type of material that Groucho was sending to FPA and the other columnists. In a piece called "Boston Again" Groucho wrote, "There is a statue of Paul Revere on the Common, but none of his horse. This was an affront to American horsemanship and should be corrected. Everybody remembers Man o' War, but who remembers the jockey?" Writing about Chicago in the column "The Outside World," he commented that "the famous Lake Michigan drinking water now has the combined flavors of chlorine, drainage canal, iodine and lake flounder. It is soon to be bottled and marketed as near beer." Witticisms of this sort would continue to appear under Groucho's byline in a variety of publications for the next several years, usually as contributions to the other people's columns.

Writing in the *St. Louis Post-Dispatch* in 1927, Groucho claimed that "I have received several good offers to conduct a humor column, but so far I have refused them all. I realize how difficult it is to be funny and I believe that the place for me to be funny is on the stage. There I do not have new material for every performance and my voice and mannerisms add to the comedy. Conducting a column I would not have these and I would have to be funny in cold type and far too often to suit me."* In a 1939 guest column written for Ed Sullivan, Groucho wrote, "How can anyone do this every day? What is there happening in the world important enough to fill up this much white space every 24 hours! Why don't they just leave it blank and say Harpo wrote it?"

Even if Groucho had ruled out his own column, by 1928 his byline was appearing frequently, and over much more substantial pieces of work. By this time most of Groucho's magazine and newspaper work was written in the first person, and most of his essays were autobiographical. By 1929 Groucho had begun to carve out his own style, based on a combination of his stage persona and the writing styles of some of his favorite humorists.

In the early part of 1929 the Marx Brothers were filming *The Cocoanuts* in Astoria during the day and were appearing on Broadway at night in *Animal Crackers*. In spite of the demands on his time, Groucho managed to have some of his writings published during this period. In his May 4, 1929, *New Yorker* essay called "Buy It, Put It Away, and Forget About It," Groucho poked fun at the stock market. Published several months before the stock market crash, the piece was an ironic forecast of the doom soon to come to Groucho and other investors. Years later Groucho would claim that he began to suffer from insomnia as a result of the crash and would rarely find it as humorous as he did in that early *New Yorker* piece. A more innocuous subject in Groucho's writing during this time was to be found in a series of

---

*[Years later Groucho would at least consider writing a column. *Newsweek* reported on October 27, 1941, that "the rumors that Groucho Marx may turn columnist are true. He has been dickering with Bell Syndicate." *Variety* reported on October 9, 1944, that Groucho was preparing a new syndicated column, "Marx Remarks." "Marx Remarks" later became the title of a column written by Groucho's daughter Miriam for the newspaper at Bennington College a few years after the *Variety* report.]

essays that were published in *College Humor*. These essays would form the basis for Groucho's first book, *Beds*.

The publication of *Beds* in the fall of 1930 filled Groucho with pride. He wrote in the introduction to the 1976 edition of the book, "It was the thrill of my life, a fellow with little education and a tall blonde stenographer joining such immortals as Shakespeare, Tolstoy and Longfellow. I could well imagine afterlife behind the pearly gates, discussing with them such topics as tall blonde stenographers." Sales figures for *Beds* are unavailable, but on November 1, 1931, the *Columbus Dispatch* claimed that *Beds* had "already sold over 25,000 copies in the short time it has been on the bookstands." However, in 1976 Groucho wrote that "instead of buying my *Beds*, most people took to their own. During the next forty years people refused to have anything to do with *Beds*. Whole families slept standing up." *Beds* probably didn't do as poorly as Groucho claimed, but the *Columbus Dispatch* report was questionable. During the 1930s a first printing of an author's first book was likely to be around three thousand copies. Only two printings were necessary for *Beds* and in later years the original edition became a collector's item. "Not even I can afford [it]," Groucho wrote.

The *Columbus Dispatch* article, one of the few to deal solely with Groucho's literary career, also reported that Groucho was at work on a follow-up to *Beds*. It was to be a history of practical jokes through the ages, to be titled *Wags*. The article concluded that Groucho had "compiled a list of about one hundred examples of the fine art of ribbing," and that "his publishers are enthusiastic about the outline of the work which he has given them and are fully confident that the publication will be another big seller." *Wags* was never published, but Groucho's contributions to national magazines became more frequent after the publication of his first book.

Beds was a playful look at the various things that people do in bed. All the things, that is, except one. When asked about *Beds* in 1976, Groucho told his biographer, Hector Arce, "It was about people not fucking." Groucho was probably inspired by the then-current proliferation of sex manuals, and the parodies they spawned. James Thurber and E. B. White had collaborated on *Is Sex Necessary?*, and even contributed to an imitation of their parody called *Whither, Whither, Or After Sex, What?*. At the time of its publication, *Beds* was merely one of the many books on the market to have fun with the sexual mores of the period.

Arce's biography, *Groucho*, was written with Groucho's complete cooperation and asserts that *Beds* (as well as Groucho's second book, *Many*

Happy Returns) was ghost-written by Arthur Sheekman. While Sheekman was involved with both books, Arce probably overstates his contribution. *Groucho* is thoroughly researched in regard to most aspects of Groucho's career, but Arce devotes only a few paragraphs to Groucho's writing and doesn't say much about Groucho's first two books other than to assert that Sheekman wrote them. Arce acknowledges that portions of *Beds* had previously appeared in *College Humor* and quotes Groucho as saying that it only took him one week to write the book. Arce's conclusion about Sheekman might have been different had he gone a little further in researching the genesis of *Beds*. In the September 1930 issue of *College Humor* (which contained the first installment of *Beds*), editor H. L. Swanson wrote, "The only way I ever got Groucho Marx to write about wild Beds he has known was to hang around backstage at *Animal Crackers* every night until the show broke, and then pounce upon Groucho in his dressing-room." *College Humor* was based in Chicago, and Swanson was referring to the Chicago run of the show. It was during this engagement (December 22, 1929, through March 1, 1930) that Groucho first met Arthur Sheekman. Sheekman was a columnist for the *Chicago Times* who had come to the theater to interview Groucho. They became friends instantly and Sheekman's interview turned into a guest column written by Groucho. They remained friends until Groucho's death in 1977. (Sheekman died in 1978.)

Soon after they met, Groucho and Sheekman collaborated on some sketches for a Broadway revue called *Three's a Crowd*. This is a credited collaboration. Swanson's comments indicate that *Beds* was originally conceived for *College Humor* and that it became a book later on.* While the exact nature of Sheekman's work on *Beds* remains a mystery, the fact is that the four essays published in *College Humor* are somewhat different from the versions that appear in the book. That Groucho paid Sheekman for his work on the book comes out in their letters from the period. Sheekman's work on *Beds*

---

*[Two books (*The Marx Brothers: Their World of Comedy* by Allen Eyles and *The Marx Brothers: A Bio-Bibliography* by Wes D. Gehring) incorrectly state that *Beds* was serialized in *College Humor* in 1929. *Beds* actually appeared in the magazine in four installments: September 1930, November 1930, December 1930 and January 1931. Note that the November 1, 1931, *Columbus Dispatch* article refers to "the short time it has been on the bookstands." Farrar & Rinehart announced the publication of the book in the November 29, 1930, issue of *Publishers Weekly*. It is possible that *Beds* wasn't widely available until sometime in 1931.]

was most likely to shape the magazine pieces into the book, the work of an editor rather than a ghost writer.

Sheekman's correspondence with Groucho reveals much about his involvement in Groucho's literary endeavors after *Beds*. In some telling instances, key portions have been deleted from the published versions of Groucho's letters to Sheekman. Not coincidentally, *The Groucho Letters*, published in 1967, was edited by Arthur Sheekman. The most obvious fact that comes out in reading the original letters from the Library of Congress collection is that Sheekman was having difficulty in his own writing career. It also becomes clear that Groucho occasionally used his influence to help his friend. In a letter dated February 19, 1940, Groucho wrote, "I was extremely gratified to know that [Max] Gordon liked the play. This morning I spoke to George [S. Kaufman] and told him to do everything he could to help you." The play was *Mr. Big*, which Sheekman wrote in collaboration with Margaret Shane. Later in the same letter, Groucho wrote, "I have told a number of people in Hollywood about it (not the idea), but just the idea that Kaufman may do it—that kind of propaganda may be good for you, considering your present Hollywood status."

Sheekman's "Hollywood status" apparently changed at various times during his career. Initially, Groucho invited him to come to California in 1931 to work with several other writers on *Monkey Business*. His early days in Hollywood would be spent working mostly on Marx Brothers projects. Before working on *Duck Soup*, Sheekman moved to New York in 1932 to work on Groucho and Chico's radio show, *Flywheel, Shyster and Flywheel*. Upon his return to Hollywood, Sheekman worked on the screenplays of two Eddie Cantor films, *Roman Scandals* and *Kid Millions*. He also worked on a Shirley Temple film, *Dimples*. It's worth noting that on both *Kid Millions* and *Dimples*, Sheekman worked with screenwriter Nunnally Johnson. Johnson was one of Groucho's closest friends. There is a strong possibility that Groucho's influence helped get Sheekman these jobs. Sheekman moved back east again in the early forties to work on *Mr. Big*. Sheekman's second move to Hollywood in 1945 resulted in some steady employment on good projects. The screenplays for *Wonder Man*, a Danny Kaye film, and *Welcome Stranger* with Bing Crosby had to be considered choice assignments. Other more famous writers who came to Hollywood in the thirties would have relished the opportunity to work on films of this quality. Writers such as F. Scott Fitzgerald and Nathanael West found themselves assigned to low budget B pictures with no major stars upon arriving in Hollywood. Sheekman usually found work on quality films during this time, but there were also sometimes lengthy stretches when he simply couldn't find work on any film. This is probably what Groucho meant when he referred to his friend's "present Hollywood status."

Groucho's assistance probably had some role in getting Sheekman's play produced. *Mr. Big* bounced around quite a bit before coming to the stage. On March 4, 1940, Groucho wrote, "It's too bad about the play, but those things constantly happen and I guess you have to expect them. As you suggest, I'll phone George Bye [Groucho's literary agent] and see if there is a dollar to be made via the magazine route." On June 12 Groucho asked again, "What's happened to your play? Is it going to disappear like Dewey at the Republican convention?"

Mr. Big finally appeared on Broadway, but not without cost to Sheekman's reputation. Producer Lee Shubert had agreed to bring the show to Broadway. Later, George S. Kaufman offered to direct it with Max Gordon acting as producer. Sheekman, who years later wrote in *The Marx Bros. Scrapbook* that having Kaufman direct a play was "the nearest thing to an insurance policy in the theater," decided to go with Kaufman and Gordon. Shubert promptly sued Kaufman. In an out-of-court settlement, Shubert was given seventeen and a half percent of *Mr. Big*, which didn't amount to much since the show opened to unanimously unfavorable reviews. It closed after seven performances—a rare flop for Kaufman during this period. Kaufman summed up the experience as only he could: "It's a pleasure to lose money for [Shubert]." There is no way of knowing how this episode affected Groucho's relationship with Kaufman and Gordon, but it certainly didn't help Sheekman's career.

Apparently Sheekman had some difficulty selling magazine pieces at this time as well. In a letter dated December 19, 1941, Groucho remarked that Norman Krasna (Groucho's friend and sometime collaborator) had read a letter of Sheekman's, "thought it was wonderfully written and couldn't understand why you weren't able to sell comedy stuff to magazines under your own name." In that letter, Groucho also admonished Sheekman with the following advice: "I've been telling you this for years, but I'll repeat it again—four or five amusing pieces or stories by you would get you quicker Hollywood recognition than any other avenue of entrance." In spite of this advice, Groucho continued to help Sheekman pursue those other avenues of entrance by mentioning, in the same letter, that Harpo had spoken to Samuel Goldwyn about putting Sheekman to work on a "story of some kind." That some of Sheekman's magazine pieces got into print under Groucho's byline becomes apparent from reading the unedited correspondence between the two of them. However, what also becomes apparent is that this situation arose out of Sheekman's inability to sell his material rather than from Groucho's inability to write quality humor.

The letters indicate that Groucho's essays from this era fall into three categories: first, pieces written by Groucho with no input from Sheekman at all. In a July 1, 1940, letter to Sheekman, Groucho asked, "Did you see that little piece I wrote for *Reader's Digest*?" On March 17, 1941, he wrote, "My drool is coming out in next week's issue of *This Week* so cancel your subscription now." Clearly Sheekman could not have had anything to do with a piece that he was told to look for.

The second, and probably largest, category of Groucho's essays of this period consists of those written by Groucho and sent to Sheekman for editorial assistance. On July 20, 1940, Groucho wrote, "I'm enclosing a copy of the piece I wrote. Probably another page or so is needed to complete it, but our starting date [for filming *Go West*] came and I just haven't had time to finish it. Let me know what you think of it and be honest because any other kind of an opinion would be of no value to me. I won't attempt to influence you by telling you the reactions I've already had, so for the love of God tell me the truth." * Shortly thereafter, on October 10, Groucho wrote, "I received your suggestions on my piece—I'm glad you liked it, if you did—you're probably right about the beginning. I'll do it over again." By the time Groucho wrote to Sheekman on July 25, 1942, it appears that some sort of formal financial arrangement had been made regarding Sheekman's suggestions. On that date Groucho also wrote, "I'm writing an unfunny piece on insomnia and I'll send it in a week or so, I hope, for you to read—I'd like your opinion, proofread—correcting all the glaring illiteracies and, otherwise, do a fine polishing job."

The remainder of Groucho's essays from this period fall into the third category, Sheekman compositions with varying degrees of input from Groucho. The level of Groucho's contributions to the articles in the third category

---

*[In the same letter Groucho again asked for a progress report on *Mr. Big* and wrote, "Send me the script—perhaps I can be of some help on it." It would seem that Sheekman also received editorial help from Groucho. In at least one other instance, Groucho acted as a "play doctor." He advised James Thurber and Eliot Nugent to "scrape off the easy gags and reveal the seriousness underneath" their play *The Male Animal*. According to Thurber's biographer, they took Groucho's advice.]

ranges from actually suggesting the topic and drawing up an outline to simply rewriting a few paragraphs for the purpose of injecting his own style into the piece. In a July 10, 1940, letter Groucho wrote, "I think you ought to try another political piece—a campaign thing—for *This Week* or some other magazine. This will be an extremely hot subject for the next few months and I think you should take advantage of it. If you'll write to me, I'll try to jot down a few items that you could complain about." Presumably, the chain of events would continue with Sheekman sending an essay to Groucho for his approval and whatever rewrites were needed. On May 29, 1940, Groucho wrote, "Received your piece and looked it over." In these letters to Sheekman, Groucho always referred to a piece as either "my piece" or "your piece." The letter continued, "I thought the piece was good . . . and I'll send it to Bye and see if he can sell it . . . I'll just rewrite a couple of paragraphs in your piece—not that I can improve them, but perhaps they'll sound a little more like me. Your style is becoming increasingly like that of an Oxford essayist and less like the brash, illiterate style of your correspondent." Groucho was concerned enough about this arrangement to take the care to at least make the piece somewhat his own.

Groucho really had no need for this entire enterprise. Surely he was happy to have Sheekman's occasional help with editorial matters, but the appearance of Sheekman pieces under the Groucho Marx byline did not really benefit Groucho. He gave the money to Sheekman and had no trouble getting his own work published. In a letter to his one-time family doctor, Sam Salinger, Groucho wrote, "I'm constantly implored by most of the important national weeklies to contribute to their pages." This was no doubt true. A star of Groucho's stature didn't need to be a particularly good writer to get his material published. The fact that he was good just made him that much more desirable a contributor. The principal reason for Groucho submitting Sheekman's work to magazines as his own was that it made Sheekman's material easily marketable based on Groucho's celebrity. Sheekman couldn't have been altogether happy with the arrangement, but the reality was that he was periodically unemployed and the use of Groucho's name brought in occasional paychecks. Sheekman's income from the pieces that were published under Groucho's name can be calculated, to some degree, by examining their letters. It seems that Groucho paid Sheekman the full amount for any collaborative piece regardless of whether Groucho had suggested the topic or rewritten portions of the piece. So it is not quite fair to call Sheekman

Groucho's ghost writer. A more apt description of their literary relationship at this time is that Groucho occasionally fronted for Sheekman and offered him the services of his literary agent, while each offered the other editorial advice. The reasons for some of their collaborative efforts not being credited as such remain unexplained, but Groucho was never shy about crediting his collaborators, and in every other case he did so.

The dedication page of Groucho's 1959 autobiography *Groucho and Me* pays tribute to the six writers whom he considered to be his biggest influences: Robert Benchley, George S. Kaufman, Ring Lardner, S. J. Perelman, James Thurber and E. B. White. During the thirties and forties, Groucho's written work began to show the signs of these influences—particularly Benchley. That Benchley's work had a major effect on Groucho's writing style is not surprising. Benchley influenced practically every twentieth-century humorist. Thurber even wrote in the introduction to his 1933 book *My Life and Hard Times* that a humor writer's worst fear was "that a piece he had been working on for two long days was done much better and probably more quickly by Robert Benchley in 1924." Groucho's essays from the early thirties are Benchley-like in style and tone, but remain mostly autobiographical. A familiar Benchley method was to write as a speaker or educator delivering a lecture. (Indeed, he was so successful at lecturing in print that Benchley made the transition to the screen starring in a popular series of comedy short subjects beginning in 1928.) Groucho adopted the lecturer's role in print easily. In "My Poor Wife" Groucho offers advice to any woman who might consider marrying a comedian: "Dear, dear reader, you are now going to hear about the curse of my profession. When a man is in the comedy business, people expect him to be comical at all times. A violinist can leave his fiddle at home; a pianist can forget to bring his music; but a comedian has no excuse. If he isn't conspicuously funny, he's regarded as a rather dull and disappointing fellow." With this explanation he recounts his "worst offenses in after working hours comedy because I want you to know the extent of my wife's grievances." In the same essay, Groucho also offers some comments about his literary heroes: "Ring Lardner is one of the wittiest men in America; certainly he is the most humorous. But when he's away from his typewriter, Ring is content to be as solemn as a New England preacher dedicating a new chapel." About George S. Kaufman he wrote, "[he] is another of America's first wits; and he too is considered a grave gent by people who meet him for the first time."

Stylistically Groucho didn't draw much from Lardner or Kaufman, although the humor is obviously similar. Neither did he take much from Thurber or White. But his admiration for them was unwavering. The same cannot be said of his admiration for S. J. Perelman. To say that Groucho's relationship with Perelman had peaks and valleys is to understate the case. Perelman was one of the team of writers, along with Arthur Sheekman, who came west in 1931 to work on *Monkey Business*. Groucho was an early admirer of Perelman, having written a blurb for the dust jacket of the author's first book, *Dawn Ginsbergh's Revenge*, in 1929. In an open letter to Perelman, Groucho wrote, "From the moment I picked up your book until I put it down, I was convulsed with laughter. Someday I intend reading it."

Perelman had first been approached by Groucho to write a Marx Brothers radio show in collaboration with Will B. Johnstone. Johnstone had already written a hit Broadway show, *I'll Say She Is*, for the Marxes in 1924. Perelman would later write in *The Last Laugh*, a posthumously published memoir, that his and Johnstone's ideas for the radio show developed into *Monkey Business*: "'Listen,' said Groucho after a whispered colloquy with his brothers. 'You fellows have stumbled on something big. This isn't any fly-by-night radio serial—it's our next picture!'"

Perelman also worked on another Marx Brothers film the following year. That film, *Horse Feathers*, would mark the end of Perelman's career as a Marx Brothers writer, but he and Groucho maintained a tenuous friendship for the rest of their lives. Although there were times when the two exchanged bitter jibes in the press, they still socialized. In one interview Groucho paused during a tirade against Perelman to interject that he had dined with him recently. Their correspondence, some of which has been published in *The Groucho Letters* and in *Don't Tread on Me: The Selected Letters of S. J. Perelman*, is cordial, funny and often congratulatory. Perelman sometimes refers to Groucho as "Cuddles" in his letters. At some point, however, there was a break in their cordiality. Nat Perrin, another member of the *Monkey Business* writing team, suggested in an interview published in *The Marx Bros. Scrapbook* that the schism occurred as a result of "one or two articles written by Perelman." The articles, although not specifically cited by Perrin, are most likely "Week End with Groucho Marx" (*Holiday*, April 1952) and "The Winsome Foursome—How to Go Batty with the Marx Brothers While Writing a Film Called *Monkey Business*" (*Show*, November 1961). The *Holiday* piece does contain a few cheap shots, but would hardly qualify as an example of character assassination. The *Show* article, beginning with its title, is largely unflattering. At one point Perelman describes his terror at the reading of the first draft of the script. After nearly two hours, Perelman finished the reading. According to the article, Groucho then got up and said, "it stinks," and walked out. Perrin suggested that those articles "may have clouded Groucho's vision on the subject of Perelman's contributions to the two films that he worked on."

In a 1970 interview with *Take One* Groucho was asked, "Didn't S. J. Perelman write for you?" "Not a great deal," Groucho answered. "There's a strange thing about that man. When he was riding high on the *New Yorker* and anybody asked him if he'd worked with the Marx Brothers, he'd say, 'A little bit. Not very much.' Now that he isn't so successful anymore and his name isn't on the front page, when he gives an interview he says 'I wrote pretty near all of two of their movies,' which is a goddamned lie. As a matter of fact he worked with four other writers and he wasn't very good for us. He wasn't a dramatist. He could write funny dialogue, but that's very different from writing drama." Perelman, in an interview broadcast on public television in July 1966, answered the inevitable question about working with the Marxes by saying, "In essence it was an experience no worse than playing piano in a house of call." Perelman had grown weary over the years of being asked about his association with the Marx Brothers and found it annoying that his other work was often overlooked as a result of his work on those two films. In later years he would describe the Marxes as capricious, boorish, disorganized, ungrateful and megalomaniacal. In *The Marx Bros. Scrapbook*, Groucho simply called Perelman "a son of a bitch." Eric Lister, a friend and traveling companion of Perelman's, actually titled a memoir of his travels with the writer *Don't Mention the Marx Brothers: Escapades With S. J. Perelman*. Lister wrote, "He had been bored with the Marx Brothers saga albeit he admired their best work, especially the two films on which he worked. When meeting strangers he would hiss in my ear, 'Don't mention the Marx Brothers.'"

Despite the harsh words Groucho still admired Perelman's writing and read all of his books. Late in his life Groucho would soften his personal criticism. In *The Groucho Phile*, he summed up their stormy relationship with a short passage that evaded any controversy: "In recent years the press had concocted a feud between S. J. Perelman and me, no such feud ever existed. Sid has often been asked about writing for the Marx Brothers and I have often answered questions concerning his contributions to our films. What Sid and

I both agree on is that he is a great writer with a brilliant comic mind that didn't always mesh well with the lunacies of the Marx Brothers."

Perelman's influence on Groucho's writing is difficult to assess. They both began publishing their magazine work at around the same time, and in many cases in the same magazines.* Their senses of humor were very similar. Perelman's biographer Dorothy Herrmann noted in *S. J. Perelman: A Life* that Groucho was occasionally confronted with the accusation that he had mimicked Perelman's style and had even copied his physical appearance. To this Groucho replied, "I was doing this kind of comedy long before I met S. J. Perelman." What is clear is that they had a profound effect on one another's careers. Groucho's success on the stage and screen made Perelman's style of writing, whether original or not, fashionable. Perelman's success as a writer no doubt influenced Groucho. It would have been a strong influence if only in the sense that Groucho admired Perelman enough to want him to write for the Marx Brothers. For Groucho it surely didn't end there. Many of his essays can be called "Perelmanesque." But Groucho would probably have countered such a contention by calling Perelman's work "Grouchoesque."

During the early forties, as the Marx Brothers' film career was drawing to a close and his radio career floundered, Groucho became very prolific in his writing. He expanded his range of subjects to include topical matters and even wrote several pieces about the American war effort. His primary topic, however, continued to be the one he knew best: himself. For several of the war pieces, Groucho adopted another familiar Benchley form. The titles alone look as if they've strayed from a Benchley table of contents. By Groucho's own admission, "How to Build a Secret Weapon," "How to Be a Spy" and "How to Crank a Horse" could hardly be compared to such Benchley classics as "How to Be a Detective," "How to Train a Dog" and "How to Avoid Colds," but they are among Groucho's best work of this period.

The early forties also found Groucho at work on a play in collaboration with Norman Krasna. Groucho and Krasna had worked together before, having written the screenplay for the 1937 film *The King and the Chorus Girl* (under the working title "The Grand Passion").

---

*[Perelman actually started as a cartoonist for *Judge*. His first article appeared in the September 18, 1926, issue, about a year after his first cartoon was printed in the magazine. Groucho's first magazine piece appeared in the February 21, 1925, issue of *Judge*.]

Work on the screenplay took place during the filming of *A Night at the Opera* in 1935. In an interview done for Charlotte Chandler's book *Hello I Must Be Going: Groucho and His Friends*, Krasna states that Groucho made it clear at the time that he hated the way the film turned out. The critics, on the other hand, were very kind. *Time* said, "the fact that Groucho Marx receives screen credit as co-author with Norman Krasna . . . may to some extent account for the picture's utterly amoral and pleasantly lucid lunacy."* Groucho apparently was unhappy with Mervyn LeRoy's direction. (It is unclear how he felt about the film's advertising campaign, which featured a photograph of Groucho in costume with the words "he wrote it" displayed prominently.)

The King and the Chorus Girl was Groucho's only produced screenplay, but it was not his only attempt. During 1937 he collaborated with Paramount screenwriter Ken Englund on a screenplay based on his own story idea about the adventures of a madcap runaway heiress. Englund recounted the story of their brief partnership in an article in *Daily Variety* on October 31, 1972. Groucho proposed the project to Englund during a chance meeting in a Beverly Hills candy shop, telling him that he had a "hilarious idea that will make cinema history." Englund quotes Groucho as saying, "We can toil an hour or two every night—no more. And even if we don't sell it, it'll give us a dandy excuse to get away from our wives and children." Like Groucho's other collaborative efforts, the work on the project proceeded with Groucho writing verbally and Englund at the typewriter. According to Englund, Groucho strummed his guitar and ad-libbed dialogue.

This unproduced screenplay, *Madcap Mary Mooney*, was written as a starring vehicle for Carole Lombard, who would have played an Amelia Earhart–type heroine. The story concerned Mary flying off on a scientific expedition and pretending to be lost so that she can be made love to by her handsome co-pilot. Groucho was able to inject a good deal of political and social satire into the story by having Mary engaged to a dull United States senator. In one scene on the Senate floor there is a motion to replace the

---

*[Motion Picture Academy records indicate that three other writers made uncredited contributions to the screenplay. Academy policy stated that contributions of less than ten percent need not be credited and all three writers agreed that they were not entitled to screen credit for their work. Arthur Sheekman had done some work on the story outline and Sherman Rogers had worked on converting the outline into the screenplay. Julius J. Epstein, who eight years later would win an Academy Award for the screenplay of *Casablanca*, contributed some dialogue.]

eagle as the country's national emblem. The replacement suggested is the seal: "The eagle has been known to snatch infants from their cradles and to kill sheep and other helpless animals, while the seal is known for his good nature and is loved by all children. It is the only animal smart enough to balance a ball on its nose, act in vaudeville, and, as an emblem, it would show the world that we are a peace-loving nation."

The fate of *Madcap Mary Mooney* was decided in a most unusual manner. Englund wrote, "The day we delivered our hilarious masterpiece to Paramount, Amelia Earhart tragically disappeared at sea." Norman Krasna called *Madcap Mary Mooney* "one of the funniest, most unsaleable stories ever written!"

Groucho's other collaboration with Krasna began in the summer of 1940. In a July 20, 1940, letter to Arthur Sheekman Groucho wrote, "in about six weeks Krasna and I are starting to write our musical."* By the time the show opened on Broadway, it was no longer a musical and eight years had passed. *Time for Elizabeth* was originally to be a starring vehicle for Groucho. He wrote to Sam Salinger in 1941, "I've taken the fatal step and definitely burned my bridges behind me. [The Marx Brothers had announced their retirement from making films together that April.] I'm writing a play with Norman Krasna—an idea we've had for two years. If we write it well, I expect to play it in New York with none of the familiar accoutrements . . . it's a straight play with some comedy, I hope."

Apparently the play went through many changes and even long periods when they stopped working on it. In fact, the original title, *Middle Ages*, was even scrapped. On December 19, 1941, Groucho wrote to Sheekman, "My play with Krasna is proceeding. We are making substantial changes and it will either emerge as the great play of 1942 or we'll tear it up immediately on its completion and deny that we ever wrote it." By 1944 Krasna had written another play entirely on his own. *Dear Ruth* was a big success and Krasna was very candid about the fact that it was based on the Groucho Marx family. He told Charlotte Chandler, "Groucho is the judge, Groucho's wife Ruth is the Ruth in the play, and the children are Arthur and Miriam. That family really meant a lot to me. I practically lived with them for a while as part of their family. They made me feel so much at home until I

---

*[Press releases from the spring of 1940 had announced that Groucho and Krasna were at work on a musical with a score to be composed by Jerome Kern and Ira Gershwin.]

was going there for dinner several nights a week." As for *Time for Elizabeth*, Krasna said it "was written over a number of years. Neither Groucho nor I was in any special hurry. Originally the part was for Groucho, but we did it with Otto Kruger. The lines were written to have been Groucho's and I think the play would have been a success on Broadway if Groucho had done it. Groucho got an entirely different reaction when he finally did *Time for Elizabeth*. Nobody else could get that reaction with the same lines." Groucho began performing the play in summer stock productions in 1952 and in 1964 filmed it for television.

Asked what it was like to collaborate with Groucho, Krasna provided a valuable insight into their work process: "I did the work at the typewriter while Groucho paced around and talked." The same procedure seems to have applied to some of Groucho's work with Arthur Sheekman. A May 1931 letter to Sam Salinger begins, "It is midnight. I just got through shooting a couple of scenes, and while I am getting undressed, Sheekman is taking this letter down." Sheekman proceeds to inject his own comments into the letter and indeed they are very Groucho-like. This system probably worked well, as Groucho's mind obviously worked faster than he could type. Since Krasna and Sheekman were both full-time writers, Groucho no doubt counted on them to take care of small details, such as typing. The same was true of his short partnership with Ken Englund.

Throughout the forties, Groucho was a fairly regular contributor to *This Week*, the magazine supplement to the *New York Herald-Tribune*. He also wrote frequently for *Variety* and occasionally for other magazines such as the *Saturday Evening Post* and *Liberty*. During 1941 Groucho began work on his second book. As was common in his work of this period, he was aided on the project by Arthur Sheekman.

As with *Beds*, Sheekman's exact contributions to Groucho's second book, *Many Happy Returns*, are unclear. The fact that the book was written during the period in which Sheekman was polishing some of Groucho's magazine pieces suggests that his contributions were greater than in the case of *Beds*. A March 11, 1941, letter refers to an advance payment of $500 by Groucho to Sheekman. While it is not certain that the advance was for *Many Happy Returns*, it is likely. When payment for a magazine piece was discussed in one of the letters, Groucho was always specific, either about the magazine or the subject of the piece. The timing also works out. The letter was dated about one year before the publication of the book.

The only reference to the book as a work-in-progress comes from another letter from Groucho to Sheekman. The letter, dated December 19, 1941, refers to the Japanese invasion of Pearl Harbor only twelve days before. The book was near completion at this time and since the book was a spoof directed at the Internal Revenue Service, Groucho was concerned about seeming unpatriotic. He wondered if it was wise to publish a guide to income tax evasion in the face of a national emergency. He wrote Sheekman, "Simon & Schuster wired me that they're using the title *Many Happy Returns*. I agree with you that there should be some recognition in the book of the current situation. Perhaps a word about Defense Stamps—maybe coupling it with the Stamp Act of 1776. You might say that the Stamp Act was: Two fellows came out and stamped on the stage and finished with a song." That particular item didn't make it into the book, but it indicates that *Many Happy Returns* probably fell into the category of Groucho's work with Sheekman in which Groucho fed Sheekman ideas.

Groucho did acknowledge the war in the Pacific in *Many Happy Returns*: "Our President has asked me to say nothing about military and naval matters. Other people, obviously of smaller stature, have merely asked me to say nothing. But I would not be true to myself if I did not express the opinion that, to win the war, taxes are even more essential than such rousing, unifying songs as 'We're the Chaps Who Won't Take Naps Till We Slap the Japs Right Off the Maps, Baby.'" At the end of the book Groucho writes that "to bring *Many Happy Returns* up to date, you need only tear out pages 9 to 89 and replace them with U.S. Defense Bonds." In another nod to the war effort, the book's cover illustration features Groucho slamming Hirohito, Hitler and Mussolini with a mallet marked "Income Taxes."

Like *Beds* before it, *Many Happy Returns* did not climb to the top of the best seller list, in spite of an unabashed publicity campaign by the author. In a letter to *Variety* Groucho wrote, "I have been plugging for your throwaway for many years and it's about time you turned around and helped boot this book of mine into a best seller." The reviews were lukewarm at best. The *New Republic* reviewer offered a typical complaint: "Groucho Marx in print is not so funny as he is in person, but anybody other than Groucho Marx who was as funny as Groucho Marx in person would have been bounced into the receiving ward at Bellevue long ago." The book sold only five thousand copies, prompting Groucho to later remark, "I only write first editions."

In the late forties, as the Marx Brothers got back together for a couple of films and as Groucho started to appear in movies without his brothers, his published writings became more infrequent. When Groucho became a success on radio, and later on television in *You Bet Your Life*, the few essays and comic pieces he wrote were generally publicity pieces related in some way to the show. A September 1950 piece called "King Leer" appeared in television listings around the country to promote the impending debut of the television version of *You Bet Your Life*: "TV presents a completely new set of problems to me. In my 35 years in show business, I've learned the intricacies of the stage, then the movies, then radio. Now comes television. I can't even learn how to turn it on." Groucho's attitude toward the new medium was not enthusiastic: "I must say I find television very educational. The minute somebody turns it on, I go into the library and read a good book." As his show became a hit, however, his attitude changed and he often wrote guest columns for local newspaper television columnists. A July 11, 1951, *Variety* piece bemoaned the excessive number of commercials in most shows. Careful not to bite the hand that fed him, Groucho added, "My comments are necessarily brief and cautious for in my profession, it is extremely hazardous for a comedian to outrage the sponsor, for without the commercial he hasn't got a job, and without a job, he is hardly a comedian."

Most of Groucho's written work during the fifties was television-related. In 1958 he collaborated with *You Bet Your Life* writer Robert Dwan and television producer Hal Kanter on a script for a proposed television special called *Groucho on Laughter*. Never produced, the show was to be a forum in which Groucho could examine the American comedy scene and perform a few musical numbers. The script carries the subtitle "A One Hour Comedocumentary."

His success on *You Bet Your Life* returned Groucho to the national spotlight and opened a few doors of opportunity in his literary career. Always a voracious reader, Groucho often had authors appear on his show to promote their books. In nearly every case Groucho had read the guest's book and usually had some kind words. In April of 1957, John A. S. Cushman, the managing editor of Little, Brown and Company, began a correspondence with Groucho, ostensibly to thank Groucho for his help in promoting some of the firm's books. Cushman used the opportunity to court Groucho for the purposes of Little, Brown publishing his autobiography. Cushman wrote on April 16, "we are very much interested in publishing a book of yours. We think it would give great pleasure to American readers (and I hope you, too) if you would write your story so that it would be available in book form. I don't believe there would be any other book quite like it!" In a May 22, 1957, letter Cushman suggested that Groucho should have the help of journalist Pete Martin, who had written a piece about Groucho for the *Saturday Evening Post*. Martin had also co-authored the memoirs of several show business figures, including Bob Hope. Cushman had actually gone so far as to contact Martin's agent. He did qualify this by writing, "Nevertheless we still think that G. Marx has something of his own to write about in his own style." Groucho wrote back on May 31,1957, "About me writing a book, I'll think about it. But if I should do a book, I'll write it. Nobody writes as badly as I do—but, at least it would be my own. I don't believe in ghosts—except around four in the morning when I start thinking of too many things."

Groucho and Cushman met that summer while Groucho was appearing in a summer stock production of *Time for Elizabeth* in Rhode Island. In a September 18, 1957, letter Cushman wrote, "Everyone here hopes that you will jot a few things down this fall for your book. I hope you won't worry about writing it too much. It ought to be more fun than worry-making, and you shouldn't concern yourself about putting a polish on it too early. I thought Mr. Dwan's idea of jotting down incidents separately without trying to build it up chronologically might be a good idea. On the other hand, sometimes it is easier just to start at the beginning and see how far you can go." In the same letter Cushman suggested dictation as a method for getting material down on paper, noting that Winston Churchill and John P. Marquand had dictated their books.

By the time Groucho had written to Cushman on May 29, 1958, he had apparently gotten started on the book that would become *Groucho and Me*. Again scheduled to meet Cushman during his summer stock tour, Groucho promised to "bring along a few pages of this hopelessly illiterate saga" and warned that "it will take Webster himself to untangle my immortal words." Cushman had to feel the sting when he was informed that fall that Groucho had decided to publish his autobiography with a new company instead of Little, Brown. The company, as *Newsweek* reported on March 30, 1959, would be a partnership consisting of, among others, Bernard Geis, Art Linkletter, John Guedel (the producer of *You Bet Your Life* and Linkletter's television show) and Groucho. Groucho was to be a five-percent partner in the firm. Originally called Star Press, the company would later become known as Bernard Geis Associates. The new company's books would be distributed by Random House. *Groucho and Me*, published in the fall of 1959, was one of their first publications.

The book begins with Groucho discussing the state of the publishing industry and how he came to write his autobiography: "The trouble with writing a book about yourself is that you can't fool around. If you write about someone else, you can stretch the truth from here to Finland. If you write about yourself, the slightest deviation makes you realize that there may be honor among thieves, but you are just a dirty liar." Later in that first chapter he writes, "I still can't understand why I let the publishers talk me into tackling this job. Just walk into any bookstore and take a look at the mountain of books that are currently published and expected to be sold. Most of them are written by professionals who write well and have something to say. Nevertheless, a year from now most of these books will be on sale at half price. If by some miracle this one should become a best seller, the tax department would get most of the money. However, I don't think there's much danger of this. Why should anyone buy the thoughts and opinions of Groucho Marx? I have no views that are worth a damn, and no knowledge that could possibly help anyone."

Groucho's speculation that *Groucho and Me* would not be a best seller was no doubt based on his previous track record. *Beds* and *Many Happy Returns* certainly hadn't sold well, and the length of time between the publication of *Many Happy Returns* and the appearance of *Groucho and Me* may indicate that Groucho had doubts about his commercial potential as an author. He need not have worried. The sales as well as the reviews for *Groucho and Me* were very good. One review that must have been particularly gratifying for Groucho appeared in the *Times* of London. While pointing out that Groucho may not be as funny on paper as he was in person (by then a common theme in reviews of Groucho's books), the critic noted that Groucho "wisely adopts a spare and springy style which adds weight to the book's dedication." Writing in the *New York Times Book Review*, *Variety* editor Abel Green was careful to note that *Groucho and Me* was not ghost-written, calling the book a "simon-pure, self-written memoir." Green, whom Groucho surely respected, concluded that the book may not be as polished as it could have been, but it was better as a result.

After the publication of *Groucho and Me*, Groucho's magazine writing tapered off dramatically. Some excerpts from the book were reprinted in various publications, but most of his original pieces from this period are letters to the editor. Perhaps the success of *Groucho and Me* had convinced him to concentrate his efforts on another book. *Memoirs of a Mangy Lover* was published in the fall of 1963.

For his fourth book, Groucho collected a group of short comic essays, mostly about love. While most of the essays were written specifically for the book, seven had previously appeared in magazines, albeit in slightly different versions. For example, a three-part piece called "The Outline of Love," which appeared in *Liberty* in June of 1933, was edited and updated for inclusion in the book and was retitled "The Unnatural History of Love." This was a common practice among humor writers. Most of Perelman's and Thurber's books were collections of their magazine work.

When a reviewer in the *New York Times Book Review* expressed doubt that Groucho had actually written *Memoirs of a Mangy Lover*, angry publisher Bernard Geis fired back. In a letter in the December 15, 1963, issue of the *Review*, Geis wrote, "Groucho Marx has always stated publicly that he writes his own books. The absence of any acknowledgement to a collaborator indicates that this statement is correct or that Mr. Marx is misrepresenting the truth. I can vouch for the fact that he has indeed written every word of this book and every other book that bears his name." Geis went on to quote from James Thurber's *New York Herald-Tribune* review of *Groucho and Me*, in which Thurber stated that Groucho wrote in "a swift, expert and uniquely witty style," and that there was "nothing ghostly or ghosted in anything Groucho wrote."

Groucho himself had something to say about critics when, in its February 8, 1964, issue, the *Saturday Review* allowed him to review his own book. He wrote:

> Given about three yards of sheer effrontery, any Groucho Marx could have written this book. But the naked truth is that I am the only Groucho Marx who did. To review a book of this stature—ah, there is a reef on which any ship of fools might well founder. Consider for a nonce or two the dazzling intrepidity with which the author has braved the boudoirs of dallying damsels and the caddish gusto with which he tells all (a phrase dear to any publisher's heart). It is enough to give one pause, and what better thing could any reviewer give? In his previous book, *Groucho and Me*, he had a thing or two to say about critics and their unrestrained power. He pointed out that no other clan was granted such immunity to throw knives, or had such power when it did. Did you ever hear of a farm critic coming out and saying

"Farmer Snodgrass's corn is not up to last year's crop." Or, "Another year's crop like this one and he'll be back digging sewers for the county asylum."

Groucho's irreverent criticism wasn't confined to his own work. He had also reviewed a few books for the *New York World Telegram* in 1950. Of a book called *Snobs* by Russell Lynes he wrote, "I have read this book from cover to cover and I can say without fear of contradiction that it is approximately 9 inches long, 5 inches wide and wears yellow pointed shoes." In the same review Groucho wrote, "I think most book reviews are too long. The last book review I wrote was 112 pages longer than the book. In fact, I was so busy writing the review, I never did get around to reading the book."

Groucho's review of *Memoirs of a Mangy Lover* appeared in John G. Fuller's "Trade Winds" column. In the same column, Fuller wrote about Groucho's relationship with his editors. Calling Groucho's attitude toward his copy editor irreverent, Fuller cites some choice Grouchoisms. On a question regarding a word change, Groucho wrote, "You say you don't care for 'tubercular' and prefer 'tuberculous.' Personally, I wouldn't care to have either." When queried about an altered quotation, Groucho answered, "What my secretary does with the classic phrases I dish out is beyond my control, but you must realize she has only been in this country for twenty-seven years. Incidentally, she is quick to inform me that she went to Northwestern University, where I understand you are now majoring in trivial corrections." Fuller claimed to have gained access to Groucho's correspondence with his publisher and editors through a "secret agent." He reports that, along with his irreverent comments, Groucho's final message to the editor who worked on his manuscript was, "At any rate I want to thank you for going through this assorted nonsense." It seems that Groucho saved his most irreverent comments for his publisher, Bernard Geis, to whom he wrote, "My best to your wife, who if she had waited a while longer, might have married a success."

Memoirs of a Mangy Lover would, with a few rare exceptions, mark the end of Groucho's comic writing. The majority of his writings after 1963 would be autobiographical. His later books dealt with his life and career in much more accurate and sober terms. Of course, anything that Groucho wrote was inherently humorous, but during the sixties he left the Benchley influence behind and moved into another area. Content during this time to appear on television occasionally as an elder statesman of comedy, Groucho no longer felt that he had to prove himself as a performer. Perhaps this logic can be applied to his written work as well.

When the Library of Congress requested Groucho's papers in October of 1965, he told the *New York Times*, "I have all these letters because for twenty-five years I had a secretary named Dorothy Bigliani who wouldn't throw anything away. She thought they were funny." That his letters would be of interest to anyone came as a surprise to Groucho. He was honored to comply with the request, and often mentioned it in interviews. In the *New York Times* interview Groucho also took care to point out again that he did not use the services of a ghost writer. He summarized his forty-year writing career by saying, "I've always been a part-time, on-the-fringe writer."

The publicity generated by Groucho's donation of his papers to the Library of Congress resulted in much public interest in the writings of the self-proclaimed "part-time writer." The publication of his fifth book, *The Groucho Letters*, in February of 1967 was one of Groucho's proudest accomplishments in either literature or show business. He rarely missed an opportunity to point out that not only had his letters been published, but that they were in the congressional library. Arthur Sheekman wrote in the introduction to the book, "As P.S. 84's [sic]* most prominent drop-out, Groucho was of course impressed by the Library of Congress's request for his papers. After all, he had spent less time in academic classrooms than in the classroom act called 'Fun In Hi Skule.'"

Simon & Schuster's advertising campaign for *The Groucho Letters* trumpeted it as "a great event in American letters." It was different from many collections of letters in that it contained letters both to and from Groucho, and his correspondents were among the wittiest and most famous people in the world. The book includes letters from, among others, T. S. Eliot, S. J. Perelman, Booth Tarkington, James Thurber and E. B. White. In spite of the impressive array of Groucho's pen pals, many critics found the book somewhat less important than did Simon & Schuster. *Esquire* called the book "a sore disappointment" and Groucho "a facetious bore." Echoing the usual complaint about Groucho's writing, the *New York Times* said that Groucho's wit "doesn't survive passage to the printed page," but qualified the statement by saying that they did not "miss the moustache, the cigar and the other props." Criticizing the book's haphazard arrangement (actually Arthur

---

*[Groucho actually attended P.S. 86.]

Sheekman's doing, not Groucho's), *Playboy* commented that "reading *The Groucho Letters* sometimes seems like wading through a waste basket—but it's worth the wading." Some critics were kinder, but most of the reviews were not good. This didn't stop people from buying the book, which has had numerous reprints over the years and remains in print in English as well as in several foreign languages.

In spite of its structural flaws, *The Groucho Letters* contains some first-class Groucho, such as his letter to the Governor of Idaho in which he wrote, "Thanks for the potatoes. Would have thought you'd have stuck a piece of butter in each one." There are a few letters, particularly those to the Warner Bros. legal department concerning *A Night in Casablanca*, that could almost be classified among Groucho's comic essays. Concerned that the Marxes were infringing on their copyrights for the film *Casablanca*, Warner Bros. requested a plot outline from Groucho. Groucho replied, "I play Bordello, the sweetheart of Humphrey Bogart. Harpo and Chico are itinerant rug peddlers who are weary of laying rugs and enter a monastery just for a lark. This is a good joke on them, as there hasn't been a lark in the place for fifteen years." In another letter Groucho assured Warner Bros. that "the average movie fan could learn to distinguish between Ingrid Bergman and Harpo. I don't know whether I could, but I certainly would like to try."

Groucho didn't write much in the seventies, but he was persuaded to pen an introduction for Richard J. Anobile's book of Marx Brothers photos and dialogue, *Why A Duck?*. The introduction makes it clear that Groucho had not lost his ability to write a funny essay. He wrote, "As for this Richard J. Anobile and his butchers who are editing *Why a Duck?*, they actually had the nerve to tell me I'm getting a 'trifle wordy.' The insulting bastards! Of course I'm getting wordy! Have they forgotten that I'm getting paid by the word? Just because I'm a sensitive dreamer who knows nothing about money, and cares less, they're trying tell me that 'Ha ha ha ha ha' is one word! I'd like to remind this Mr. Anobile that if there are any words he doesn't consider worthy of *Why a Duck?* they will immediately be snapped up by the *Hot Rod Monthly*."

Groucho and Anobile developed an association through the *Why a Duck?* experience that led to a collaboration on a book of Groucho's recollections. *The Marx Bros. Scrapbook* is merely a collection of interview transcripts and could hardly be considered a book written by Groucho, although it is credited in that manner. Groucho apparently didn't realize that it was Anobile's intention to print the interviews verbatim and attempted to stop the book's publication through a $15 million lawsuit. He was not successful and the book was published in the fall of 1973.

That fall also saw the end of an ad campaign which featured Groucho's final comic essay. Teacher's Scotch Whiskey ran a series of celebrity endorsements in the early 1970s. Groucho's ad ran in the fall of 1973 in both *Playboy* and *Esquire*. It recalls his written work of forty years prior, leaning toward the style of his early *New Yorker* and *This Week* pieces: "[Harpo] once had a horse who finished ahead of the winner in the 1942 Kentucky Derby," he wrote. "Unfortunately, the horse started running in the 1941 Kentucky Derby. And as far as ladies go, Harpo's ladies always went. As a matter of fact, they went a lot faster than his horses. Although his horses were a lot prettier."

The remainder of Groucho's written work, with the exception of the introduction he wrote for the 1976 edition of *Beds*, was the result of a partnership with Hector Arce. Arce was initially hired to collaborate with Groucho on a book about *You Bet Your Life*. *The Secret Word Is Groucho* was published in the spring of 1976. The narrative is Groucho's. To Arce fell the job of organizing Groucho's thoughts and those of the many *You Bet Your Life* staff members who were interviewed for the book. During the course of his research, Arce became very close to Groucho and it was agreed that he would write an authorized biography (*Groucho*, published in 1979).

Arce also assisted Groucho in the preparation of what would be the last book to bear his name. *The Groucho Phile: An Illustrated Life* is an oversized scrapbook of photos and clippings with running commentary by Groucho. Arce wrote the introduction in which he offered insight into his collaboration with Groucho. After delivering the first draft of *The Secret Word Is Groucho*, in which Arce had supplemented some of Groucho's witticisms with some of his own, he heard nothing from Groucho for several days. Arce wrote, "Finally, one morning he called me to his room. One of the great comic writers of his time looked at me and gently said, 'You shouldn't try to write funny.'"

Recent studies of the Marx Brothers have ignored Groucho's written work, usually making casual mention of his books but offering no further study of the larger body of work. In *The Marx Brothers: A Bio-Bibliography* Wes D. Gehring takes notice of Groucho as a writer and theorizes that in his writings Groucho was part of the antiheroic movement in American humor. To arrive at this conclusion he draws the appropriate parallels to Benchley, Thurber and Perelman, pointing out that Groucho often placed himself as the frustrated antihero in his essays. This is partially accurate. Groucho regularly portrayed himself as the hapless victim of whatever his subject was. However, a broader look at what is certainly a larger body of work than what Gehring considered reveals that Groucho just as often wrote as a social commentator and a critic, using his essays as a forum for his opinions. The antiheroic elements in Groucho's writing can surely be considered the natural extension of Groucho's screen persona brought to the printed page. Not to recognize the other facets of his writing is to oversimplify Groucho's literary efforts.

When considered collectively, Groucho's written work cannot be dismissed as merely the typical writings of a successful entertainer. Many of Groucho's show business contemporaries published their memoirs and other books. Groucho was a genuine humorist and, in spite of critics who felt short-changed by getting his humor on paper as opposed to the stage or screen, Groucho's written body of work stands up alongside the work of those humorists he first considered his idols, but grew to call his friends and finally earned the right to call his peers.

Robert S. Bader
New York City
April 1993

ACKNOWLEDGMENTS

This book has been a work-in-progress since I was a boy. As a result there are many people to thank for their help and support.

First and foremost, my parents, Sandy and Morty Bader, deserve special thanks. Many parents would have thought it unusual that their adolescent son practically lived at the library. Mine probably did, but they kept their mouths shut.

Without the help of a small band of rabid Marx Brothers fans, this would be a very different book. It also would probably have been published years earlier. Paul Wesolowski, Matt Hickey and Charlie Kochman are most definitely four of the three musketeers.

Groucho had Al Shean, and I too had a favorite uncle. Isaac Deutsch was the first person in my life who understood just how much a seven-year-old boy could love the Marx Brothers. I saw many of their films for the first time on outings with Uncle Isaac. I suppose I should also thank my Aunt Stella for letting him out when those films were playing.

Thanks must also go to Charlotte Gusay, a fine literary agent and a good friend. Charlotte's help went far beyond the services of an agent and she was instrumental in the creation of this book, as were Betsy Uhrig at Faber and Faber and Robert Finkelstein, the executor of the Groucho Marx estate.

I wish there were a way that I could mention the name of every member of the staff of the central branch of the Queens Borough Public Library. Much of the research for this book was done there and I rarely found a need to go elsewhere. When I did, I found equally competent staffs at the main branch of the New York Public Library and the Lincoln Center Library of the Performing Arts, the Manuscript Division of the Library of Congress in Washington and the Margaret Herrick Library of the Motion Picture Arts and Sciences in Los Angeles. Thanks also to Wendy Shay for her assistance with the Groucho

Marx Collection at the Archives Center, National Museum of American History, Smithsonian Institution in Washington.

The editor and publisher gratefully acknowledge that all pieces by Groucho Marx appearing herein are reprinted with the permission and cooperation of Groucho Marx Productions, Inc. In addition, the editor and publisher are indebted to the following for permission to reprint the pieces in this volume:

"Up from Pantages" copyright © 1928 by The New York Times Company. Reprinted by permission.
"We Stand Corrected" copyright © 1929, 1957 The *New Yorker* Magazine, Inc. (formerly The F-R Publishing Corp.).
"Press Agents I Have Known" copyright © 1929, 1957 The *New Yorker* Magazine, Inc. (formerly The F-R Publishing Corp.).
"The Return of the Four Mad Prodigals" copyright © 1929 by The New York Times Company. Reprinted by permission.
"Bad Days Are Good Memories" reprinted with permission from the *Saturday Evening Post* copyright © 1931.
"Mackeral for Xmas" © 1936 Reed Business Information, a division of Reed Elsevier, Inc. Reprinted by permission.
"Buy It, Put It Away, and Forget About It" copyright © 1929, 1957 The *New Yorker* Magazine, Inc. (formerly The F-R Publishing Corp.).
"Life Begins for Father" reprinted with permission from the July 1940 *Reader's Digest.*
"Uncle Julius" reprinted by permission of the *Hollywood Reporter.*
"Yes, We Have No Petrol" © 1942 Reed Business Information, a division of Reed Elsevier, Inc. Reprinted by permission.
"Your Butcher Is Your Best Critic" © 1943 Reed Business Information, a division of Reed Elsevier, Inc. Reprinted by permission.
"Groucho Marx Gives Kidding-on-the-Square Pitch for Hosp Shows" © 1944 Reed Business Information, a division of Reed Elsevier, Inc. Reprinted by permission.
"Many Happy Returns" reprinted by permission of Omni International, Ltd.
"That Marx Guy Again" © 1934 Reed Business Information, a division of Reed Elsevier, Inc. Reprinted by permission.
"Groucho Marx Insists 'Variety' Plug His Book" © 1942 Reed Business Information, a division of Reed Elsevier, Inc. Reprinted by permission.

"Groucho Marx Rebuttals" © 1942 Reed Business Information, a division of Reed Elsevier, Inc. Reprinted by permission.

"Dear Simon & Schuster" reprinted by permission of the *Hollywood Reporter*.

"Groucho Marx's Back-to-the-Soil Movement Flivs" © 1943 Reed Business Information, a division of Reed Elsevier, Inc. Reprinted by permission.

"Groucho's New Idea" © 1943 Reed Business Information, a division of Reed Elsevier, Inc. Reprinted by permission.

"Letterature" reprinted by permission of the *Hollywood Reporter*.

"And That's Why Groucho Is Not Going Into Vaude" © 1944 Reed Business Information, a division of Reed Elsevier, Inc. Reprinted by permission.

"Groucho Clears It Up" copyright © 1946 Time Inc. Reprinted by permission.

"And That's Why I Won't Imitate the Four Hawaiians" © 1946 Reed Business Information, a division of Reed Elsevier, Inc. Reprinted by permission.

"An Apology," The *Nation* Magazine. Copyright © 1950 The Nation Company, Inc. Reprinted with permission.

"This Theatrical Business" copyright © 1929 by The New York Times Company. Reprinted by permission.

"One of the Marks to Shoot At" copyright © 1934 by The New York Times Company. Reprinted by permission.

"Movie Glossary" reprinted by permission of the *Hollywood Reporter*.

"Night Life of the Gods" © 1940 Reed Business Information, a division of Reed Elsevier, Inc. Reprinted by permission.

"Grouchoisms" reprinted from the *New York Post*, July 12, 1947. Reprinted with permission.

"Run for Your Career, Boys" reprinted by permission of the *Hollywood Reporter*.

"Whenever I Think of Scotch I Recall the Immortal Words of My Brother Harpo" advertorial for Teacher's Scotch reprinted by permission of Hiram Walker & Sons, Inc., Farmington Hills, MI.

"Just Another Anniversary" © 1944 Reed Business Information, a division of Reed Elsevier, Inc. Reprinted by permission.

"When An Act's Successful" © 1919 Reed Business Information, a division of Reed Elsevier, Inc. Reprinted by permission.

"The Small Time's Season" © 1920 Reed Business Information, a division of Reed Elsevier, Inc. Reprinted by permission.

"Alibis" © 1927 Reed Business Information, a division of Reed Elsevier, Inc. Reprinted by permission.

The editor and publisher apologize for any errors or omissions in the above list and would be grateful to be notified of any correction that should be incorporated in the next edition or reprint of this volume.

EDITOR'S NOTE

In compiling this collection, I took great care not to include material written by others under Groucho's byline. Several published pieces were obviously written by either press agents or studio publicity people. Authorship of at least one article has been claimed by Groucho's son Arthur. Groucho didn't care for ghost writers, but publicity pieces related to Marx Brothers films and similar pieces written to promote Groucho's radio and television shows did often carry his byline while not actually being written by him. None of this material has been included here.

This book and its six sections have, in a sense, been titled by Groucho. Charlotte Chandler's 1978 book *Hello, I Must Be Going: Groucho and His Friends* contains a page of suggested but unused titles for that book. Groucho's suggestion, *Groucho Marx and Other Short Stories*, was appended by composer Marvin Hamlisch to make the full title, which has been appropriated for this collection.

The first section, "The Gus Sun Also Rises," takes its name from the first piece in it, "Up from Pantages." The Gus Sun circuit was one of the many small-time vaudeville circuits that Groucho played early in his career. "Homicide on the Range," as *Variety* reported on October 18, 1944, was to be the title of a book Groucho was writing about the wild west. *Variety* also reported, on August 30, 1944, that Groucho was writing a book about his experiences visiting army camps called "Forward Marx." It's likely that these reports, while obviously untrue, were based on information provided by Groucho since, as will become clear, he never hesitated to write to *Variety* to correct an inaccurate report. Several of Groucho's letters to *Variety* are included in the section titled "Jamison, Take a Letter." This section takes its name from a line in *Animal Crackers* and is thus really the creation of George S. Kaufman and Morrie Ryskind, but it's a safe bet that Groucho would have no problem with that. "Marx Remarks," as noted in the introduction, was the name of Groucho's rumored syndicated column in 1944. "The Schweinerei," the section added to this new edition, takes its name from an act the Marx Brothers staged in the fall of 1930. For an engagement at New York's Palace Theater and a short tour of RKO theaters, the brothers presented a revue consisting of excerpts from their three Broadway shows, *I'll Say She Is*, *The Cocoanuts*, and *Animal Crackers*. The German word "schweinerei" literally translates to "mess" and Groucho named this act in deference to the colloquial use of the German word, which during his childhood referred to the scraps a butcher used to make sausages.

Four of Groucho's other books rely, in part, on previously published material. *Memoirs of a Mangy Lover* reprints, in one form or another, seven magazine pieces. "What This Country Needs" is the only one included in this collection. Most of the original magazine piece, however, does not appear in *Memoirs of a Mangy Lover*.

Although *Groucho and Me* does not actually contain reprints of any articles, Groucho borrowed several anecdotes from his previous works for that book. Portions of "Mackerel for Xmas," "Uncle Julius," "Bad Days Are Good Memories," "Why Harpo Doesn't Talk," and "Sh-h-h-h!" were used in *Groucho and Me*. These pieces appear here in their complete and original form. Furthermore, "Uncle Julius" appears in its entirety, as does "Grouchoisms," in *The Groucho Letters*.

Finally, *The Groucho Phile* reproduces the original clippings of eight articles. One of them, "That Marx Guy, Again," appears herein. Also reprinted in *The Groucho Phile* is the original draft of "Run for Your Career, Boys," which is included here as it appeared in the *Hollywood Reporter*. For the most part, the material in this collection is appearing in book form for the first time.

A NOTE FROM THE AUTHOR

MARX OF HUMOR

This is the first time I have ever attempted to write a humorous article for a magazine.

Now, after looking that paragraph over, I feel encouraged, it's not bad; there are chemical traces of humor in it, nothing sensational, mind you, but traces of something that if kept up will make this an article.

Here this letter is still in its infancy, and I have about run out of material. I can think of lots of gloomy things, my visit to the dentist every other day, the inroads radio is making into the gross receipts of the show business, the money I owe my wife for last month's rent, but nothing real humorous.

It's a funny thing the peculiar impressions the average layman has about professional humorists. Invariably they visualize them as lean, cadaverous, skulking creatures, with pencil and paper, ever on the alert for the elusive joke, pun and whatnot, that they can incorporate in their story or play.

As far as I am personally concerned this is a myth, a fallacy without any foundation. I get all of my jokes out of the popular joke books and I find they are immeasurably better than any I could possibly think of.

Julius H. Marx

Judge

February 21, 1925

PART ONE

The Gus Sun Also Rises

Up from Pantages

When "Up from Pantages" was published, the Marx Brothers were about to begin rehearsals for their third Broadway show, Animal Crackers. *Like* I'll Say She Is *and* The Cocoanuts, Animal Crackers *would have a long run on Broadway.*

There is no denying the fact that I am getting old, particularly if you take a look at me. Although I believe I still have a few years to go, I have reached the point in my career where I can look back at what is known among show people as My Twenty Years Before the Footlights, which is equivalent to Gerard's Four Years in Germany, and the time is rapidly approaching when I will be known, if at all, as Groucho Whiffen Marx, the grand old man of musical comedy.

After this, of course, will come a dinner at the Green Room Club, with possibly a bust of Joseph Jefferson from the class of "Uncle Tom's Cabin," then oblivion, and a few years later the inevitable book of memoirs called, in this case, "The Gus Sun Also Rises." This book will have its usual phenomenal sale, and may even hit the hundred mark. Seventy-five copies of this masterpiece will be purchased by the author as birthday gifts for his immediate family, and the other twenty-five will be used to keep the window in the attic from falling down.

Looking back twenty years, I can remember playing a movie and vaudeville house in the business section of Jacksonville, Florida. It was a long, dark, narrow hall, filled with folding yellow chairs, the kind that are used by undertakers to make the mourners more uncomfortable, and by politicians for their pre-election rallies. It wasn't really a theatre, but a gents' furnishings store that had been converted into a theater simply by removing the counters, shelves and some of the rubbish, and by installing an electric piano.

There was no stage. There was, however, a long, narrow platform about as wide as the scaffolding used by painters and stone masons, and it was on this precarious ledge that most of the performance was given. If the act involved dancing, acrobatics or anything strenuous there was a brief intermission to enable the performer to jump to the floor for that part of the act.

The dressing room was large and roomy and had perfect ventilation. It was, in fact, a trifle too roomy, as it comprised the whole backyard and was shared alike by a grocer, a butcher and a blacksmith. It was not much for privacy but great for congeniality and comradeship. One had for companions a crate of chickens, three pigs that were about to be slaughtered, some horses waiting to be shod, two girls who later became known as the Dolly Sisters and a covey of the largest rats that ever gnawed at an actor's shoes.

The program consisted of four turns. At least that was the manager's contention, but actually there were only two acts. The manager built up the bill by advertising the mechanical piano as an act, and also a reel of the most flickering film that ever ruined an audience's eyes.

The first performance began at noon and then every hour on the hour until midnight, or longer if the business warranted it. The manager was a Greek who had been in the theatrical business only a few months—just long enough to master such a childish profession—and he had therefore set himself up as critic, censor, master of ceremonies, stage manager, ticket chopper and, frequently, bouncer.

We had named ourselves the Nightingales, a title that certainly bore no relation to our singing, but it promised much and in those days, bookings were made on promises. The opening performance Monday found us Marxes singing lustily to what we imagined was a spellbound and enraptured throng. We had just arrived at the point in the chorus where we hit the big harmony chord, the chord which was supposed to put the song over with a bang, when we heard a terrific noise which might have come from a wild bull, but which turned out to be the manager running down the aisle, waving arms, head and hands, and shouting: "Stop it! Stop it, I say! It's rotten. Hey, you fellers, you call that singing? That's terrible. The worst I ever heard. My dog can do better than that. Now you go back and do it over again and do it right or you don't get a nickel of my money, not a nickel."

Embarrassed and red faced, we slunk to the side of the stage, too dazed to utter a word of defense. We were certainly the saddest-looking nightingales that ever chirped a song. While we cowered in the corner, the Florida Belasco announced to an audience which was entirely too sympathetic to suit us that these hams—pointing to us—could sing rotten in Tampa, could sing rotten in Miami and, if they so desired, could sing rotten in St. Petersburg, but when they sang in Jacksonville, the biggest and best town in the state, they would have to sing on key or they wouldn't get any money. Ordering us back to the stage, he jumped off the ledge and ran up the aisle to hearty applause and vocal encouragement from the local music lovers. Apparently there was no more than the usual amount of discords on our second attempt, as there were no interruptions, except the customary jeers and catcalls which always accompanied our musical efforts.

In Orange, Texas, we lived at a wormy-looking boarding house run by a landlady who looked like a cross between one of the Whoops Sisters and a coach dog. Her rates were five dollars a week—a little high, she conceded, but she set a grand table, easily the best in Texas.

If it was all the same to us, she would prefer her money in advance. We held out for four and a half apiece, and after much general haggling we compromised on four seventy-five, this to include laundry.

For our first meal, which she announced as lunch, we had chili con carne, bread and coffee. This was not an unusual lunch for Texas and we thought nothing of it. The chili was good—everybody makes good chili down there—but the coffee was terrible. It may have been good to the last drop, but I never got that far; the first drop was awful. That evening for dinner we had chili and a depressing-looking vegetable which we finally agreed to call okra, and for all I know may still be known by that name. The following morning for breakfast we had bacon and chili, and for lunch we each had a big bowl of steaming chili.

What the baby of song and story is to its mother, what the saxophone is to a jazz band, what Gilbert was to Sullivan—those were all nothing to what chili was to this landlady. It was her pièce de résistance, her monument to Mexico with a low bow to all of Central America. By Thursday, despite the fact that we still had a healthy equity in the $4.75 we had paid in advance, we had retreated to the general store in the village and there rounded out the week on canned goods, dried fruits, brick cheese and Coca-Cola.

Later on that season we played an open-air theatre in Gulfport, Mississippi. It was just a short way as the wind blows from the swamps of Louisiana, and was set in a clearing in the woods. It had the appearance of an early frontier fort and we later discovered it was just about as safe. The wind had been blowing steadily from the marshes all day and by show time that night the air was black with blood-hungry mosquitoes, which, if they had been labeled like asparagus, would have been known as the giant variety extra size. The dressing room had sides and a floor, but a thrifty management, knowing the actor's love for the great outdoors, had decided that a roof would be superfluous, and had therefore taken that lumber and with it built a few extra benches for the customers. This was fine for the manager and the customers, but hard on the performers. The make-up lamp on the shelf acted like a village church bell calling the faithful to the meeting house, and these faithful fell on us, hook, line and stinger. Like thousands of miniature monoplanes they swooped down, while we, armed with towels, socks, rolled up newspapers and fans, tried vainly to repel them. It was like trying to stop a cyclone.

Stung beyond endurance, our screams of anguish finally brought the manager on the run, and we told him, between slaps, fans and curses, that, wedded as we were to our art, we would have to abandon it for the time being unless something drastic was done in the way of relief. The manager promised us that he would return in a few moments with a remedy that he had used for years, a remedy that had never failed. Then, leaving us, he rushed out to mollify an audience that was threatening to tear down what theatre there was, unless the promised and advertised entertainment was forthcoming.

In a few moments he was back with a half dozen smudge pots filled with pitch and pine, and which when lit quickly drove out the man-eating insects. We got dressed and went out on the stage, puffed and swollen, but still the Nightingales and still singing off key.

While singing our opening song we smelled smoke, and were happy because of it, figuring the more smoke, the less mosquitoes. But by the time we came to our third song we noticed a certain warmth in the rear that we realized could not be entirely due to the Southern climate, and when we came to our last song, we saw the audience rushing out of a theatre that was entirely in flames. We rushed after them, happy that we had lost the mosquitoes. But we also had lost our wardrobe and our trunks, and we later discovered we had lost the manager with what salary was coming to us.

New York Times
June 10, 1928

We Stand Corrected

During the Broadway run of Animal Crackers, *Groucho had three pieces published in the* New Yorker. *(The third was actually published a few weeks after the show had closed on Broadway, but* Animal Crackers *played on the road for several more months.)*

Forty-Fourth Street Theatre,
New York
Monday, January 28, 1929

To the Editors of The New Yorker:
Dear Editors,

Three-fourths of my brothers called my attention to the fact that the last issue of your esteemed gazette stated that Governor Alfred E. Smith had seen but four shows to date, namely, "Whoopee," "Scandals," "Three Cheers," and "Street Scene." I'll give you just twenty-four hours to retract that statement before I call on you and horse-whip you within four or five inches of your life.

Stack your Bibles, bring on your notary public! I can prove that Governor Smith attended a performance of "Animal Crackers." I know because I saw him smile at Zeppo, snicker at Chico, chuckle at Harpo, and roar at me. When he wasn't roaring at me, he was guffawing; when he wasn't guffawing, he was helpless with mirth; when he wasn't—I could keep this up for hours but I won't.

Regarding your inaccurate statement regarding Mr. Smith's playgoing activities, you may say for the Marx Brothers that we don't give a damn, or rather, four damns. But I know how proud Governor Smith is of his record of having always supported any issue benefitting the public and the Marx Brothers.

In return, we are just as proud of having always supported Mr. Smith and the Alert Clipping Bureau. During the recent election, we were back of Governor Smith to a man, despite the charge made that he was a Marxian Socialist. (The only Socialist ever in our family was a second cousin, Plumbo Marxo, a plumber.)

On Election Day, 1928, we cast three votes for Governor Smith. They were signed Chico, Zeppo and Groucho Marx. Harpo was the man behind the Silent Vote.

To return to the point in question, after witnessing the performance of "Animal Crackers," Governor Smith called on us backstage, the tears still coursing down his cheeks. Tears of merriment, that is.

He recalled the first time he had seen us—during the Democratic Convention in June, 1924, when we were appearing in "I'll Say She Is." He even remembered a wheeze I pulled. At that time Governor Smith was trying to oust ex-Mayor Hylan. It seems like yesterday when I heard myself saying in my eager young voice (I was just twenty-one at the time) that Governor Smith's favorite song was the "Hylan Fling." Maybe that wouldn't panic you in this sophisticated era, but it was considered pretty funny way back in good old 1924.

If you're a man, you'll eat your words and print this retraction on the cover of your magazine with illustrations by Peter Arno and life studies of the Marx Brothers in their dressing rooms or at home, curled up before a hot fire with an engrossing book, or vice versa.

Yours for more haste and less speed.
Groucho Marx

The New Yorker
February 2, 1929

Press Agents I Have Known

"Press Agents I Have Known" was Groucho's sixth New Yorker *piece. At the time it was written, the Marx Brothers were spending their days in Astoria, Queens, making their first film,* The Cocoanuts. *After the day's shooting they would rush back into Manhattan to perform* Animal Crackers *on Broadway. They maintained that hectic schedule for about two months.*

The little fellow climbed upon my lap and tugged me gently by the beard. "Tell me, grandfather," he said, "about your first press agent."

I gazed into the fire. Unknowingly, the child had touched a tender spot. It had been years since I even thought of the affair. But now something within me stirred. My whole body seemed on fire. I seemed to catch a faint odor of hyacinth. Ah, youth! Those moonlit nights! Those first interviews! Those passionate scenes! Those notes! Those notes—

(From the Spokane *Spokesman*)

Groucho Marx, a member of the Four Marx Brothers, spends his spare time collecting pipes. He now has 762 pipes of all sizes and varieties. When asked about his hobby, Mr. Marx said slyly, with a twinkle in his eye, "Yes, I collect pipes. Let me show you a rare piece of lead pipe."

I claim to be an authority on press agents. As soon as I have finished my present opus, "My Fifty Years on the American Stage," or, "From Weber and Fields to an Institution," I intend to write the long-awaited work, "Press Agents I Have Known, or Regretted." These few notes will constitute my introduction:

First of all, there is the stunt press agent. The fellow who pops into your dressing-room, all smiles, and says, "What are you doing tomorrow afternoon?"

"Fixing the coil on my still," I say, all hope abandoned.

"Oh, no, you're not," he insists cheerily. "You're going to sit on top of the flagpole on the Paramount Building with a sign on your back: 'Hello Mars! The Marx Brothers in "Animal Crackers" send greetings.'"

"But my lumbago—"

"It's all arranged. I'm going to have fourteen reporters, a flock of cameramen and the ship-news reporters. What a break it'll be! It'll go all over the world! For the good of the show!"

That always gets me. I don't know why it should after all these years, but it does . . . After I get vertigo reaching the top of the Paramount Building, I find that the reporters have been called away to cover a big fire and the flock of cameramen consists of two disagreeable little fellows who seem quite bored with the whole proceeding.

"Climb a little higher," they tell me. "Can't you do better than that?—this will make a terrible picture."

They probably figure that if I climb any higher they won't have to use their plates at all. They are right about one thing. It makes a terrible picture. Two weeks later, the press agent comes bounding into the dressing-room, waving the evidence of his genius. The picture is published on page 34 of the *Billboard*. That's the way it goes all over the world. The caption reads:

CLIMBS FLAGPOLE
G. Merks, of the Three Merks Brothers, vaudeville acrobats, climbed the Paramount flagpole last month to pay an election bet.

Let's consider another species—the press agent who keeps phoning you: "Wait until you see what I have to show you! Articles in seven newspapers and each one different!"

They are. He finally struts around to show you the stories. The first one starts: "*Les frères Marx, maintenant*—" (That's all I can read—it's in the Paris *Matin*.) The next article begins: "*Die Marx Brüder*," and is in the Berlin

Tageblatt. You get the idea—he gets us swell publicity in some of the world's greatest newspapers, including the Stockholm *Svenborgen*, the Portugal *Estrada*, and the Riga *Raschgitov*. Nice little articles for the scrapbook, to read before the fire some rainy night.

Then there is the highbrow press agent who spends weeks interviewing me. He corners me for hours at a stretch to ask me such questions as, "But, Mr. Marx, don't you feel that Pinero was undoubtedly influenced by Aeschylus?" I'm all a-twitter when he tells me he has placed the interview. It finally appears in the *Dial*, which comes out once a month and is great for business.

Then there is the fellow who has been a circus press agent and can't forget his early training. He's a dangerous character. No weather is too bad for him to lead you out to Central Park to be photographed with the animals. After risking my life trying to appear as if I were teaching a hippopotamus to sing (the press agent cleverly gets the hippopotamus to open his mouth by holding out a frankfurter—from the other side of the fence), the animal always gets the credit. The picture appears with the hippopotamus covering seven-eighths of the space and my picture looking like the frankfurter. And the caption reads:

> CHARLIE, CENTRAL PARK HIPPO, RECEIVES CONGRATULATIONS ON HIS THIRD BIRTHDAY. Picture shows Charlie receiving the best wishes from one of his admirers, a well known Broadway hoofer.

And then there is the press agent who *schmeichels* you into doing his work. "Mr. Marx, I could get stories about you in any paper in New York, but I know perfectly well I can't write as well as you can. So why don't you dash off one of your brilliant articles for the *Times*, a clever autobiography for the *Sun*, and one of your screamingly funny pieces for the *American*. I'll take them around myself to make sure they get in."

Then the press agent who never gets you in the papers unless you play at least three benefits a week and appear at the opening of a new butcher shop to throw out the first chop.

And the press agent who gets you all steamed up about the story he landed for you in the *Tribune*.

"What's it like?" you ask, all agog.

"Wait till you see it."

He finally sends you a copy. The story runs like this:

Among those present at the dance of the Mayfair Club at the Ritz on Saturday night were Eddie Cantor, Mary Eaton, Gertrude Lawrence, Beatrice Lillie, Walter Woolf, Peaches Browning, Ethel Barrymore, Will Rogers, Lenore Ulric, Alice Brady, Katharine Cornell, Tammany Young and one of the Marx Brothers.

I mustn't forget the press agent who gets such wonderful publicity for himself. After getting me all on edge about the interview he has landed, I buy a paper and read the following:

AN INTERVIEW WITH GROUCHO MARX
BY ALAN J. WURTZBURGER

I'll admit that I was terribly excited when I knocked on Mr. Marx's door, ready to interview him. My heart pounded rapidly. Then I recalled the time I interviewed Otis Skinner, my tête-à-tête with Pavlova and my heart-to-heart talk with Doug Fairbanks.
So I walked boldly in. Mr. Marx received me cordially and after asking me to sit down, admired my cravat. "I always wear that tie when I'm interviewing a celebrity," I told him, to make him feel at ease. "I'll tell you an interesting story about that cravat—"

And so on for two columns about that fascinating fellow, Alan J. Wurtzburger.

All these varieties of press agents are pretty bad, but the fellow I had last spring was positively vicious. He used to drop into my dressing room, smoke my cigars, and spend his time, not in interviewing me, but giving me advice on the market. The only things worse than my cigars were his tips. He was the reason I had to spend the summer delighting audiences in motion-picture houses.

Maybe I'm unduly hopeful, but I'm still looking for a press agent who will get me some publicity without making me roller-skate down Broadway to demonstrate that STAGE STAR SOLVES TRAFFIC PROBLEM BY SKATING TO THEATER. I want a press agent like Hoover's got. Look at the stuff that chap landed for Hoover during the election. And I'll bet Hoover didn't climb any flagpoles either.

The New Yorker
March 9, 1929

The Return of the Four Mad Prodigals

The Marx Brothers had opened at the Palace Theater in New York the week before "The Return of the Four Mad Prodigals" was published. The two-week engagement marked their return to the vaudeville stage. Their act was essentially a portion of Animal Crackers, *which had its final Broadway performance the week before. They were paid $7,000 a week, which made them the highest paid act ever to play the Palace.*

It doesn't seem possible that it could be merely a coincidence—the day after the Palace announced "The Triumphant Return of the Marx Brothers for a Limited Engagement," Radio-Keith-Orpheum stock dropped 10 points.

Be that as it may, it was with great delight that I realized that, after eight years on what has been whimsically called the legitimate stage, the Marx Brothers were returning to vaudeville. I expected to find things greatly changed during that period. But some things were the same as ever:

There are still as many children running up and down the aisles in vaudeville shows as there were eight years ago. During tense dramatic scenes, especially, games are considered quite the thing by the younger set.

Then, there are the same old jokes that were sprung eight years ago, and they are greeted with the same laughter by the same audiences. Why, when we were breaking in our act a week ago Saturday at the Madison Theatre in Brooklyn I actually heard a team pull a brand-new joke which began like this: "Who was that lady I seen you with?" And it got a pretty good hand, at that.

Seriously, I hadn't been playing in the Palace ten minutes before I noticed one thing about vaudeville audiences. They get the point of a joke much sooner than do musical comedy audiences. They laugh much quicker. And also stop much quicker.

I also observed that the members of the acts and the leader of the orchestra still twit one another with the same extemporaneous dialogue that has been carefully rehearsed three hours before the show.

And the same speeches when the act gets a couple of encores—"How can we ever thank you? It's so good to be back at the Palace." But the best speeches the audience never hears. These are made on the way to the dressing rooms when the act doesn't get its two encores.

Some things, however, are radically different from the days when the Marx Brothers were sensations in such sketches as "On the Mezzanine," "Fun in Hi Skule" and other problem plays. Among the changes I have noted in vaudeville are:

The performers dress much better today than they did eight years ago. Instead of wearing a pair of spats, they wear two pairs.

And they talk differently. In the old days they'd grab you and tell you what a riot they were in Findlay, Ohio, and how they wowed them in Des Moines. Now, all you hear is "We don't know what to do—Vitaphone wants us to make a short but Movietone is after us to do a full length."

The nature of the acts is a little different today than formerly. No longer do bills open with acrobats in white tights. They still open with acrobats, but they come out in evening clothes and the only indication that they are acrobats is the resin marks on their trousers. Nobody suspects they are acrobats, except the entire audience.

And what has happened to the trained seals? I met a seal backstage whom I hadn't seen since we were playing Pantages time. As Walter Winchell says, he immediately slipped me a fin and told me how disgusted he is with the profession. All that seals can do now is to hang around waiting for Yuletide, when they can dig up a little trade acting as Christmas Seals.

One thing I dislike about the Palace is the fact that the stage door is so narrow that we have to bring Heywood Broun* in the front, like a baby grand piano.

---

*[New York newspaper columnist and certainly the largest member of the Algonquin Round Table crowd.]

After the show, in the old days, the actors used to rush to the nearest one-arm lunch for a load of ham and eggs. Now they all rush to Reuben's to find out how many sandwiches have been named after them.

In conclusion, it certainly is wonderful to be back with our old friends at the Palace. What a welcome I got from the stage hands, especially one fellow with a remarkable memory. Think of remembering a small sum like $10 for eight years!

New York Times
April 21, 1929

Bad Days Are Good Memories

"Bad Days Are Good Memories" was published as the Marx Brothers' third film, Monkey Business, *was about to be released. The Marxes had recently relocated to California, and* Monkey Business *was their first film to be made in Hollywood. Three of the Four Marx Brothers returned briefly to New York in August of 1931 to make a two-night guest appearance in the Howard Dietz–Heywood Broun Broadway revue* Shoot the Works. *Oddly, in a curtain speech following their number, Groucho expressed gratification that the three brothers could get along without the fourth. This was the first public hint that Groucho, Harpo and Chico would someday be working without Zeppo.*

"Bad Days Are Good Memories" would later become a valuable reference source on the Marxes' vaudeville days for their various biographers and would even be used by Groucho, who borrowed a couple of anecdotes from the article for Groucho and Me *in 1959.*

"And what," asked the young newspaper reporter, as he took a chair in my dressing room and set fire to his pipe—surely tobacco could not have given off such an aroma—"and what is the happiest memory of your life?"

"The happiest memory," I said, "is of a time when I was a boy actor, stranded in Colorado, hungry and broke."

"And did you actually enjoy being hungry and broke in Colorado?" the gentleman of the press wanted to know.

"It was dreadful," I assured him. "It was misery. That's why the memory is such a happy one."

And before I could explain the paradox, the reporter laughed. Not, of course, that he was amused by the remark; he wasn't in the least. His chuckle was merely a gesture of courtesy, a bow to my years as a professional comedian.

But I was in earnest. It only happens about once in twenty years—well, twice if you're going to quibble—that I want to talk about memories, and here was one of the times. When I tried to point out why I delight in remembering the least agreeable experiences of my life, the reporter only laughed again. Then he promptly changed the subject. Did I think the talkies would ever replace the stage? Well, that was a pretty personal question and I'd have to talk it over with my wife. Did I plan to play Hamlet? No, we couldn't think of playing any town under 100,000—not with road conditions as they are. And thus the conversation was dragged away from the subject of memories. Now don't think I'm going to be so easy this time. You may laugh if you like, but you're not going to change the subject. I'm here to talk about memories, and nothing—except possibly a hurricane, or maybe the editor—can stop me.

For me, a happy experience does not necessarily mean a happy memory. On the contrary, I am sometimes jealous of my past.

If I enjoy recalling the days when my diet was regulated—and oh, how rigidly!—by my purse, it is because such recollections add a zest to such a simple thing as a well-cooked, well-served dinner. On the other hand, if I get no pleasure in remembering how I once was able to consume, with ecstatic gusto, four or five hot dogs at one sitting, it is because I can't do that any more.

No, the eating of five consecutive hot dogs is not a particularly important accomplishment—I mention it only as an easy symbol, as the first example that comes to mind; and because I still feel rather ill from the effects of one handsome Frankfurter eaten at lunch two hours ago.

What I'm trying to say is that boiled mutton is pretty poor stuff to a man with caviar memories.

I'm not one who looks back with a wistful yearning at the good old days of the theater. When I think of my early years as an actor, I think mostly of tawdry boarding houses; jobless weeks—even months; wages that barely paid for the simplest requirements; and of theater managers who thought nothing of bringing your act to distant towns, then canceling you after the opening performance.

Canceling was the dread of every small-time performer. It meant that after you had traveled miles, at your own expense, for three or four days' employment, you were likely to be dismissed after the very first show. For in those days the manager was the czar of his theater. If he didn't happen to like your songs, or jokes, or the way you combed your hair, he could cancel without a moment's notice.

In the dressing rooms—where there were dressing rooms; I can remember changing my clothes in a yard back of a theater—we would come across signs like this: Don't Send Out Your Laundry Till the Manager Sees Your Act.

But canceling wasn't the manager's only prerogative. If your work displeased him during any performance, he assumed the right to fine you any amount that struck his fancy. When you were found smoking in your dressing room, that usually meant a fine of five dollars—and a fight on pay day, because actors never accepted the fines very willingly.

The actors' associations, and the improved contract laws, have put an end to the powers of despotic little theater men. Now, when an act is engaged for a week, it gets paid for a week. It is the booking man's duty to know what it is he's engaging before the contract is signed.

But I'm wandering a little from my subject . . . Here are the ten happiest memories that occur to me—heartbreaking little experiences that have done something to make my later years more pleasant.

1. Sometimes when the audience likes our performance and there is laughter and maybe applause, I like to think of that night—that horrible night—we were known as The Three Nightingales: my brother Gummo, who has since quit the theater to become a manufacturer—and if business doesn't improve, he'll soon quit being a manufacturer—a soprano; and myself. Harpo, Chico and Zeppo had not yet gone on the stage.

I know now, as I faintly suspected then, that The Three Nightingales were not very good. At any rate, the managers seemed to agree that we did not belong on the two main programs which were given each day in the leading vaudeville theaters. We were among the beginners or second-raters—or both—who appeared, four times a day, on the fill-in programs which kept the theaters going from one o'clock to eleven at night.

When The Nightingales came out to sing, there was seldom anyone in the audience, for apparently our reputation had preceded us. So it was very depressing, singing our snappy ditties and amorous ballads—songs we had rehearsed for hours—to a dead silence. Did I say silence? Well, I was thinking only of applause. The house wasn't actually silent, because we could always hear—even when we sang—the footsteps of the boys who walked up and down the aisles putting chocolate in the slot machines that were attached to the backs of the seats.

"Love me," I'd sing out very coyly at our soprano, and there'd be a loud, disconcerting clunk as another empty candy box snapped open, ready to be refilled. It was most discouraging.

But finally our Big Opportunity came. One of the two-a-day acts had failed to arrive and the manager of Keith's Boston Theater—it was then known as the Cradle of Vaudeville—told us we were going to be used in this main evening performance. If we were good, it meant that we'd be two-a-day players from then on.

It was 8:10. The audience was in the theater. I think it was the first audience we had seen in about six weeks.

"It's a cinch," Gummo said to me, and I shook his and the soprano's hands.

She patted us both on the shoulder, and I could feel her hand shaking nervously.

Well, the orchestra struck up the introduction, a thrilling sound; the soprano walked on the stage alone, to sing the verse of "Love Me and the World Is Mine." And Gummo and I, taking turns looking through the peek hole at the side, could see that the audience was at least interested. When the verse was finished, Gummo and I, slickly attired in white yachting outfits, with artificial flowers in our lapels, marched in from opposite sides of the stage to join in the chorus with our trick harmonies and barber-shop chords, which we thought were pretty hot.

The chorus of "Love Me and the World Is Mine" jumps from B flat to C, and the soprano inadvertently leaped to E flat. And she leaped alone; for Gummo and I had rehearsed the chorus in C, and no soprano was going to get us to change.

The audience laughed—more at our comic nervousness than at the botching of the song—and we went on singing, vaguely hoping that a bolt of lightning would suddenly appear to strike us all dead, or that our soprano would change her mind and return to the key of C.

Never before had I known such anguish; for, besides the humiliation of being laughed at—even the musicians were laughing—we knew that our chance to become two-a-day players was being tossed away by a note and a half. It was sad, bitterly sad; because if there is one talent that young people have in common, it is a talent for suffering.

And so the next week found us at the Howard Theater in Boston, where the second-rate variety acts went on before, between and after the burlesque shows. For that week, the manager had booked the Jeffries-Johnson fight films and, because there was no other place for us on the program, it was decided that we were to do our singing during the showing of the films.

We were—let's face it—the vocal accompaniment for a prize-fight picture. And while the audience was yelling at the fighting gladiators on the screen the three broken Nightingales were chanting, "How'd you like to be my sweetheart?"

A miserable experience . . . a happy memory.

2. What success we have had with our screen comedies has been all the more gratifying because of that unhappy venture, years ago, when we decided to produce a picture of our own.

Chico, Harpo, Zeppo and I each contributed $1000; and similar amounts came from the author, Jo Swerling, and two friends who would rather be nameless, although their names are Al Posen and Max Lippman. To be sure, the art and business of making movies were profound mysteries to all of us, especially to Jo, who, maybe because of this, has since become a celebrated Hollywood author. But our lack of knowledge and experience did not keep us from going ahead. And go ahead we did—to Fort Lee, New Jersey, where somehow or other the picture got itself finished.

I was the old movie villain, Harpo was the Love Interest—and these weren't the only things wrong with the production, which, I'm rather ashamed to say, was called Humor Risk.

So the seven cheerless producers gathered in the projection room with notebooks, cigars and heavy hearts. None of us was very hopeful about the proceedings, but we said, without really believing our words, that, "You can't tell until an audience sees it. We'll get the thing previewed in some theater around New York and then we'll know if we've got a picture or not."

But we knew what we had, and so did the managers who viewed Humor Risk. Not one of them wanted the picture shown in his theater. We even offered to pay a small rental, but the managers seemed to be too considerate of their audiences. It was Chico—it's always Chico—who found a weak-willed exhibitor in the Bronx who was willing to let us show our picture in the afternoon, when the audience consisted mostly of backward children.

"The Marx Brothers in Humor Risk" . . . The title was flashed on the screen, and the seven producers were seated in their chairs, waiting for the verdict of the children. "Children," we told ourselves, "have an instinct for drama . . ."

It must be true, because never before—or since—have I seen so many screaming children run up and down the aisles. When the picture began Benny, in the fourth row, would recognize Sammy sitting in Row L, and the two would shout hello's, and then join in running up and down the aisles. Unless it was wholly imagination on my part, I think that the manager ran with them.

And so the preview was over. The producers, actors, author and director walked out of the theater, saying not a word.

"What'll I do with the film?" said the weak-willed little manager, who was now man enough to be ashamed of his weakness. "What d'ya want me to do with the film?" he repeated, when he heard no answer.

I think he was being polite; for he knew very well what to do with the film.

And so, silently and sadly, we walked out into the afternoon and—for several years—out of the movies. We tried to forget Humor Risk, but it remains one of those memories.

3. No, I'll never forget the humiliation of that night in Washington Courthouse, Indiana. My brother Harpo had become an actor, joining Gummo and me in The Three Mascots, which was heralded as one of the Three Big Acts on the local bill.

Besides the Mascots, the Three Big Acts consisted of a lantern-slide troubadour and an unmanned player piano, which performed its entertainment when the manager put a nickel in the slot.

Not surprisingly, the lantern-slide singer became temporarily drunk, and the manager hurried backstage to ask if one of us could take his place. I was about to volunteer, when Harpo, who had never sung a solo note in his life, stepped in ahead of me.

It was an embarrassing spectacle. The song was of the 'neath-the-old-cherry-tree-sweet-Marie school, and it might have been all right if Harpo had known either the words or the tune. But perhaps the mellowness of years makes me exaggerate in Harpo's favor. The performance would have been sordidly frightful even if Harpo had known the words or the tune, because Harpo happened to be possessed of the worst singing voice I had ever heard.

When the song was finished, the manager came backstage and fined us five dollars for Harpo's work. "It'll take six months to get the bad odor out of this house after that song," he said, quite frankly.

We refused to pay the fine; but when pay day came around, the manager held out five dollars of the seventy-five dollars due us—salary for the performers, who were required to pay their own railroad fares out of this allotment. My mother sent for the chief of police, who turned out to be the theater manager's brother-in-law. He fined us another five dollars for disturbing the peace.

The ten dollars in fines amounted to the surplus we would have had after our expenses were paid. So it was a week before the Mascots had any spending money.

4. It had every indication of being a perfect week. For one thing, there was six days' work ahead of us—three days in one Pennsylvania town, and three in another, a town about eight miles away. And to the strolling small timer, six days of consecutive work was something pretty close to a week of paradise.

The first town began as a pleasant engagement. To be sure, nobody actually agreed with the ads which described our act—now called Fun in Hi Skule—as An Artistic Screamingly Funny Howling Masterpiece; still, on the other hand, the manager hadn't canceled us and the audiences refrained from throwing things.

Then the blow fell. It was on the night before we were to leave town; an epidemic of smallpox had been discovered, and no one was permitted to enter or leave the town. Here was a problem. The epidemic was serious, but so was our need of work. Besides, we were still too young to regard a quarantine as reason enough for depriving the good people of the next town of Fun in Hi Skule. We decided that we'd get to that town if we had to walk, with baggage in hand—and that's precisely what we had to do. When the town was sound asleep, we sneaked out of our boarding houses and hiked the eight miles to our next theater.

I can remember our mood of high triumph as we entered the theater—I think it was called the Bijou, because in those days most of the smaller variety theaters were called Bijou. We were still weary from the walk when we gave our opening performance, with the manager sitting in the first row, glowering at us.

When the act was over, the manager came backstage and told us we were through, canceled, unwanted. After we had walked eight miles with our baggage—through the mountains too!

We were too disappointed to argue, too amazed to protest, and much too tired to fight. Finally I managed to say, "Well, you've got to pay us for this one performance."

"Say," he said, "you're lucky not to get run out of town."

And now, as I recall the jokes and antics in Fun in Hi Skule, I think that maybe he was right.

5. From there we went to Asbury Park, New Jersey—completely broke. After our week's board had been paid in advance—six dollars for each of us—there was not a nickel—and I mean that literally—in the troupe.

Oh, the things we wanted to buy as we walked along the boardwalk from our boarding house to the theater! There were ice-cream cones; rich, juicy hot dogs; and pop corn—beautiful, molasses-covered pop corn!

It was the molasses-covered pop corn that cast the most powerful spell. For three days I walked by the pop corn stand, each time pausing for a look. On the fourth day I had not the strength to walk by.

I went through my pockets, although I knew very well that my only treasure was a fountain pen, which had been given to me on my thirteenth birthday. I adored this pen; it was the first gift I had ever received. As owner of this pen, I was envied by all the youngsters in Gus Edwards's act Kountry Kids, which was appearing on the bill with us.

I examined the pen; I looked again at the pop corn. The choice was not easy to make. Still, a choice had to be made.

"I'll give you this fountain pen for some pop corn," I heard myself saying to the man who presided over the stand.

"Can it write?" he asked. And I, resenting a little the impertinence of his skepticism, showed him that it could. I wrote my name on a paper bag, and how beautifully the ink flowed!

"All right, here you are," he said. I watched the pen leave my hand. There was still time to alter my decision. But my will remained weak. Besides, there already was a handful of pop corn in my mouth. It was food for the gods; it was ambrosia for a child actor. I ate it slowly.

But that night I was far from happy. I missed the fountain pen. And even now I would give anything to have it back.

6. My first experience on the stage was, I think, my saddest. I was fifteen years old when I saw an ad in the New York World saying a boy singer was wanted for the LeRoy Trio. Well, I had done some choir singing; my uncle, Al Shean—later of Gallagher and Shean—was an actor, and I was ambitious.

So I walked the four miles from Ninety-third Street to a tenement near Second Avenue and Twenty-eighth Street to display my qualifications before Mr. LeRoy. These consisted of a slightly changing voice and the rudiments of tap dancing.

Mr. LeRoy led us job seekers to the top of the tenement, where we sang and danced for him on the tin roof. Johnny Morris, an actor now in Hollywood, was immediately hired for his buck dancing, and LeRoy was considering me for the third member of the Trio. He liked my voice.

"Know any ragtime?" he asked, and I didn't quite know what he meant. I knew that ragtime had something to do with singing, so snapping my fingers, I sang The Palms, which I had just learned in the choir. And I was hired, with a salary of four dollars a week and board.

LeRoy hadn't told us that our first jump would be to Denver, and that we'd have to sit up for three nights in day coaches. But we didn't much care. It was worth a few discomforts to become an actor. Nor had LeRoy told us that we were going to be female impersonators.

Still, four dollars a week was four dollars a week, and even female impersonating was acting. We were now professionals; we were now of the theater, and we actually liked LeRoy's curious whim which required Johnny and me to have LeRoy Trio printed on our hatbands.

The Denver engagement was the first and last of the LeRoy Trio—at least so far as Johnny Morris and I were concerned. It began unfortunately. On the opening performance Morris missed a few steps of his buck-dance routine, and the manager fined the act twenty dollars, which was about half of what LeRoy got for himself and his company. Remember, LeRoy had paid our railroad fares, and his own, too, to Denver.

At the end of the week there were no more bookings in sight. There was no money in the troupe. So, without saying good bye, LeRoy left town. Johnny was able to leave too; but I was without money—alone and discouraged and without a friend for hundreds of miles.

I was no longer a professional with LeRoy Trio on my hatband. I was now a child, and I think I cried.

The next day I was lucky enough to get a job driving a grocery wagon from Victor, Colorado, to Cripple Creek. By saving most of my salary—three dollars a week—and the few nickels I earned by singing illustrated songs here and there, I soon collected enough money to buy a ticket home, with ten dollars additional for meals. The money was tucked into my grouch bag—a chamois bag that many actors used to wear around their necks—and I said good-bye to Colorado.

On the way to the train I lost my grouch bag. I thought of three days without food, and I thought of myself being carried home starved—a deceased member of the inglorious LeRoy Trio. But fortunately there were kindly old ladies on the train. There are always kindly old ladies on trains—I think they must be provided by the railroads. From these benevolent travelers I obtained large quantities of bananas and peanuts, with an occasional sandwich too.

I returned home despondent, penniless—and with a mild rash from the excess of peanuts and bananas.

7. I remember, too, the day when my son Arthur—he was seven years old at the time—walked out on our first successful movie, The Cocoanuts, because the picture contained no shooting. It depressed me—not so much because he didn't care for the movie, but I was afraid he was going to become a critic when he grew up.

8. Then there was the time in Ohio when a woman came backstage and asked me if I wouldn't entertain at a little party she was giving in her home. I felt flattered. Besides, I had heard of actors who were paid handsomely for entertaining at parties.

When we got to the door of the woman's house, I heard a man's voice. "Get away from here!" he shouted. Then I heard a revolver shot, and it seemed that a bullet was whizzing by my head.

I was terrified as well as surprised. While running for the theater, I naively supposed the man was a maniac. And from one of the stage hands I learned that he was a maniac, but also a husband whose wife had a habit of meeting actors by telling them she wanted them to entertain at a party.

9. As the Four Marx Brothers, one of our first productions was a tabloid musical show called Mr. Green's Reception. And when I think of Mr. Green's Reception, I think of that mournful afternoon in Battle Creek, Michigan, when we gave our entire show with only four patrons in the audience, in a theater that seated close to three thousand.

10. I can never look at fish without thinking of that cheerless week in Atlantic City when The Three Nightingales were singing in the Atlantic City Garden. The salary for the act was forty dollars a week—with board. And, while the board was certainly plentiful, it consisted of nothing but fish.

That wasn't because the theater manager—he also owned the boarding house—regarded fish as brain food and healthful. He happened to keep a huge fish net right below my bedroom window, and at night I could hear my breakfast, lunch and dinner swimming into the net.

By Wednesday I detested fish. I wanted meat. By Thursday I was spending all my leisure hours in front of a roast-beef counter, sniffing at the luxurious meat which I could not buy. I began to feel something like a cannibal. I could have eaten children, or even the two unappetizing midgets who were on our bill. But instead I ate cod, halibut and flounder—cod, halibut and flounder.

On the following week I ate nothing but roast beef.

I can remember when—but hold on a moment; my young son, Arthur, is coming in with a bag of molasses-covered pop corn, and I can no longer interest myself in the past.

I say, "How's the pop corn, son?"

"Pretty good," he answers.

Pretty good! . . . As though molasses-covered pop corn could be anything but perfect! For a fraction of a second I wonder if it would be wise for me to take away Arthur's fountain pen so that he, too, will have a happy memory when he grows up. Or should I—should I take away the pop corn? No; he knows how much I like it myself.

So I resolve to tell Arthur about that day in Asbury Park when I gave up my only treasure for the delicacy that he calls pretty good . . . And while I decide that I never want him to have experiences like those, I wonder if he won't miss them a little.

"Arthur, here's a dime. Go out and get me some pop corn like yours."

The Saturday Evening Post
August 29, 1931

Mackerel for Xmas

Christmas of 1935 was an especially good time for the Marx Broth-
ers. Their first MGM picture, A Night at the Opera, *had just been*
released and was a major critical and commercial success. In
"Mackerel for Xmas," written for Variety*'s annual anniversary is-*
sue, Groucho related a tale that was a favorite of the brothers. In
fact, he told the story in print again in Groucho and Me *twenty-three*
years later. Like most fish stories, the later version is the product of
years of dramatic embellishment. "Mackerel for Xmas" is probably
much more faithful to the facts of the story.

Beverly Hills, Dec. 25.

Here I am sitting at home Xmas day, clutching the swag presented to me by
admiring friends and relatives. Pajamas and briar sets, sets of books, costly
wines, and a year's subscription to the [*Hollywood*] *Reporter* (I dare you to
print it).

What a racket. I have two cars, two kids, two servants, two suits of clothes,
two overcoats, and two pictures to make under our present contract.

I remember a Xmas day 25 years ago with mother, Harpo, Gummo and
myself. We were playing Passaic, New Jersey, at a theatre called the Bijou,
Majestic, or Family, and we were living at a boarding house which had been
highly touted to us by the Empire Comedy Four, and Pipifax and Panlo,
boarding house epicures of no mean standing. The place was conducted

by a lady called Mrs. Abernathy who had suspiciously red streaked hair, a tightly corseted figure and giant and phony earrings. The rates were a little higher than we usually paid—$8 a week double and $9 single American plan. But it was Xmas week, we had been working pretty steady, so what the hell.

Our first meal, breakfast, was around 11 A.M. and it wasn't bad. Choice of fruit, half orange, or prunes, griddle cakes and a composition that the landlady swore was coffee. We inquired about Xmas dinner. Would it be around 1 or after the matinee? Mrs. Abernathy said she always had it after the matinee as the actors were then more in the mood. We gave two shows a night and, as we didn't go on until about 8:30 for the first performance, we felt that after the matinee would be perfect. It would give us plenty of time to gorge and recuperate before we panicked Passaic with that classy act known as The Three Nightingales.

Mrs. Abernathy had two dining rooms. One was for the townspeople (mostly bachelors, with a sprinkling of school teachers and clerical workers) and the other was for the actors. This was necessary as the actors had been known to throw food at each other in discussing material priority. Some of the boarders didn't like their food served that way. Personally we didn't care how our food was served, as long as they served it.

All through the matinee we thought of nothing but the turkey, cranberry sauce and pumpkin pie that awaited at Mrs. Abernathy's. At 5 o'clock we were up and down the halls in eager anticipation of that pungent Xmas dinner. At 5:10 we were all at the table discussing routes, layoffs, agents and Albee.* At 5:30 a big dish arrived and on it was a huge baked mackerel and a dish of cranberry sauce. At first we suspected Mrs. Abernathy of having turned comic for the moment and that pretty soon this offensive dish would be removed. But there sat the mackerel and there sat us and for five minutes neither the fish nor the actors moved. And then with a bitterness too deep for violence we realized that the turkey was for the regular boarders.

The local theatregoers must have been slightly bewildered that Xmas night to see and hear five acts give a complete performance about mackerel. I doubt if a more hysterical and insane performance has ever been given in the history of vaudeville.

---

*[Edward Franklin (E. F.) Albee, with partner Benjamin Franklin (B. F.) Keith, operated the Keith–Albee vaudeville circuit.]

After the show we returned to the boarding house and sneaked into the kitchen, broke into the icebox and found the carcass of a cold turkey and cranberry sauce. So there we sat, five vaudeville acts grouped on the floor of a cold dark kitchen, ravenously eating a belated Xmas dinner.

Variety
January 1, 1936

Why Harpo Doesn't Talk

"Why Harpo Doesn't Talk" is one of the many articles that Groucho wrote for This Week, *a Sunday magazine supplement to the* New York Herald-Tribune *which was also syndicated in newspapers around the country throughout the forties and fifties. When it was written, in the fall of 1948, Groucho was beginning his second season of* You Bet Your Life *on radio while suffering through the failure on Broadway of* Time for Elizabeth, *the play he'd written with Norman Krasna. The story recalled in "Why Harpo Doesn't Talk" is a Marx family legend and was told by Groucho many times. He'd written an article about the incident for* Variety *eight years earlier and would later retell the story in* Groucho and Me.

'Twas the week before Christmas—now don't get excited. This isn't going to be a story about Santa Claus. This is a story about Harpo, Chico, Zeppo and me.

It happened back during the wormier days of vaudeville in one of those soft-coal towns in Illinois, where if your street ensemble didn't include a small miner's lantern on top of your cap, you were eyed with considerable curiosity.

The theater was no Radio City Music Hall. It seated, uncomfortably, about 500 people. The dressing rooms were in a damp, dimly lit cellar underneath the stage, containing very little heat and a minimum of plumbing.

Our show was a tabloid music comedy. It was advertised as a magnificent Broadway production, differing from the original only in the cost of the tickets. Actually there were other differences. Our company consisted of four men, eight girls and ourselves. Our salary for the entire company was $900 a week, which meant that for three days we would pull down $450.

Early Thursday morning I walked in to rehearse the orchestra. Since I was the only one of the boys who didn't know an eighth note from a bank note, I never quite understood why I was delegated for this job. In later years I realized it was because I was the only Marx Brother who could be routed out of bed before noon.

I was a jaunty sight as I walked through the stage door that morning. I had a genuine imitation diamond stickpin in my tie, a cane in my hand, and between my lips the best five-cent cigar money could buy.

As I strolled to the mailbox to see if that redheaded dame from Bloomington was coming on to see me, a burly figure appeared out of the darkness.

"Hey, you!" he shouted. "Don't you see that sign? It says, 'No Smoking.' That'll cost you five dollars."

Flicking the ash off my cigar, I replied in my iciest tone: "Who, may I ask, are you?"

"Who am I?" he bellowed, "I'm Jack Wells, the manager and owner of this theater. We have rules here and that sign is one of them."

"What sign?" I said, a little puzzled.

"What sign!" he roared, and pointed, in the gloom, to a tiny NO SMOKING poster tacked high on the wall, almost out of sight.

"Why don't you hang the sign in a closet?" I asked. "Then you can be sure no one'll see it."

"Oh, a wise guy, eh! That crack'll cost you another five."

This repartee was beginning to run into money. Reluctantly tossing my stogie away, I left Wells and started rehearsing the music. These were the days before actors' unions. Every theater manager was a little king, and his fines were as absolute as Supreme Court decisions. Some managers collected almost as much revenue through this petty larceny as they did through the box office.

The more I thought about Wells and that $10, the madder I got—especially when I thought about the $10. I was still burning when the rehearsal was over. Back at the hotel, I woke up the boys, after quite a struggle, and told them what had happened. They were purple with rage. However, I don't think they were as angry over the fine as they were over the fact that if I hadn't had the run-in with Wells they could still be sleeping.

We held a council of war and decided we wouldn't go on unless Wells rescinded the fine.

The curtain was scheduled to go up at two-thirty. At two o'clock we were all in our dressing rooms in the cellar. We donned our stage clothes, slapped on our make-up, and when we were all ready, sent for Wells.

Together we weren't afraid of him. There were four of us. We were young and full of hell, and besides, each of us carried a blackjack. A few moments later Wells appeared. Chico, the eldest, acted as spokesman. Taking a firm grip on himself, and gulping a trifle, he said, "Mr. Wells, unless you cancel that ten-dollar fine, we're not going on."

Wells was furious. He wasn't accustomed to mutiny. He said, "Listen, you guys. I have rules in this theatre, and one of the rules is NO SMOKING. I caught your brother Groucho smoking, and I fined him. That's the law of this theater, and it stands!"

Chico hollered out to the company, "Okay, everybody, take off your make-up and costumes. We're not going to give a show."

By this time the orchestra had played the overture four times, and a houseful of tough theater-lovers were stamping and shouting for the curtain to go up.

Wells was getting nervous. He was part of the town and he couldn't afford this. He knew we had him.

"Now, wait a minute, boys," he whined. "You can't do this to me. Those people came to see a show."

We answered, "We came to give a show, but as long as the fine stands, we don't go on. Take your choice."

We, too, were bluffing. We couldn't afford the loss of three days' salary. Then Harpo, the Neville Chamberlain of his time, spoke up.

"I'll tell you what," he said. "We'll take ten dollars and you take ten, and we'll combine it and throw the whole twenty in the Salvation Army Christmas pot on the corner."

"You can throw all your salary in the Christmas pot," said Wells, "but they don't get any of my dough."

Out front the stamping grew louder and the yells more threatening. Wells listened with alarm.

"What do you say?" Chico taunted him. "Does the Salvation Army get the money?"

Wells eyed us murderously, but rather than lose the afternoon's receipts, and perhaps his life, he surrendered and the show went on.

We were leaving Saturday night for our next jump, and by the time our last show was over we had about 40 minutes to get dressed, pack, load the scenery on tracks, get to the depot and check our baggage.

In the midst of all this confusion, two of Wells's stooges staggered in and dumped four big canvas bags on the floor.

"What's that?" we asked.

"That's your salary," one of them said. "Mr. Wells sends his regards."

Each bag contained $112.50 in pennies, but we had to make sure. We also had to catch a train, so as quickly as possible we counted one of the bags and measured it up against the other three. We could only hope that Wells hadn't loaded the uncounted bags with slugs.

We barely made the train, and as it pulled out of the depot, we stood on the track platform watching the town and theater recede into the distance.

Then Harpo, the pantomimist, raised his voice, and above the clatter of the train, bellowed:

"Good-bye, Mr. Wells. Here's hoping your lousy theater burns down!"

We thought it was just a gag, till next morning—when we discovered that during the night, Jack Wells's theater had been reduced to ashes. From then on we decided not to let Harpo talk—his conversation was too dangerous.

This Week
December 12, 1948

PART TWO

Homicide on the Range

My Poor Wife

"My Poor Wife" was published during a particularly busy time for the Marx Brothers. The film version of Animal Crackers *had been released in the fall of 1930 and the Marx Brothers would soon sail for Europe. Their appearance at the Palace in London got rave reviews, which helped erase the memory of a lukewarm reception during their visit to London in 1922. Groucho and his family (first wife Ruth, nine-year-old Arthur and three-year-old Miriam) were living in a ten-room, two-story stucco house on a wooded acre in the fashionable Great Neck section of Long Island. Groucho's Great Neck neighbors included* New York World *editor Herbert Bayard Swope, Ring Lardner and, for a brief time, Chico and his family. Regular weekend visitors to Great Neck included George S. Kaufman and Marc Connelly. Surrounded by his family and the writers he most admired, Groucho would later recall that these were among his happiest days.*

The lady—a new acquaintance—tittered as she was leaving our house. Turning to my wife, she said:

"If laughing makes people fat, how do you manage to keep your figure? Why, you must spend most of the time in hysterics, having a comedian for a husband."

My wife smiled, or rather tried to smile, and I felt ashamed. I knew how many times Ruth had heard the jests, wisecracks and puns that I had uttered during the evening, and I wondered how long her beautiful patience could last.

How often (I couldn't help thinking), how often she must have wished she had married a plumber or an undertaker, who, although he might talk shop at home, would hesitate to work at it after hours! I had seen my wife wince when I told the story (again) about the Scotchman who painted red stripes on his son's thumb so the child would think he had a peppermint stick. She had heard the story five (possibly six) times before, even though it was, I still hope, new to our guests. She had even laughed a little during the second and third recitals of the anecdote. And the second time she had actually directed the conversation to small talk about thrift.

But there are limits to human endurance . . . Oh, I know that a theater usher has to hear the same jokes as often as two and three hundred times a year (when the show's a hit); but then that's the usher's *job*. And I doubt that my wife could have been happy as an usher.

Then why, you ask (and it's about time you were taking an interest in what I'm saying), why do I tell and retell these trifling japes and nifties? Why don't I become a quiet, unclownish husband like Mr. Smith, the grocer, or Mr. Jones, who delivers our coal?

Dear, dear reader, you are now going to hear about the curse of my profession. When a man is in the comedy business, people expect him to be comical at all times. A violinist can leave his fiddle at home; a pianist can forget to bring his music; but a comedian has no excuse. If he isn't conspicuously funny, he's regarded as a rather dull and disappointing fellow.

Let a stage clown go to a party and completely forget his profession, and people will say: "Oh, he's all right behind the footlights, but isn't he uninteresting when you meet him? I supposed he just isn't a natural comedian." Whereupon the poor man develops a first-class inferiority complex and begins slinking down alleys for fear that a mad critic will bite him.

There are, of course, a few men—men braver than I—who are in the business of being funny and yet will not hesitate to indulge in a quipless evening, no matter how many eager auditors are around them, hopefully waiting for something to laugh at.

Ring Lardner, for example, is one of the wittiest men in America; certainly he is the most humorous. But when away from his typewriter, Ring is content to be as solemn and unfunny as a New England preacher dedicating a new funeral chapel. I have spent evenings with Lardner when he didn't say one funny thing. I have spent evenings with him when he didn't say anything at all.

George Kaufman is another of America's First Wits; and he, too, is considered a grave gent by people who meet him for the first time. "Great playwright," they say of George, "and a funny writer, but he didn't say one amusing thing all evening."

And I ought to cite Ed Wynn, too, among the heroic gentlemen in the comedy business who can (when away from the theater) puff at their pipes and ask whether Radio [RKO] is likely to go up a few points during the next day and how do you think the Giants will hit the old apple around next season?

Courageous men, Lardner, Kaufman and Wynn. How my wife must envy their wives!

Not, of course, that she wasn't sufficiently warned before our marriage. Ruth was a dancer (I might add, a *good* dancer; in fact, I'd *better* add a good dancer) in our vaudeville act when we met; and, although I tried to keep her from hearing me repeat my off-stage comedy in our courtship days, I wasn't altogether successful. You see, we were almost constantly together. And I was weak. I couldn't always resist making fresh use of a good anecdote, or what I considered a snappy bit of repartee, whenever there was a new listener to hear it.

The wedding itself might have changed Ruth's mind, but it didn't. It was the only comical wedding I have ever attended.

We were married in Ruth's home in Chicago; and of course my brothers (also in the comedian business) were present. Harpo was in a particularly mirthful mood.

Just as the clergyman—he was a most dignified old gentleman—began to say the words that were to make Ruth my wife and permanent audience, he coughed and made a funny noise with his throat.

Unfortunately, it was just such a sound as that which served as a signal for a comedy bit in our show. On the stage, when the straight man did an "er-r-r-r," Harpo would pretend to become frightened and would quickly fling himself under the carpet.

Yes, it happened at the wedding. The clergyman had no sooner cleared his throat than Harpo was under the carpet; the wedding became giddier than any skit I have ever seen in the revues. Everybody but the clergyman laughed.

As Harpo left his hiding place under the rug, Chico began wishing me luck in Italian dialect, and Zeppo asked the preacher if it would be bad taste for him to sing a little ditty about his yearnings for Alabammy.

I, of course, had no part in these monkeyshines. It was my wedding, a solemn day in my life. A day of dignity. And it's only because Ruth's memory isn't as good as mine that she says I answered the preacher in Moran and Mack fashion.* Oh, I might have walked up to the altar doing a modified fox trot (I was rather proud of my dancing in those days) but I did not—I most certainly did not—talk like Moran and Mack.

For my part, I can only wish that my comedy during our married years had been easier for Ruth to bear. To be sure, she has never once complained. More often than not, in fact, she has encouraged me.

I can remember (with no pride at all) remarking that I could tell the age of a chicken by the teeth. "But a chicken *has* no teeth," Sam Harris—I think it was Sam Harris**—said, and I replied: "No, but I have." There was a round of laughter in the room.

Personally, I thought this a pretty terrible crack, but the Marxes believe that the customer is always right.

The next time we had chicken for dinner, and a few friends at the house, I found myself saying once more that I could tell the age of a chicken by the teeth. And it was Ruth—Ruth herself—who said, "but a chicken *has* no teeth."

But to be perfectly honest with you, I must confess that I brought up the subject of a chicken's age three or four days later . . . And it was four months before my wife served chicken again. She said she had grown tired of poultry, but down in my heart I knew.

It is with honest humility that I am citing my worst offenses in after-working-hours comedy, because I want you to know the extent of my wife's grievances. I can remember when Reigh Count—or was it Man o' War?—won the Kentucky Derby in the rain, and the papers referred to him as a good mudder. And I said, "And does the mudder eat his fodder?"

---

*[George Moran and Charlie Mack were a popular vaudeville minstrel act who performed in blackface and affected stereotypical black speech.]
**[Sam Harris was a prominent theatrical producer whose many hits included *The Cocoanuts* and *Animal Crackers*.]

Well, George White,* who was present at the time, had won a few nickels on the horse. Consequently he was in good humor at the time. He laughed. And you can't guess how laughter can spoil a comedian. The next night, when Reigh Count was mentioned again, Ruth said—very slyly I thought— "he's an awfully good mudder, isn't he?" Dear, dear Ruth! That, I knew, was my cue. So quick as lightning—as though the thought had just struck me—I went into my little joke.

Four days later, when Eddie Cantor mentioned the Kentucky Derby, Ruth neatly changed the subject. Nothing was said about mudders and fodder.

Then there was the time when we went fishing in Long Island Sound and the man who rented the boat and fishing equipment said the bait would cost us eleven dollars. I said it would be cheaper to cut up the children for bait; and Ruth became annoyed. She said it wasn't a nice thing to say; the man might take me seriously; and . . . anyway, I knew she was right. But my objection to the remark was that it had fallen pretty flat. The boatman merely stared at me and held out his hand for the eleven dollars.

I am not, to be sure, *always* weak. Only a month ago when the grocer talked about the "pesky kids" who swiped cherries from the stand in front of his store, I restrained myself from asking if a pesky was a skeleton key in Russia. And never—may I never hear another laugh if I'm lying to you now—have I said that the best way to tell a bad egg is to break it gently.

Because I wear a painted mustache and a comical costume on the stage and in the movies, I seldom am recognized by strangers. Which is quite a handicap (or maybe a blessing) for some of my off-stage comedy.

You see, people are always a little quicker to laugh at a professional funny man than they are at a person in another profession or business. When we moved to Great Neck, I went to one of the village confectioners and asked for some candy for the children.

"Just a few dainties to make the kiddies sick," I told the clerk and he gave me a frigid stare—and the candy.

A month later, after the confectionery man had learned that I was a comedian I happened to drop in for more candy.

"The kiddies want to get sick again," I said, and the clerk shook the counter with his laughter. Surely this wasn't a funny remark. Certainly it wasn't any

---

*[George White was a vaudeville dancer, writer and producer, well-known for the *George White Scandals* revue shows.]

more amusing than when I had said a similar thing before. But the fact that I was a comedian made a difference.

Now this confectioner chuckles when I merely walk into his store. He has, I think, a frustrated yearning to be some comedian's "straight man," or foil.

Ruth has no such wish.

For ten years she has been listening to my oft-repeated flippancies; she has heard me say the same things again and again—serious things as well as skittish.

Even all this—all that I have been telling you—Ruth has heard before.

I'm sorry for my wife.

Collier's
December 20, 1930

Holy Smoke

One of the great passions of Groucho's life was cigar smoking. Apart from the cigar's inherent usefulness as a prop on stage, Groucho truly enjoyed a good smoke. "Holy Smoke" was written in early 1930 while the Marx Brothers were performing Animal Crackers *in Chicago. This was around the same time that* Beds *was written. Groucho had five essays published in* College Humor *in the early thirties. The serialization of* Beds *accounted for four of them, with "Holy Smoke" being the other.*

Smoking was originated by the American Indians, who settled all their arguments by smoking the pipe of peace. Their system was simple and effective: when one tribe was sore at another, they'd invite the rival *mispocha* over for a tobacco *klatch*. After the hostile tribe had spent several evenings smoking the pipe of peace, the home team found themselves with enough coupons to secure a dozen Indian blankets. Through the ages, this system has been preserved almost intact by American businessmen, who use the same method to settle their disputes. When they have an argument on hand, the rival magnates get together, light cigars and blow smoke in each other's faces.

Smoking was introduced in England by Sir Walter Raleigh, who was taught by the Indians how to blow rings. He returned to England and blew rings for Queen Elizabeth, who was so impressed that she immediately promoted Raleigh to the post of Chief of Room Service. In this capacity he continued to blow rings—one ring for ice water, two rings for bed linen, etc.[1] The system is still in vogue in the palace to this day.

Pipe smoking made its appearance in Ireland in 1066, the same year that clay was discovered. In 1067, every Irishman above the age of twenty-one was telling the gag about the advantage of a clay pipe—when you dropped it, you didn't have to bother about picking it up. By 1068, all England was laughing at the joke.

Twenty years later smoking was introduced in Scotland. The Scotch, true to their tradition, not only smoked their pipes but also played them.

Since these pioneer days there has been a great development in the art of smoking. Some years ago, ex-Vice President Marshall got himself famous,[2] and many boxes of cigars, by stating that what this country needed was a good five cent cigar. Conditions have changed radically since then. What this country needs today is a good five cent cigar with a twenty cent filler.[3]

Briggs afterward immortalized this idea with his cartoon, *When a Filler Needs a Friend.*

During the Civil War, smoking gained in popularity because of Ulysses S. Grant, who was devoted to the weed, as tobacco is often called (but not by cigarette manufacturers).

If Grant had lived today,[4] he would find himself greatly in demand. His picture would be used in all the magazines, a blindfold over his eyes, accompanied by this sort of testimonial:

> *I'll fight it out with this cigar if it takes all summer!*
> "During the winter of 1864, I noticed that many of my soldiers were coughing. This is serious in wartime, as it gives the enemy a good idea of your position, to say nothing of your health. I passed out a fresh supply of smokes and soon there wasn't any more coughin' in the camp.[5]
> (Signed) Ulysses S. Grant."

---

1. And one Ring for Lardner.
2. And was the only vice president who ever did.
3. My address is Great Neck, L.I.
4. There would be no Grant's Tomb.
5. He probably meant there wasn't any more coffins in camp.

Holy Smoke

By GROUCHO MARX

SMOKING was originated by the American Indians, who settled all their arguments by smoking the pipe of peace. Their system was simple and effective: when one tribe was sore at another, they'd invite the rival *mispocha* over for a tobacco *klatch*. After the hostile tribe had spent several evenings smoking the pipe of peace, the home team found themselves with enough coupons to secure a dozen Indian blankets.

Through the ages, this system has been preserved almost intact by American business men, who use the same method to settle their disputes. When they have an argument on hand, the rival magnates get together, light cigars and blow smoke in each other's faces.

Smoking was introduced in England by Sir Walter Raleigh, who was taught by the Indians how to blow rings. He returned to England and blew rings for Queen Elizabeth, who was so impressed that she immediately promoted Raleigh to the post of Chief of Room Service. In this capacity he continued to blow rings—one ring for ice water, two rings for bed linen, etc.[1] The system is still in vogue in the palace to this day.

Pipe smoking made its appearance in Ireland in 1066, the same year that clay was discovered. In 1067, every Irishman above the age of twenty-one was telling the gag about the advantage of a clay pipe—when you dropped it, you didn't have to bother about picking it up. By 1068, all England was laughing at the joke.

Twenty years later smoking was introduced in Scotland. The Scotch, true to their tradition, not only smoked their pipes but also played them.

Since these pioneer days there has been a great development in the art of smoking. Some years ago, ex-Vice President Marshall got himself famous,[2] and many boxes of cigars, by stating that what this country needed was a good five cent cigar. Conditions have changed radically since then. What this country needs today is a good five cent cigar with a twenty cent filler!

Briggs afterward immortalized this idea with his cartoon, *When a Filler Needs a Friend*.

During the Civil War, smoking gained in popularity because of Ulysses S. Grant, who was devoted to the weed, as tobacco is often called (but not by cigarette manufacturers).

If Grant had lived today,[4] he would find himself greatly in demand. His picture would be used in all the magazines, a blindfold over his eyes, accompanied by this sort of testimonial:

I'll fight it out with this cigar if it takes all summer!

"During the winter of 1864, I noticed that many of my soldiers were coughing. This is serious in wartime, as it gives the enemy a good idea of your position, to say nothing of your health. I passed out a fresh supply of smokes and soon there wasn't any more coughin' in camp.[5]   (Signed) Ulysses S. Grant."

These testimonials apply not only to the army, but also the navy. Nowadays a sea captain can't get his papers until he passes his blindfold test. Think of the opportunity missed by the cigarette manufacturers by not having Captain Lawrence say in type: "Don't give up the ship—I left my ciggies in my cabin."

Moreover, if the testimonial hounds had been on the job in the good old days, posterity would be richer by pictures of Lincoln freeing the slaves between puffs and Eliza crossing the ice, accompanied by a pack of greyhounds and a pack of cigarettes.

Some twenty years ago the highest honor actors could hope for would be to have a cigar named after them. But in this effeminized day, actors, alas, are well satisfied to have sandwiches named after them.

In the last ten years, the smoking situation has undergone a decided revolution. Old fetishes and shibboleths have been overthrown: a new order of smokers rules the land.

Smoking has always been the greatest problem American men have been called upon to face. For years they have waged a fierce campaign, a campaign to convince their wives that ashes are really good for the rugs. For years we men have been struggling in vain to remove the tobacco crumbs from our overcoat pockets. A friend of mine, also a Scotchman, has the right idea. He lets the crumbs accumulate for three years—as who doesn't? At the end of this time, he cuts out the pocket and smokes it.

The matter of accessories is another tremendous problem which smokers have to face without flinching. No man is

[*Continued on page 129*]

[1] And one Ring for Lardner.
[2] And was the only vice president who ever did.
[3] My address is Great Neck, L. I.
[4] There would be no Grant's Tomb.

¶ Reading from left to right: the author, sizing up the Amalgamated Alfalfa situation.

[5] He probably meant there wasn't any more coffins in camp.

These testimonials apply not only to the army, but also the navy. Nowadays a sea captain can't get his papers until he passes his blindfold test. Think of the opportunity missed by the cigarette manufacturers by not having Captain Lawrence say in type: "Don't give up the ship—I left my ciggies in my cabin."

Moreover, if the testimonial hounds had been on the job in the good old days, posterity would be richer by pictures of Lincoln freeing the slaves between puffs and Eliza crossing the ice, accompanied by a pack of greyhounds and a pack of cigarettes.

Some twenty years ago the highest honor actors could hope for would be to have a cigar named after them. But in this effeminized day, actors, alas, are well satisfied to have sandwiches named after them.

In the last ten years, the smoking situation has undergone a decided revolution. Old fetishes and shibboleths have been overthrown: a new order of smokers rules the land.

Smoking has always been the greatest problem American men have been called upon to face. For years they have waged a fierce campaign, a campaign to convince their wives that ashes are really good for the rugs. For years we men have been struggling in vain to remove the tobacco crumbs from our overcoat pockets. A friend of mine, also a Scotchman, has the right idea. He lets the crumbs accumulate for three years—as who doesn't? At the end of this time, he cuts out the pocket and smokes it.

The matter of accessories is another tremendous problem which smokers have to face without flinching. No man is free from this evil. If he hasn't a smoking jacket, he has a pouch;[6] if he hasn't a pouch, he has a lighter; if he hasn't a lighter, some one is sure to give him one.

Smoking jackets quietly disappeared when lighters were invented. Only a millionaire can afford to own a smoking jacket and maintain a lighter. The upkeep of a lighter is terrific. In the first place, lighters quickly get out of style, to say nothing of getting out of order. Lighters, in the good old days, were substantial. A good two pound lighter was the order of the day and men had to have leather pockets built in their suits.

These heavy models grew passé, however, and nowadays the latest lighters tend to slender lines and beveled ruching. A man would be as embarrassed to pull out a 1924 model lighter as he would be to carry around one of those gold tooth-picks which were all the rage some years back.

In the gay Twenty-twos and Twenty-threes, lighters went in for fancy initials. In the blithe Twenty-fours and Twenty-fives, futuristic designs were *de rigueur*. In the carefree Twenty-sixes and Twenty-sevens, wind protectors reared their ugly heads. And in the frolicsome Twenty-eights and

---

6 The pouch was introduced in Australia by the kangaroo.

Twenty-nines, lighters completed the cycle by again reflecting the utilitarian motif.

I can still remember the days when lighters were primarily lighters. Now
they are primarily wardrobe trunks. No self-respecting lighter is complete
without a watch, a mirror, a nail file, a compass, a calendar, a corkscrew
and a can opener. The latest models, I am informed by Poiret, will also have
toothbrush holders. They will also once more have the small wick which was
finally retained by the fashion experts after a heated argument.

It has been pretty generally accepted that bachelors are behind the great
increase in smoking. Several years ago, smoking fell off considerably and
bachelors scurried about in great alarm, holding conferences and appoint-
ing committees to do something about the decrease in smoking. This struck
at the very roots of bachelorism. For if there was no smoking, how could
bachelors have reveries? And if there were no reveries, what would be the
fun of being a bachelor?

Happily, however, we can report that smoking is more popular than ever,
and as a consequence, the Field Secretary of the United Bachelor Brother-
hood tells us that 1929 will be a bumper year for reveries.

Be that as it may, smoking isn't what it used to be. In the days of my youth,
if Father caught little Willie stealing a smoke behind the woodshed, he'd
caress him with a hairbrush or a razor strap. Nowadays, when he catches
him, he merely grabs the kid's coupons.

Which brings us finally to the greatest evil in present day smoking—coupons. Coupons represent a tremendous departure from the day when beautiful
reproductions of actresses were enclosed in each package of cigarettes. These
pictures, beyond all question, constituted Early American Art. Each man was a
collector and didn't need Sir Joseph Duveen to tell him when he had a real masterpiece. Coupons can never take the place of the good old cigarette pictures.

Nowadays they don't give art studies with cigarettes, but they give everything else, except tobacco. You can get a good gift from the coupons but
you can't get a good smoke from the cigars. In fact, most of the cigars are
so bad these days, it would be much better to save the cigars and smoke
the coupons.

College Humor
February 1930

Buy It, Put It Away, and Forget About It

"Buy It, Put it Away, and Forget About It" was Groucho's seventh and final New Yorker *piece. The premiere of the Marx Brothers' first film,* The Cocoanuts, *would come a few weeks after its publication in the spring of 1929. The stock market crash, in which Groucho lost $250,000, would not occur until October. The Marx Brothers had been paid $100,000 by Paramount for filming* The Cocoanuts *and were each earning $2,000 a week during the Broadway run of* Animal Crackers. *At the time of the crash the brothers were in Baltimore, opening a one-week run of the show at the Maryland Theater. George S. Kaufman had invested $10,000 in a stock based on a tip from Groucho and Harpo. When he lost his entire investment he remarked, "Anyone who buys a stock because the Marx Brothers recommended it deserves to lose $10,000."*

I come from common stock. I always planned to begin my autobiography with that terse statement. Now that introduction is out. Common stock made a bum out of me.

Between the ages of sixteen and twenty-six my interests were devoted to the drama, music, painting, literature, and the Arts. I was a dilettante, a classicist, a philosopher, a bookworm. For years I read no farther back in a newspaper than the sporting page. To me, the financial sheet was only a page to remove mud from my shoes. No more. I use the editorial page now. The financial sheet is sacred.

It all started when I got tired of being advised by my friends to buy some stock, put it away, and forget about it. It seemed harmless, so I thought I'd humor them—like trying their favorite remedy for breaking up a cold. It sounded easy enough to buy some stock, put it away, and forget about it.

For my first stock, I selected Anaconda Copper. I got the tip from a clerk in a hardware store when I went in to buy a copper kettle for my Great Neck hovel. "Have you any copper kettles?" I asked, my thoughts far, far away from the world of finance.

"We have an excellent stock," he replied—significantly, I thought.

"How much is this kettle?" I asked, trying to draw him out.

"Fifteen dollars," he said, knowingly.

"Why so expensive?" I asked.

"Anaconda high price of copper."

That settled it. I'm influenced by such things and that's all there is to it. I rushed to the street and, in more time than it takes to tell it, was at the broker's. Here a nice, accommodating young vice-president took me under his wing and gave me some advice.

I didn't buy the Anaconda after all. He advised against it. He let me in on something special, even taking me over in a corner to tell me about it. That's how I happened to buy Mack Truck. For the trifling sum of sixteen thousand dollars, I became one of the principal bag-holders.

"Now, put this away and forget about it," the broker told me.

I did. That is, I put it away. But I couldn't forget about it. Every night I would pace the floor wondering if the back of the bookcase was a safe place to keep the stock. Moreover they wouldn't let me forget about it. My broker kept phoning me. "Don't worry, old boy," he would say, "things will come out all right—we look for a sharp reversal any day now—it's bound to rise sooner or later to where you bought it."

Each day I learned a new reason for the stock's latest slide. Call money, gold reserve, brokers' loans, or even the Federal Reserve statement. (And there I was living in a fool's paradise, thinking, in my innocent way, that the Federal Reserve was encamped in Plattsburg!)

Then came the big slump of last fall. (Why is it always a big slump? I'd like to see a good little slump before I cash in my chips.) Mack Truck skidded with the rest. The stock went down, down, and—down. I wasn't more terrified than usual but I feared the president of the company might be worried. So I wired him: "DON'T WORRY OLD BOY AM STILL BEHIND MACK TRUCK."

The wire must have fallen into the hands of a wisecracking sales manager, because the answer read: "IT'S BETTER TO BE BEHIND A MACK TRUCK THAN IN FRONT OF ONE STOP HAVE YOU SEEN OUR 1929 MODEL."

By this time I owned several other stocks. The virus was in my blood. My hunger for information became insatiable. I hung over the ticker every day. Pretty soon I saw spots before my eyes. Not only spots, but numbers. Not only numbers, but fractions. I went to an oculist. He diagnosed it as a pernicious case of ticker eyes.

I was occupying a divan in a broker's office one morning when a portly gentleman walked by me. "That's Louchheim Minton," whispered the fellow-sufferer in the next chair.

Minton stopped to confer with another portly gentleman.

"Who's he talking to?" I asked.

"Hirsch Lilienthal," I was told.

Two of the greatest financiers in the country! A chance to get some real information! I decided to eavesdrop. I wriggled up next to them and got an earful. All I could hear them say was "Chrysler—wonderful—marvellous—Chrysler—magnificent—Chrysler."

That was enough. I sprinted to my broker and implored him to buy me a thousand shares of Chrysler before it went up.

I could have walked on my hands and still been in plenty of time. It didn't go up. After it had dropped sixteen points that afternoon, I became pretty annoyed. Minton and Lilienthal must have purposely given me a run around, I thought. Oh, if I could only lay my hands on them!

As luck would have it, I saw Louchheim Minton enter the same broker's office the next day. In a stride I was at his side.

"Are you Louchheim Minton?" I demanded fearlessly.

He nodded.

"Didn't I hear you praising Chrysler yesterday afternoon?" I almost shouted.

"Yes," he said affably, "you certainly did. I think he's America's greatest violinist."

The New Yorker
May 4, 1929

Our Father and Us

When "Our Father and Us" was written, the Marx Brothers were preparing to film Cracked Ice, *which after several rewrites would become their fifth film,* Duck Soup. *On March 9, 1933, the Marx Brothers broke their ties with Paramount and briefly negotiated with United Artists. They quickly returned to Paramount to film* Duck Soup, *but it would be their last film for the studio and their last with Zeppo.*

The previous fall Groucho and Chico had starred in a radio series for NBC. Flywheel, Shyster and Flywheel *ran for twenty-six weeks and had its final airing on May 22, 1933. By this time much had been written about the Marx Brothers' legendary mother, Minnie, but little was known about their father, Sam. Ironically, Groucho's affectionate memoir was published just a couple of months before Sam's death on May 11, 1933.*

He is seventy-two years old now, but his hair is still thick and black; his mustache is still trimmed in the sprightly Menjou manner, and his gay Chesterfieldian wardrobe remains the envy of all his five sons—Chico, Harpo, Gummo, Zeppo and I.

Ever since we've been children, we have regarded him as a sort of sixth brother. We've called him Frenchy—partly because he could speak only French when he first came to this country from Alsace-Lorraine, and partly because of his passion for dancing, lively neckties and good cooking.

I sat looking at my father at dinner the other night, when the entire family was gathered at my house. Frenchy was the most dapper man at the table; there was scarcely a wrinkle on his face, and his appetite was better than mine. We talked about things theatrical, and business conditions, but Frenchy was only mildly interested. He was wondering which of us boys would take him on for a game of pinochle.

"Darling," he said to Chico, "maybe after dinner we get out the pinochle deck, huh?"

Chico, now the business manager of the family, smiled; he had an important engagement. He was going to play bridge.

"But maybe," he suggested, "Groucho would like a game." "Groucho is no good at pinochle," said Frenchy rather sadly—much as Joseph Conrad might have sighed, "My son cannot write." To Frenchy, my own shortcomings at pinochle have been one of the minor disappointments of his life.

However, Chico put off his appointment for an hour, and Frenchy was elated. Chuckling as he shuffled the cards, he winked at me to indicate that he was going to give Chico the trimming of his life. I looked on, without paying any attention to the game. I was thinking of the extraordinarily picturesque life the Old Man has led.

His story, I thought, is the story of a happy pinochle-player—a philosophic fellow who has looked at life from behind a deck of cards. and when the cards were running, found life very pleasant. Depressions have come and gone—gone and returned—during his lifetime; but Frenchy has only worried when his partner was melding four aces and a hundred and fifty in spades.

Not that pinochle has been Frenchy's only career. He has been a tailor, a salesman, a manufacturer, and—what's vastly more important—a cook and housekeeper, looking after the feeding of a large flock of stage-struck sons, while his wife served (far better than anyone else could have done the job) as their manager.

During our early years in the theater, when my mother was camping in the booking-managers' offices, informing anyone who would listen that her sons had got a lot of laughs in Aurora, or that they had taken four bows in Freeport, Frenchy was at home preparing a dinner.

There was a perfect understanding between my mother and my father. When it was definitely decided that our work (when we could get it) was in the theater, a field completely foreign to Frenchy's experience, my mother became our manager. She had come of a theatrical family; her parents had been strolling magicians and musicians in Germany, and her brother Al (Al Shean, later of Gallagher and Shean) was already in vaudeville, and something of a success. So Frenchy looked after the cooking; it was his own suggestion.

And what a cook he was! His *Kügel* (plum pudding, our favorite dish) became the talk of the booking offices—and the talk wasn't only ours.

There were times when that *Kügel* got us work. For when a booking manager was only half-sold on the potentialities of the Marx Brothers, Mother would invite them over to dinner. And as he sat purring over the ambrosia that was Frenchy's pudding, Mother found her job easy. Before the dinner was over, she usually got us the assurance of a few weeks' work.

When we were living in Chicago, and playing (now and then) the five-a-day houses, Frenchy would come into our dressing-room after the final matinees, with a big basket of food. There was scarcely enough time to go out for dinner, and even if there had been enough time, there probably wasn't enough money. Anyway, no restaurant could provide roast chicken or *Kügel* like Frenchy's.

After dinner was over and it was again our turn on the stage, Frenchy would pack his basket and rush out into the audience to provide his "prop" laugh, which nearly always proved infectious. He spent most of his spare hours in our theaters, roaring at our jokes, which he knew quite as well as we did. The prop laugh was designed not only to lead the rest of the audience to laughter, but also to fool the managers, who unfortunately soon became as familiar with Frenchy's mechanical merriment as we were.

So, at Mother's suggestion, Frenchy began hiring "boosters." A group of boosters, as they were called in those days, was a paid *claque*—theatergoers brought in to applaud and laugh at their employer's entertainment.

The players had to buy the tickets for the boosters, and sometimes pay them an additional dime for their time. I can remember when our act opened at the Majestic in Chicago. It was our Opportunity, our first experience on the Big Time.

"I'll go out and get some boosters," Frenchy volunteered at the dinner table.

"Get fifty," my mother said.

This large order astonished Frenchy, but he saw the wisdom of it. Furthermore he was rather proud of his proficiency in hiring talented boosters. He hoped we had forgotten the sad afternoon when he brought in those six boosters who, mistaking an earlier act on the bill for ours, yelled and stamped their feet to express approval, and remained perfectly silent when we were performing our antics. That time our act was canceled after the opening matinee. Maybe even the boosters couldn't have saved us—but Frenchy blamed himself. Later he was more careful in instructing his professional laughers and handclappers.

So Frenchy brought in the fifty boosters, and such laughter and applause I have never heard since. And we remained on the Big Time. It was, my mother used to say, Frenchy's *Kügel* that got us the job; and his boosters that kept it for us . . .

Dinner at home—it was always something of a festival. While Frenchy was in the kitchen, getting ready the dessert, my brothers and I would be gathered around the piano, rehearsing. We would try out new jokes and sing new songs, under Mother's direction.

And Frenchy, hearing a tune that he liked, would come out of the kitchen in his apron, and perhaps carrying a large spoon that always managed to leave a few drippings of whipped cream on the carpet. He would offer a gag for the act, knowing perfectly well that it wasn't going to be accepted. But he didn't mind. Let others provide the family's comedy, so long as he could supply its *Kügel*.

If Harpo remarked, at dinner, that he had had a good luncheon at the White Front Restaurant, Frenchy was faintly resentful. He disliked hearing anyone else's food commended. It seemed like a subtle affront to his own culinary accomplishments. He would sit down at the table, and while eating a plentiful meal himself, would glance out of a corner of his eye to see how the dinner was going. True, he delighted in hearing that some one had praised our act, but he liked also to hear a nice word for his pot-roast and potato pancakes. Above all, he liked to see all the food consumed; and invariably it was.

Then followed the hurried business of clearing the table and doing the dishes, a chore in which my mother always assisted. If Frenchy raced through the job as though he were being timed by a stopwatch, it was because a Mr. Hempelmeyer, next door, was coming over for a little session of pinochle. And if Mr. Hempelmeyer or another crony couldn't come over, one of us boys would be expected to stay in for the game. Chico and Harpo were Frenchy's favorite opponents. Gummo and Zeppo were too young for the game, and I (may heaven forgive me for it!) could not get pinochle through my head.

I was too occupied with learning the current popular songs, and their parodies. Wasn't I the tenor of the act, and hadn't that booking man promised Minnie Marx that her sons would be given a route if Groucho would learn a few new parodies?

Once, in touring small time houses around Chicago, we were to play in the old Pekin Theater, on south State Street. This was a colored neighborhood house; and I, unfortunately, had forgotten to alter my principal parody, which had something to do with the approaching Johnson-Jeffries fight. In my ditty I had been vocally assuring my listeners that Mr. Jeffries would knock the tar out of Mr. Johnson, a prediction that was not altogether accurate.

Well, here we were, going into the Pekin Theater, and Jack Johnson was going to be in the opening audience. That meant a busy morning for me. I had to rewrite the parody, to predict that it would be Mr. Jeffries who would have the tar knocked out of him, and not Mr. Johnson.

I can still see Jack Johnson, a big ebony hulk of a man, sitting in the front left box, in a white silk shirt, with huge muscles bulging out of sleeves that were rolled up. Frenchy was in the audience with a half-dozen colored boosters, who laughed even before we said our jokes.

As I finished the first chorus of the pugilistic prediction, the phony applause of the boosters was completely unnecessary. The house shook like thunder, and Johnson, his face a large grin, was turning around, bowing to the audience.

But I had been careless; I had neglected to change one line of the second refrain. And as I approached this line, I grew panicky. How I had overlooked it during my morning's rewriting, I don't know. Anyway, there I was, about to utter a bit of sentiment to the effect that the heavyweight crown would remain on Jeffries's head. The rhyme made it impossible for me to transpose the names. So I stood there, silent and confused, while the orchestra went on playing.

Frenchy knew I was in trouble. He signaled to his boosters, who were sitting with him, and they started their bedlam of applause and cheering, which went through the house like a hurricane. Johnson was applauding too. There was no need for me to go on. I made a little speech; Jack Johnson made a little speech, and the act was "in," so far as the Pekin Theater was concerned . . .

It was when we were very young, and living in New York, that Frenchy was in the tailoring business. He was not a particularly distinguished craftsman, because, as I have said, his heart was in pinochle and in cooking.

Occasionally he got customers, and occasionally these customers paid him for the clothes he made—but not often. Sometimes when Frenchy went out to collect some money that was due him, the delinquent customer would give him a pinochle game instead of cash; and Frenchy would feel that the trip had not been altogether in vain.

Poor collections was not Frenchy's only problem. For, what with one thing and another, Chico (the oldest of us boys) was becoming in need of funds. And unfortunately for the tailoring business, Chico had learned that, if you took a new pair of pants to a pawnshop, a man would lend you two dollars and fifty cents.

After that, Chico made frequent trips to the pawnshop. Obviously Frenchy had to regain the pants. So Chico would be given a whipping, and the two dollars and fifty cents necessary to get the trousers out of hock. Chico didn't really care for the whippings; but he was no coward, and two dollars and fifty cents was two dollars and fifty cents in any man's pocket.

Pants-hocking became one of the major problems of Frenchy's tailoring establishment.

Later my father began to make suits with two pairs of pants—one for the customer and one for Chico to hock. That, I believe, was the origin of the two-pants suit in America.

Frenchy has always fancied himself a business man. There were times when he convinced himself, usually with unfortunate results, that he had just as much talent for commerce as he had for cards and cooking.

Once he opened what was meant to be a fashionable tailoring shop at Fifth Avenue and Fifty-first Street in New York. The shop might have been successful if a bakery hadn't been opened across the street—a bakery with fancy white ovens, where you could look through the window and watch the bakers at work. This spectacle fascinated Frenchy.

We knew that if we didn't find him in his tailoring place, he would be across the street, looking in the bakery window. We knew that, but Frenchy's customers didn't. That is, if we can assume that there *would* have been customers . . . The first crowd to come into Frenchy's shop were the men who came to take away the counters, the sewing-machines and the show-cases.

In Chicago, Frenchy was persuaded (by a gentleman who wanted to go in business with him) to open a suit-pressing shop. For four hundred dollars they could buy a machine that would press twenty suits in an hour. So the place was opened, and the proprietors spent the first hour experimenting with the machine. They pressed the same suit of clothes twenty times, and were happy to find that the apparatus was all that the salesman had said it would be.

But it so happened that the partner, like my father, had an avocation. His was crap-shooting, just as Frenchy's was pinochle. The partner used to leave in the morning with a pair of dice in his pocket; a few minutes later my father would saunter out to the cigar-store near by, where a pinochle game was always available. It was only three weeks later, when a man came to call for the pants-pressing machine, that the firm was unceremoniously dissolved.

After that came other business ventures. There was, for example, the cafeteria that Frenchy opened in New York—and closed in Dallas, two weeks later. (The rest of the family was touring the Texas towns of the Interstate Circuit, and Frenchy was becoming lonesome. So he joined us in Dallas, and from there he closed the restaurant by mail.)

In making this deal, Frenchy felt (as Bernard Shaw would, too) that he had earned one thousand dollars; because the loss was only one thousand dollars, and he had expected to lose twice that much.

As a business man his success was something less than sensational, but what of that? There is probably no one in the world who can produce *Kügel* or biscuits like Father used to make. And I know of no one—not even Chico—who can make a better score at pinochle.

Redbook
March 1933

Life Begins for Father

During the 1940s, Reader's Digest *ran a series of testimonials for the magazine by well-known public figures. When Groucho was asked to write one in 1940, he used the opportunity to write about his son Arthur. Arthur, nineteen at the time, was a highly ranked amateur tennis player and had been a member of the 1939 Junior Davis Cup Team. Groucho would be pleased a few years later by Arthur's decision to pursue a writing career of his own.*

The first time I saw my son he was wrinkled, toothless and bald. In fact he looked then about the way I look now; but anyway he was mine, or half mine, and I told him I loved him and would be a father to him.

He quickly went through the oatmeal, high-chair and three-wheel bike period, and before I knew it he was reading his own funnies, smoking chocolate cigarettes and demanding a weekly allowance. Those were great days for me and my ego. For the first time in my life I had someone to talk to. Oh, I had talked before—chattering had been my racket for years; but now I was talking to someone who was listening attentively, and even seem impressed by what I said. It was wonderful. He looked upon me as a combination of "Information Please," "Mr. Chips," and the *Encyclopaedia Britannica.*

The years flew past, and then one gray day I sensed he wasn't listening any more. I realized the jig was up. Frantic, I began looking around for ways of supplementing the sketchy education I had absorbed in 25 years in vaudeville—and then I discovered—The Reader's Digest. Inside of six months the pains had all disappeared—but so had my son. He, too, had discovered the fountain of knowledge and was up in his room with his own copy of The Reader's Digest, secretly boning up on life, liberty and the pursuit of happiness.

The complete collapse occurred one evening at the dinner table, where I customarily sounded off on the topics of the day. As I adroitly wove each new subject into the conversation, my son would nod his head sagely and say, "That's right, Dad. I read that in The Reader's Digest."

For a time it looked as though this would put a stop to our talks. But then something happened. We found how to turn talk into conversation. There are lots of evenings now when the facts and ideas given in a Digest article start real discussions—conversational marathons that run on and on, long after we've left the dinner table. The whole family joins in. We discuss this and argue that, and before we know it we have all gotten a new outlook on the world around us.

Teaching us how to pro and con The Reader's Digest is the biggest contribution my son has made to the Marx household since he first consented to wash the family car.

Reader's Digest
July 1940

Uncle Julius

During the 1940s Groucho was an occasional contributor to Irving Hoffman's Hollywood Reporter *column "Tales of Hoffman." "Uncle Julius" was written as Groucho awaited the birth of his third child, Melinda. Groucho had married for the second time on July 21, 1945, and the following January* Newsweek *reported that Groucho and his new wife Kay were expecting a baby.*

The story of the Marxes' Uncle Julius was told again in Groucho and Me *and later would be a part of Groucho's concert performances in 1972. It can be heard, in part, on the concert recording "An Evening with Groucho."*

Dear Irving,

Between strokes of good fortune I have been toying with the idea of making you my impending child's godfather. However, before doing this officially, I would like to see a notarized statement of your overall assets. I don't intend to repeat the unhappy experience that befell my parents late in the 19th century.

At that time there was an Uncle Julius in our family. He was five feet one in his socks, holes and all. He had a brown spade beard, thick glasses and a head topped off with a bald spot about the size of a buckwheat cake. My mother somehow got the notion that Uncle Julius was wealthy and she told my father, who never did quite understand my mother, that it would be a brilliant piece of strategic flattery were they to make Uncle Julius my godfather.

Well, as happens to all men, I was finally born and before I could say "Jack Robinson," I was named Julius. At the moment this historic event was taking place, Uncle Julius was in the back room of a cigar store on Third Avenue, dealing them off the bottom. When word reached him that he had been made my godfather, he dropped everything, including two aces he had up his sleeve for an emergency, and quickly rushed over to our flat.

In a speech so moist with emotion that he was blinded by his own eye glasses, he said that he was overwhelmed by this sentimental gesture on our part and hinted that my future—a rosy one—was irrevocably linked with his. At the conclusion of his speech, still unable to see through his misty lenses, he kissed my father, handed my mother a cigar and ran back to the pinochle game.

Two weeks later, he moved in, paper suitcase and all. As time went by, my mother became suspicious and one day, in discussing him with my father, she not only discovered that Uncle Julius seemed to be without funds but, what was even worse, that he owed my father thirty-four dollars.

Since he was only five feet one, my father volunteered to throw him out but my mother said, "Let's wait a little longer." She said that she had read of many cases where rich men had lived miserly lives and then had left tremendous fortunes to their heirs when they had died.

Well, he remained with us until I got married. By this time, he had the best room in the house and owed my father eighty-four dollars. Shortly after my wedding, my mother finally admitted that Uncle Julius had been a hideous mistake and ordered my father to give him the bum's rush. But Uncle Julius had grown an inch over the years while my father had shrunk proportionately and he finally convinced my mother that violence was not the solution to the problem.

Soon after this, Uncle Julius solved everything by kicking off, leaving me his sole heir. His estate when probated consisted of a nine ball that he had stolen from a pool room, a box of liver pills and a celluloid dicky.

I suppose I should be more sentimental about the whole thing but it was a severe shock to all of us and, if I can help it, it's not going to happen again.

The point of all this is that my present wife has an uncle named Percy. She admits that it isn't much of a name but she says that Uncle Percy is a power in the South—she has been told that in Nashville, for example, it's practically impossible to go anywhere without seeing her uncle and she is sure that were we to name the child after him, little Percy would be sitting pretty.

Unknown to my wife, I recently had her uncle investigated and discovered that Percy is a southern Uncle Julius. His big business consists of retailing O'Henry Bars at the Union Depot in Nashville. So, Percy is out!

Well, Irving, that's the story. If you are interested, let me hear from you as soon as possible and, remember, a financial statement as of today will expedite things considerably.

Love and kisses.

Yours,
Groucho Marx

Hollywood Reporter
March 13, 1946

Sh-h-h-h!

"Sh-h-h-h!" was published in the fall of 1941 amid rumors that Groucho would soon be the author of his own syndicated column. Actually, he was working with Norman Krasna on rewrites of "The Middle Ages," which would later be known as Time for Elizabeth. *Groucho told a* New York Times *interviewer in November that George S. Kaufman and Moss Hart had read the play and had made a lot of suggestions. At the same time Groucho was also putting the finishing touches on* Many Happy Returns, *which would be published in early 1942.*

Go West, the Marx Brothers' tenth film, had been released the year before. Even before the film's release Groucho had predicted that it would not be well received. In April of 1941, after shooting was completed on their next film, The Big Store, *the Marx Brothers formally announced their breakup. It was at this time that Groucho first considered becoming a full-time writer.*

As for "Sh-h-h-h!" the subject matter was very familiar to Groucho. He had been suffering from insomnia since the stock market crash in 1929. In his scrapbook, Groucho had scribbled some notes on the clipping of "Sh-h-h-h!" At one point he altered the sentence, "The insomniacs are a weird breed," to read, "We the insomniacs are a weird breed." These notes were probably written when Groucho was working on Groucho and Me, *since some elements of "Sh-h-h-h!" appear in that book.*

There are few subjects of conversation that will keep a mixed crowd interested for any length of time. If you touch on baseball, business or the likelihood of an increase in the price of long underwear, most of the women will yawn and slink over to the punch bowl. If the subject turns to facials, salad dressings or whether the new winter hats will be worn over the eye or over the hook in the closet, most of the men will start pitching pennies or wrestling with the host's Great Dane.

However, there is one subject that both sexes enjoy discussing: Insomnia.

Just let someone casually groan that he didn't sleep a wink last night and guests who have been dozing for hours blink back to life again; eager, bloodshot eyes begin searching the room for sympathetic listeners.

The insomniacs are a weird breed. They may quarrel about politics, movie stars and the potency of vitamin capsules, but they unanimously agree that there is nothing as deadly as those long hours between midnight and morning—and they'll eagerly spend the rest of the night proving it.

I don't claim to be the top man of this eerie clan but, as an involuntary owl of many year's sleeplessness, I have acquired a mass of information that may be helpful to those upstarts who have been plucking at the coverlets for a mere eight or ten years.

To begin with, what keeps you awake at night? Is it a leaky faucet, your income tax for 1938, or your children bounding in around 3 A.M. from a triple feature at your neighborhood theater?

If it's a leaky faucet, you might as well toss in the sponge. There is no one alive who can fix a leaky faucet. My bathroom tap has dribbled for eight years and in that time hundreds of plumbers and master mechanics have clumped their way into my bathroom to peer at its relentless drip. They all prescribe the same remedy—a new washer. So a new washer is installed—a nickel for the washer and $8.35 for the labor. It works perfectly all that day, but next night, as I am drifting into space, the familiar plop-plop of the leaking tap jerks me back to consciousness.

A certain comely matron living in the outskirts of Zanesville, Ohio, thought she had solved the leaking-spigot problem. One night, before going to bed she hammered a crab apple into the dripping nozzle. Unfortunately her nine-year-old son, Grunion, had seen her do it, and in the middle of the night, when all was still, the sly youngster sneaked into the bathroom and cribbed the crab apple. Later that same night the matron concluded that a leaky spigot was less of a disturbance than Grunion with the colic, so she threw the whole scheme out the window.

Not all insomniacs are alike. Some midnight bed-tossers are in agony if the night is noisy, while others require all sorts of gruesome sounds to keep their eyes shut until morning.

A friend of mine, a retail dealer in provender, and a poor sleeper to boot, has worked out an idea that he claims is unbeatable. Through a series of canny trades and shrewd purchases, he acquired two chronometers, three grandfather's clocks, an infernal machine and a basketful of assorted alarm clocks. These he has planted in various parts of his room—all ticking furiously. He admits that the racket is terrific but explains happily that it keeps him from hearing the radio next door.

Now, dear reader, the bed you sleep in is important. Do you use a soft bed, a hard bed or sleep on the floor like the Chinese?

Sleeping on the floor when half-crocked is a common practice, but how many of you have tried it when sober? It has many advantages—to begin with, you save the cost of a bed; then, there is nothing to fall out of unless you are near an open window. Also, the floor has no lumps, if it has been carefully swept. The danger of getting your foot caught in a mousetrap can be easily avoided by simply wearing overshoes—or by having a good-sized tomcat crouching in a corner of the bedroom. I'm sure I don't have to tell you how terrified mice are of tomcats.

Some people find a bath very helpful in inducing slumber. It's also an excellent way to get clean—but that's the chance you take. A friend of mine who, for some unaccountable reason, hasn't been able to sleep since the market crash in 1929, found out that if he sat in a hot tub for thirty minutes before retiring, he would quickly fall asleep. The trouble was that he always fell asleep in the bath and on three different occasions his family had to send for the emergency squad to fish him out of the water and roll him over a barrel.

Sleep is an elusive minx, and care must be taken not to frighten her away. If you pursue her too aggressively, she will turn tail and scamper off.

A girl friend of mine has a husband named Hal who hasn't slept since they were on their honeymoon. She has tried to help him by hypnotism, reading aloud to him out of the Congressional Record—but he is stubborn and insists on using his own methods, though they fail him night after night. Now, that doesn't mean that the remedies he uses are all worthless. Of course not. But some are downright dangerous. Particularly if used all in a bunch.

One evening, while playing *chemin de fer* with his wife, I watched Hal prepare for bed. This particular night, he tried Formation F-2: hot noodle soup, a mustard bath, three aspirins, ear muffs, and a black mask. The following morning, weary after a sleepless night, he staggered into the living room where his wife and I were still at our game. I had forgotten all about Hal and his sleep remedies and when this masked figure appeared, I thought it was a stick-up. Instantly, I whipped out a derringer and shot him.

He has not forgiven me to this day.

Have you tried snaring sleep with mental games? Have you tried outwitting insomnia by trickery? Good sleep-inducers are radio announcers and counting sheep. It is best to have the sheep in your bedroom, if possible. However, if you are allergic to wool (and most of the sweaters I buy seem to be) you can also court sleep by counting panthers. In many ways panthers are preferable to sheep—it is common knowledge that sheep bleat and frequently stumble as they walk; panthers, on the other hand, tread the floor silently and are smart enough to keep their mouths shut. Of course, there is some danger that the panthers may eat you, but if you have insomnia, that is really the best thing that can happen to you.

So far, we have discussed only the physical, the less aesthetic side of sleep. But what is your frame of mind and mental condition? What thoughts are you thinking as you prepare for nightie-night? Is your mind composed and at rest or is it shooting sparks and flying off into space?

If you are married, and your wife snores and looks like a wind-blown witch, you unquestionably have a problem confronting you. Let's say Ann Sheridan is your dream girl—this is just a hypothetical assumption as mine happens to be Priscilla Lane—but let's say you are thinking of Ann Sheridan. Now there is nothing wrong with that. Millions of American youths are doing that all the time. But before you go to bed, you must pull yourself together and say, "Man" (or whatever your name happens to be), "this is folly. I'm married to a loyal wife, a wife who has been a staunch helpmate and provider and who has stood by my side through fair weather and foul. I have no right to be thinking of Ann Sheridan or even Priscilla Lane."

If this doesn't work, the best thing to do is to take a hot foot bath and a cup of cocoa every two hours and, as soon as day breaks, hop out of bed and grab a train for Reno . . .

Let's see, there's an 8:45 train for Reno. It arrives at Stockton at 8:20 and leaves there at 8:21. This train doesn't carry a diner, but has a bowling alley and a Turkish bath. Then there's the 3:53 that arrives in Reno at 4:42 A.M.—or is it P.M.? Gee, I'm getting sleepy. I haven't felt like this for years. I can hardly keep my eyes open.

Say! Maybe I've stumbled on something that will make insomnia as old-fashioned as a flannel petticoat. Try it sometime. Just prop yourself up in bed with half a dozen time tables and—and—ho, hum—I just can't keep my eyes open. Good night, folks—pleasant dreams!

This Week
November 23, 1941

The Truth About Captain Spalding

Groucho first met songwriters Bert Kalmar and Harry Ruby during his days in vaudeville. Kalmar and Ruby were ex-vaudevillians themselves. Groucho admired their work and they went on to compose many songs for Marx Brothers shows and films. Groucho and Ruby would remain close friends until Ruby's death in 1974. Kalmar died in 1947. "Hooray for Captain Spalding" (sometimes spelled Spaulding), which they wrote for Animal Crackers, *became Groucho's theme song. In December of 1936, Random House published a collection of Kalmar and Ruby's best songs and "Hooray for Captain Spalding" was among them.* The Kalmar and Ruby Songbook *contained essays by several prominent writers including Franklin P. Adams, Robert Benchley, Moss Hart, Ben Hecht and Groucho, who contributed "The Truth About Captain Spalding."*

While still in their teens, Kalmar and Ruby were born in a firehouse in Pelham, New York. Many of the firemen were able to prove an alibi, and, with this as a starter, the boys quickly pounded out "The Merry Widow Waltz," "The Blue Danube Waltz," "Waltz Me Around Again, Willie" and "Won't You Waltz Me Home Again for Old-Time Sake." Before nightfall they were dubbed the waltz kings, but then so were many other composers of that time.

This, then, was New York right before the turn of the century. A big, sprawling, overgrown village with no Minskys, no sharp-eyed hawkers, and no flea circus. The flea circus was still an integral part of Ruby and remained that way until Nineteen Eleven, when the fleas finally reached Kalmar.

Kalmar now decided to quit lyric writing and attend public school, but after flunking three times, he licked his wounds and returned to his first love.

New York entranced the youngsters. The polyglot sounds of the streets, the roar of the elevated, and the towering skyscrapers seemed to give them the incentive they so badly needed and under forced draught they composed that Metropolitan Symphony that fused the cry of the city into one soul-racking wail, the chant of the ancient Hebrews . . . "California, Here I Come."

The compelling urge to compose now gripped Ruby, or Serge, as he was known to his intimates; so donning sack-cloth and ashes, he entered the Moscow Conservatory in 1916. Two years later, 1918, to be exact, he made his first appearance as a pianist in Vienna. The following morning, war was declared.

In the meantime, other composers had not been idle. Franz Molnar, a Viennese of foreign extraction, re-wrote "The Merry Widow" in march time, and people began calling him the March King. Krueger,* at that time, was known as the Match King. Not to be outdone, Kalmar and Ruby countered with "The Wedding of the Painted Doll" and the whole musical world was in an uproar. Shortly after this a group of racketeers commissioned them to do a series of tone poems for the dulcimer and, using the wood winds as a basis, they gradually cribbed nearly all of Schubert's "Unfinished Symphony."

They now withdrew from public life and concentrated on their scherzo, a pianoforte trio in A minor. After this, in rapid succession, came, "You're the Cream in My Coffee," "Tea for Two," "Cheek to Cheek," and Mozart's Sonata by Richard Strauss. Then, thumbing their noses at convention, they re-wrote "The Merry Widow Waltz" in waltz time. This so angered Molnar that he swore to expose them as frauds and for many months it looked as though a serious tiff could hardly be averted. Later on the three of them became the best of friends and to this day, they can be seen, arm in arm, striding down the left bank of the Champs Elysées, none of them whistling "Hurrah! for Captain Spalding."

The Kalmar and Ruby Songbook
December 1936

---

*[American-born Karl Krueger was the one-time conductor of the Vienna State Opera; he was known as the March King.]

PART THREE

Forward Marx

What This Country Needs

During the 1940s Groucho would often write about topics related to World War II while remaining, for the most part, non-political. At home, however, most discussions with his friends involved world events and politics. Groucho teased Morrie Ryskind about his incessant campaigning for Wendell Willkie in the 1940 presidential race, but he did vote for Willkie, stating that electing Franklin Roosevelt to a third term would set an unhealthy precedent. Four years later Groucho would support FDR, feeling that changing presidents with the country at war would be unwise.

Groucho first threw his hat into the political ring in 1932. The Four Marx Brothers were candidates for vice-president on the Will Rogers presidential ticket in a studio publicity stunt. "What This Country Needs" was written as the Marx Brothers were wrapping up the filming of Go West. *Groucho's letters from this period suggest that Arthur Sheekman made some contribution to "What This Country Needs." Groucho included a considerably shortened and retitled version of the article in* Memoirs of a Mangy Lover *in 1963.*

I want to say at the outset that I am not a candidate for anything. The Marx-for-Vice-President boom never had my support, nor did it ever get very far. It was launched by an obscure Californian who was politically inexperienced and, incidentally, very drunk.

The whole thing was nothing if not spontaneous. I was at an obnoxious little dinner party the other evening, talking about world affairs, when this fellow said suddenly, "Let's run Groucho Marx for Vice-President."

Naturally I was touched, but only for five dollars, and that came later. At the moment, I asked why I should be singled out for this honor; why should my friends want me to be Vice-President?

"Because," snarled my sponsor, "the Vice-President generally keeps his mouth shut. It might be an interesting experience for you."

So you can see that the boom didn't get a good start, which is just as well because, as I say, I'm not a candidate for any office.

But don't get me wrong. This isn't any false modesty. If somebody wants to start another boom, the Vice-Presidency is right up my alley, although I'll admit it might take a little time before I could manage to listen to the Senate every day.

I remember that about twenty years ago a Vice-President made himself famous merely by announcing that what the country really needed was a good five-cent cigar. Now that's more in my line. As a matter of fact, I've been making a few notes about what the country needs and, regardless of politics, here they are:

Frankly, I don't believe we need a $30-every-Thursday plan, because Thursday is such a bad day. In the first place, the maid is out; Junior has the car and—but there's no point to rehash a measure that's already in the ash can.

But the nation does need, for one thing, a good ham sandwich. I refer to the simple, old-fashioned (now obsolete) single-decker ham sandwich which was a national institution until the druggist, with his passion for mixing things, ruined it for us.

As an experiment, I went into a drugstore yesterday and ordered a ham sandwich.

"Ham with what?" the clerk asked.

"Coffee," I told him.

"I mean," he said, "do you want the ham-and-tuna combination, the ham-sardine-and-tomato, or ham-bacon-and-broccoli? And will you have coleslaw or potato salad?"

"Just ham," I pleaded. "A plain ham sandwich, without even tomato or lettuce."

The young man looked bewildered, then went over to the drug counter to consult with the pharmacist who glowered at me suspiciously until I fled.

That's the sort of thing the country is up against.

Another of our direst needs is a coat for carrying tobacco without making it necessary to carry a bulky, bulging pouch. It has been suggested that tailors make suits out of tobacco so that, if you wanted to fill your favorite pipe, you would merely have to tear off a piece of the material and plug it into the bowl.

This is unsound on the face of it, because a suit, with its lapels smoked off, would be highly impractical. Where would you wear your campaign button or elk's tooth?

My suggestion is that only the *vest* be made of tobacco, because the vest is an otherwise useless garment. It isn't ornamental and it doesn't give much warmth. I believe that a nice mild, Burley-cut vest, trimmed with Turkish, would add a great deal to the comforts of the American man.

In designing this outfit, some enterprising tailor could also supply another need: A pair of pants that would automatically hide at night so that your wife couldn't possibly know where you were caching your bank roll.

Making your pants vanish may sound a trifle visionary, but I have been making quite a bit of progress with the idea. I've already succeeded in making my shirt disappear, merely by sitting down at the bridge table with my wife. I know a fellow who bid two hearts with only three quick tricks in his hand, and his *wife* disappeared.

That, of course, solved his problem. He could then hang his pants out in the open at night. But this solution is not to be recommended generally, because I believe that wives have a definite place in the home. They're invaluable as mothers, and also for keeping you informed when the lady next door gets a new car, or a fur coat, or is taken out dancing. Wives are people who feel that they don't dance enough. Give them their way and you won't have to hide your pants at night, because there'll be nothing in them to conceal.

The country also needs the old-fashioned corset which was laced up in the back. It's simply ridiculous to say that the present-day girdle serves the same purpose, because it doesn't. Why, thirty-five years ago, the wasp waist meant something to a man. It gave him his daily exercise, tightening up his wife's laces. But now the girdle is here and we're becoming a nation of softies.

(My wife has just informed me that the old-fashioned, laced-in-the-back corset *is* here, so disregard the whole paragraph. On second thought, I feel that the American man exercises too much. He doesn't get enough peace and repose.)

We need two oxen in every garage. *There!* I've said it. Not that I don't realize it will mean a political break with the automobile industry (I need any kind of break I can get), but because I wouldn't be worthy of a Vice-Presidential boom if I didn't have the courage of my convictions, both of which were for parking forty minutes in half-hour zones.

That's the problem: parking! With oxcarts, our great-grandfathers had nothing to worry about. Although it took them an hour to drive six miles to the downtown shopping district, they could immediately pull up in front of any store they chose. And, while we can drive the same distance in ten minutes, it takes an hour to find a place to park. That gives the ox a clear ten-minute advantage over the automobile. Of course I realize that no ox is as good-looking as one of the 1940 sport models (the yellow, snappy job): also that it might be a little inconvenient trying to buy hay at a filling station. But we cannot overlook the fact that ten minutes saved every day amounts to 3,650 minutes a year, or sixty hours and fifty minutes. And that time, properly used—say on the radio by Charlie McCarthy—is worth approximately $250,000. And while $250,000 ain't hay, it would feed a lot of oxen.

Another national need is laundries that will send you a sheet of pins with every shirt, instead of making you pick the pins, one at a time, out of the collar or (if you don't see them in time) your neck. My own laundryman and I have an understanding. Every time he sticks me with a pin, I stick him with a bad check. His cries of anguish can be heard from Culver City to my bank in Beverly Hills.

We need, too, a vacuum cleaner that won't scare the daylights out of you by whining like a Boeing bomber whenever you try to snatch a brief four-hour nap in the afternoon. At considerable expense and bother I've managed to solve the problem in my own home but, as you will readily see, it is far from the ideal solution.

I've placed land mines around my bedroom door. (Neutrals, of course, have been warned.) Thus, if the cleaner zooms within twenty feet of my room, it'll be a good joke on our maid. The only disadvantage is that, after a direct hit, you have to get a new vacuum cleaner. And of course a new maid.

Another of the country's needs—a project nearest my heart—is a federal school for love-making. Under GMP (Groucho Marx Plan), girls would be taught to sigh like Garbo, smile like Myrna Loy and pout like Ginger Rogers, and men to moon and roll their eyes like Charles Boyer.

I'd been practicing the eye-rolling business at home, but under a serious handicap. My wife asked me to stop, because it was frightening the children. So I've resigned myself to remaining the Gary Cooper type (with spectacles). Although the resemblance between Gary and myself is often commented on, I believe he's a little too tall and has too much hair on his head. And yet I feel that he is even more the Gary Cooper type than I am.

In the theatrical world I feel that we need a chain of movie houses where there are no movies, so a housewife can get her free dishes and turkey without delaying dinner. It's getting so that some women, not having time enough to sit through two pictures, go to department stores for their crockery. This is hurting show business. Now I'm not suggesting that movies be done away with. They could very easily be shown in the dish stores and poultry markets.

I would like to see a call bureau established, so anybody who wants a fourth at bridge can get immediate satisfaction. I don't know why it is, but bridge players have a habit of convening in threes; and there is nothing in the world so futile and bitter as three bridge players.

They'll call you up and, although you insist you can't play, that you loathe the game and that you're in bed with a fever which the doctor says has a good chance of developing into pneumonia, they become savage and accuse you of trying to ruin their evening. They keep phoning until, out of desperation (and perhaps your mind), you put on woolen underwear and a mustard plaster and get to their table.

Then, after your first card is put down, your partner immediately winces. You've betrayed him. He had wanted you to lead a spade. He takes it for granted that you're an expert in mental telepathy who is maliciously lying down on the job. He assails your character, and intimates that to call you an idiot would be flattery. Why didn't you go up with your King, instead of your fever, doubled and redoubled? So you write out a check for $12.70 and trudge home to bed where the doctor smiles, very pleased with himself. His prediction has come true. You've got pneumonia, which means you won't have to be a fourth again for at least three weeks—or ever, if that call bureau is established.

One thing more. The country needs men's hats that can be neatly folded and put away in your pocket so you won't have to buy them back from the hat-check girl. In fifteen evenings out, I have paid $3.75 (at two bits a night) for the return of an old fedora that originally cost only $2.95, and for which no haberdasher would now give me thirty cents. Obviously that's bad business, and what we need in Washington are businessmen. See what I mean? . . .

"Folks, go to your neighborhood politician and ask for a nice, warm, mellow Groucho Marx for Vice-President."

This Week
June 16, 1940

Yes, We Have No Petrol

Like most Americans, Groucho spent much of 1942 worrying about the war in Europe. To do his part for the war effort, he joined Bob Hope, Bing Crosby, Cary Grant, James Cagney, Laurel and Hardy and many other stars in a cross-country tour to sell war bonds. The Hollywood Victory Caravan opened in Washington, D.C., on April 30 and played in fifteen cities before reaching its final stop in San Francisco on May 19. Groucho may have joked about the sacrifices made on the home front in "Yes, We Have No Petrol," but he was very careful never to appear unpatriotic and actually took matters such as rationing quite seriously.

The Marx Brothers had already announced their retirement from the screen and Groucho had appeared without his brothers as a semi-regular on Rudy Vallee's NBC radio show during the summer of 1942. In July, Groucho and Ruth were divorced after twenty-two years of marriage. Lonely and with few job offers, Groucho focused on his writing almost exclusively at this time.

Hollywood, Nov. 24

I have no desire to evade the gasoline visitation that is about to descend upon us, but don't you think the law is a little unfair to the unfortunate few who happen to own large and well-upholstered automobiles?

Back in the comparatively lush days of '37, a beady-eyed and persistent salesman cajoled me into purchasing an automobile that was considerably longer and heavier than what I originally intended buying. He told me, as he fondly stroked the fender of this shiny monster, that here was a job (they were all called jobs in those days) that would ride like a Pullman. As I wavered, he added as a final clincher, "Brother, this job has class!" And, from the look in his eye, it was quite evident that this was a commodity he didn't think I had a great deal of. At any rate, dazed by his eloquence and flattery, I soon became the owner of a luxury super-eight.

The salesman didn't lie—it did ride like a Pullman—but he didn't tell me that it was almost as heavy as one and that it sopped up gas as though its insides were lined with blotting paper. A good deal of my time was now spent at gas stations, steadily pouring fuel into this iron camel. It was quite expensive but still not particularly tragic. I had money and gas could be bought at almost every corner.

Then the blow fell—the Government decreed that non-essential workers (and no description ever fitted me more accurately) would be allotted four gallons a week—enough to propel the average motorist 60 miles in any direction. Gargantua or the Frankenstein Eight, as it was now called, laughed heartily at this estimate. He said that if I were to equip him with new spark-plugs, adjust his timing, give him a down-hill shove and a favoring wind, he might possibly eke out 28 miles on four gallons—but 60 miles! Ridiculous! Who did I think he was—Alsab?*

So here I am, stuck with an iron horse and 28 miles a week while my poor but fortunate friends, who were lucky enough to buy small cars, have practically unlimited mileage. I ask the Government not to discriminate against me. It is unfair and un-American to penalize me because I once was a member of the privileged classes.

This is not a complaint—this is a plea for justice! I willingly drink chicory for breakfast, eat broiled kidneys on meatless Tuesdays, wear cuffless trousers, have my salary frozen in the dead of winter, send my cook to Lockheed and play dead for the local air raid warden; I buy War Bonds, stamps, entertain at the Service Camps and know the second stanza of "The Star Spangled Banner." In return, all I ask is a fair measuring stick

---

*[Alsab was a champion race-horse, winner of the 1942 Preakness Stakes.]

for my ancient ark. If I can't get that, I hereby petition the authorities to revise the local zoning laws so that I can legally stable a pair of mules in my living room.

Variety
November 25, 1942

How to Build a Secret Weapon

"How to Build a Secret Weapon" was written as Groucho again made writing his second career. In the spring of 1943, Groucho returned to a starring role in radio after an extended layoff. He was the host and star of Pabst Blue Ribbon Town *on CBS from March 27, 1943, until June 17, 1944. He was replaced on the show by Danny Kaye when his contract wasn't renewed, apparently because be had insulted the sponsor. (Legend has it that Groucho got an elder member of the Pabst family drunk on a competitor's beer.)*

It has recently come to these shifty old eyes that the U.S. Army has announced the Bazooka as an official weapon in World War II. That pleases me moderately because the inventor of this lethal instrument is my friend Bob Burns.* It seems that this Bazooka shoots rockets at enemy soldiers, and if that doesn't do the trick, it plays a few choruses of the "Arkansas Traveler" for the *coup de grâce*—that's French for those who care for French.

Now, I'm not one to belittle such a great achievement. But truth compels me to announce that Bob Burns's Bazooka is already obsolete! It's as out of date as a porterhouse steak. You hear it from my own lips—I who have invented the Super-Bazooka. This amazing new weapon operates on exactly the opposite principle from the old one. Briefly, where Bob Burns's Bazooka

---

*[Radio comedian Bob Burns invented a trombone-like brass instrument that inspired the name of the World War II anti-tank weapon.]

shoots rockets at Nazis, my Super-Bazooka will shoot Nazis at Bob Burns. This doesn't have much to do with winning the war, but it seems like a good idea in general.

But then, the Super-Bazooka is merely one among countless other inventions of mine. For example, Marx's Military Dice. These cubes are equipped with cleats on each face and are especially adapted for use in rocky terrain. Pull up a bayonet and sit down and I'll tell you the whole gripping story of my rise to obscurity as a secret-weapon genius.

In 1937, by popular demand, I decided to retire from public life and seek what had always been my true goal—Contentment. "A loaf of bread, a jug of wine . . . " that's how Omar Khayyam put it. As far as I'm concerned you can switch the wine for a bottle of beer (you know what kind!). And while you're about it you can switch the bread for a fat blonde.

Ah, Contentment!

But soon the bugles of war aroused me from my lethargy. In rapid succession, I was rejected by the Army, the Navy, Marines, Wacs and Waves. I even tried to enlist in the Spars as a Sparring partner, but they said I was too feminine.

In desperation I offered myself to the Wags. However, at the induction test, I proved gun-shy and also bit a technical sergeant as he was examining my dewlaps.

For weeks I was utterly crestfallen, but one day I looked myself straight in the eye—not an easy trick with bifocals. "Am I a man or a mouse?" I demanded. (Readers are invited to send in their votes. All ballots marked Rat will be discarded unless there is cheese attached.) Anyway, I boarded a train and after three days on the road I arrived in Washington and went straight to the War Department.

"Lafayette, I am here!" I announced. They threw me out. I then buttonholed Secretary Stimson or General Marshall—I forget which one it was, but whoever it was, he told me that they were pretty well filled up at present. "Who are you anyway?" he asked.

"Who am I?" I parried. "Why, I'm America's greatest inventor. God, sir, have you never heard of Marx's Dropped Living Rooms for Fallen Arches?"

"Why, naturally!" he cried. "And the fact is, Mr. Marx, we have an opening for an inventor."

The opening proved to be a window on the twelfth floor. In less time than it takes to tell, I was dusting off my pants on the sidewalk.

Let me skip the next three months and also the next three paragraphs. Let us take up the story again as I enter my private laboratory one dark evening in March. The reason it's dark is that I neglected to pay my light bills during those three months we skipped. I am now gainfully employed as a secret-weapon designer on a piecework basis—$22.50 per dozen secret weapons—10 per cent off to wholesalers. This particular night I have been assigned to an especially difficult problem: how to fit three lieutenants and a light Howitzer into an upper berth. Howitzer like to try that?

I worked into the wee small hours, drinking Scotch and a certain brand of beer. Beads of perspiration started on my forehead and trickled down my face to my neck, forming a rather unbecoming bead necklace. I knew I was getting close but I attributed this to the Scotch. The first 15 attempts brought nothing at all. The sixteenth produced a formula by which high-octane gasoline could be manufactured from old shoelaces. I tossed it aside with an impatient frown. My seventeenth attempt was also a failure. But finally—finally on the eighteenth try, I captured the magic formula! Mad with excitement I flung up my hands. One hit the ceiling and the other landed in a wastebasket. I could scarcely believe my great good luck. Rushing out of my laboratory, I ran through the house in a frenzy of joy.

"Eureka!" I shouted. "Eureka!"

Eureka is my wife. She came tripping down the stairs in her nightdress and almost broke her fool neck. After she regained consciousness, I whispered the secret to her.

Here it is in a nutshell, the famous Marx Upper Berth Theory:

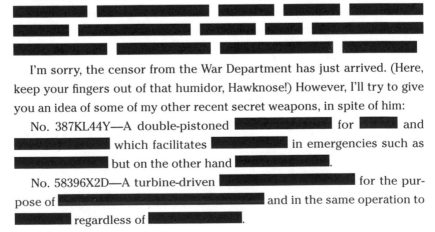

I'm sorry, the censor from the War Department has just arrived. (Here, keep your fingers out of that humidor, Hawknose!) However, I'll try to give you an idea of some of my other recent secret weapons, in spite of him:

No. 387KL44Y—A double-pistoned ████████████ for ██████ and ████████████ which facilitates ████████████ in emergencies such as ████████████ but on the other hand ████████████.

No. 58396X2D—A turbine-driven ████████████████ for the purpose of ████████████████████ and in the same operation to ████████ regardless of ████████████.

Well, what's the use of going on further? I'm sure this gives you a pretty fair idea of my work. It also gives you a pretty fair idea of the censor.

My greatest invention of all, though—my *chef d'oeuvre*—if you don't mind a little restaurant French—is as follows:

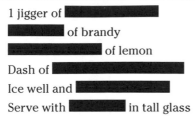

1 jigger of ████████████
████████ of brandy
████████████ of lemon
Dash of ██████████████
Ice well and ██████████
Serve with ██████ in tall glass

I call it the Marxotov Cocktail, and my plan is to lob it over into enemy trenches in individual thermos bottles. If this secret weapon affects Nazis the way it affects my friends, all our boys will have to do is march over their prostrate bodies.

I've only known one person who was strong enough to down a Marxotov Cocktail without batting an eye: it was the champion steamfitter of Los Angeles County, a Miss Diana Tiffin. It's interesting to see women emerging as the tough sex after all these centuries. It sounds incredible, but I know a man who recently married a furniture mover.

On second thought, that isn't so incredible. All women are furniture movers. A friend of mine married the most violent furniture mover I ever saw. Once I visited their home and on the third day became so confused I sat down in a potted begonia and put my feet up on the French maid.

After demonstrating the Marxotov Cocktail to a Secret Military Commission, I was deluged with honors from the government: I received the Order of the Purple Heart, the Order of Distinguished Service, and an order from the Collector of Internal Revenue to pay up my income tax or else.

Shortly after this, I received a commission to solve the vital question that is uppermost in every American's mind today, briefly: When the war is won, what shall we do with that dirty so-and-so in Berlin by the name of Adolph ████████████?

(Aw, shucks, I thought that censor had dozed off. I'm sure everyone else has. And why can't I mention ████████ anyway? Oh, well, censors are all a little queer. I'll just call ██████████████████ something else—for instance, Willard M. Schickelgruber.)

I'll tell you what we'll do with Willard M. Schickelgruber. We'll say, "Now, look here, Willard M. Schickelgruber, we're going to let you go back to your old job. For the next 50 years you're going to paper the new Pentagon Building in Washington. You can start on the first floor and paper it with paper from "Mein Kampf" and old German communiques. When those run out you can paper it with paid-off United States War Bonds. And then, Willard M. Louse, if you get through with the first floor before 50 years have elapsed, you can start the second floor!"

How's that for a peace plan? My motto is "Buy a Bond and Keep Willard M. Hitler Hanging!" (Let's see you censor that, Hawknose!)

This Week
November 7, 1943

Your Butcher Is Your Best Critic

Archibald Crossley was a well-known opinion pollster and president of Crossley Business Research Company. During the thirties and forties his name became synonymous with radio success and failure. In March 1930, Crossley began the Cooperative Analysis of Broadcasting Service, broadcasting's first ratings system. Originally referred to as the CABS, the service quickly became known as the Crossleys, in much the same way that today's television ratings are called the Nielsens.

By the summer of 1943, Groucho was starring on a network radio show and was a keen observer of the Crossleys. In the world of radio during the war years, a show (or its star, for that matter) was only as good as its latest Crossley and, of course, the latest reviews. "Your Butcher Is Your Best Critic" was written for a special radio supplement to Variety.

There are many reasons why I prefer radio to any other kind of show business. The advantages are obvious and numerous. To begin with, there is no traveling, no daily application of greasy makeup, no memorizing long strings of frequently dull dialogue, no early morning set calls and no living in bum hotels—or even good ones. In addition to this, all the sponsors are solvent.

It has, however, one disagreeable feature that can never be eliminated and, because of this, a radio comic is a fugitive and furtive character, constantly exposed to insult, humiliation and, on occasions, even danger. What I am referring to is the avalanche of gratuitous criticism that descends upon him as soon as he has completed a broadcast. This is a condition that I never encountered in the legitimate theater. True, there was criticism and it frequently was poisonous, but if the show was a hit, it was quickly forgotten. Once you got past the critics, the theater could do you no harm. The audience was composed mostly of coupon-clippers, racetrack touts and landed gentry and, unless you frequented Wall Street or Lindy's, you rarely encountered them.

Radio, on the other hand, is the poor man's theater. The price of admission is a few good tubes and a check-mailing acquaintance with the local utility company. With this meagre investment, Joe Blow (Mr. Average Man to you) automatically becomes a composite Huneker, Brooks Atkinson and Nick Kenny.*

For example—consider the butcher. We all know how difficult it is these days to buy meat. It requires money, coupons and infinite patience. Yet the steak I buy is directly affected by the butcher's reaction to my last air show. As he chips away most of the meat, leaving me a snappy piece of suet to lug home, he explains to me what's wrong with my program. This particular bloody Casanova has a yen for Virginia O'Brien and her singing, but especially for Virginia. He says, 'There's a dame with sex. Boy, would I leave my wife in a minute for her! She's got what it takes! Marx, the trouble with your show is you talk too much.' I have an answer for that but I need that meat desperately so I keep my trap shut and eventually slink out of the shop with my gristle under my arm.

The gas attendant, on the other hand, is a frustrated operatic star. His idea of an ideal program is about 20 minutes of 'Carmen' with Donald Dickson singing all the roles. If the program hasn't enough Donald Dickson, he either gives me the wrong kind of gas or absentmindedly fills my battery with steel shavings.

My barber, an ex-boy-fiddler from Long Island City, wants more of Bobby Armbruster. Waving a hot razor at my neck, he says, 'Mr. Marx, you've got a big, swell orchestra there. Why don't you use it? The Philharmonic plays an hour and a half of symphony music every Sunday and they don't use no jokes either—and they're doing all right. Why don't you get wise to yourself?'

---

*[James Gibbons Huneker was the arts critic for the *New York Sun*; Brooks Atkinson was the drama critic for the *New York Times*; Nick Kenny was the radio critic for the *New York Mirror*.]

At the broadcast, the local representative of the brewery stirs uneasily in his seat when I am up there on the stage sounding off. He is mad about commercials and smiles only when our spieler is tossing his beer pitch at the audience.

I can tell how my washerwoman likes the show by the way my woolen socks are washed. If, at the end of the day, they dangle happily on the line in their original size, she liked the program. If I see them hanging there shrunken to the size of babies' booties, she has notified me in sock language that she wasn't at all amused.

And so it goes. My critics are not Hammond, Woollcott* and Atkinson any more. My critics are now the local tradespeople and they have me in their power. If I don't click with them, they can deprive me of the necessities of life. I don't know what the solution is but if it continues, I'll either have to disguise myself as an old biddy when I do my shopping or hang a market basket on my Great Dane and send him for the groceries.

I know one thing—until I get a 20 Crossley, I'm going to steer clear of my dentist.

Variety
July 14, 1943

---

*[Percy Hammond was the drama critic for the *New York Herald-Tribune*; Alexander Woollcott was a drama critic for the *New York Times*, the *New York Herald*, the *New York Sun* and *New York World*.]

Groucho Marx Gives Kidding-on-the-Square Pitch for Hosp Shows

After making his final broadcast for Pabst, Groucho spent part of the summer of 1944 touring the nation's veterans' hospitals with Blue Ribbon Town co-star Fay McKenzie, Harry Ruby and guitarist Jose Olivera. This piece was an account of their travels.

Hollywood, Aug. 22

The first of July under the auspices of the War Department I left for the polltax section of America. These were all one-nighters and included many cities that hadn't seen me in the flesh since I was a starry-eyed juvenile.

There were four of us. Fay McKenzie, known throughout the San Fernando Valley as the Panther Woman, supplied the beauty and allure. Fay was well equipped for this junket. She was born in a theatrical trunk in Sioux City and lived in it until she was 17 years old. Then one day her folks opened the trunk to get out some clean handkerchiefs and, to their surprise, they discovered little Fay nestling there, reading "Lady Chatterley's Lover" (the unexpurgated version). She then had four years at the Pasadena Playhouse, four years at U.S.C., four years at U.C.L.A., and three years as cheerleader for the Green Bay Packers. Fay is a normal, healthy girl. She is crazy about marshmallows toasted over a Girl Scout, and sleeps in her pajamas.

Then there was Harry Ruby, the mad composer and mediocre ballplayer. Alec Woollcott, in describing Ruby, said, "He looks like a dishonest Abe Lincoln." Ruby doesn't look that good and never will, for along with his other eccentricities he has lately taken to wearing a raincoat that is a replica of the one worn by Hitler during the Brown Shirt Riots in Vienna. Despite his looks, Ruby has composed the music for many successful musical shows and his song hits are played wherever there is a dead mike.

The fourth member of this moth-eaten group was a Brazilian guitarist who answers to the name of Jose Olivera and practically anything else. I was curious about his early life and how he became such a wonderful guitarist, but whenever I questioned him he closed up and would only emit a series of South American grunts. One night, however, I plied him with reefers, and as the room thickened with smoke, he suddenly broke down and told me everything. It seems that he had spent his apprenticeship with a cluster of Latins thumping a guitar in back of Carmen Miranda and her hat, and though he liked her singing he hated fruit. Day after day, year after year, he had to watch her hat with the fruit bobbing up and down in front of him. He was slowly going mad and vowed that, at the first opportunity, he would make a break for freedom. He bided his time and one night in Montevideo, while Carmen was writhing through a particularly intricate rhumba, he slipped out the back door and fled towards the harbor. Ironically enough, he stowed away on a fruit steamer that was running bananas up the Amazon and, in less time than it takes to tell—three months to be exact—he arrived at Rio de Janeiro disguised as a fruit salad. The rest is history and can be found in any standard history.

Before I quit this nonsense, I want to say that this is not written to impress or acquaint America with our patriotism. There was nothing heroic about our tour. Where we went there was no shooting, except occasionally when they didn't like our act. But the Purple Heart Circuit means a lot to the boys in the hospitals. As the head doctor at the Lederman Hospital in San Francisco told me, "The important thing is not that you put on a show, what is important is the psychological value the entertainment has in short-circuiting the boys' mental processes. It's a distraction of inestimable value and cannot be measured in terms of just songs and jokes. When a show is advertised to appear, it is discussed for days before it arrives, and long after it is gone, they still talk about it. From a curative standpoint it contributes an element that no medicine can supply."

And that is why Marx's Moth-eaten Manikins—Fay, Harry, Joe and I—headed south for Uncle Sam.

Variety
August 23, 1944

How to Be a Spy

"How to Be a Spy" was written in the early part of 1946 as the Marx Brothers' twelfth film, A Night in Casablanca, *was about to be released. It was their first in five years. In the spring of 1945 Groucho had begun appearing as a semi-regular on Dinah Shore's NBC radio program. His final appearance was broadcast on May 16, 1946.*

The public may be surprised that I am able to write on the subject of espionage. As a matter of fact, the public may be surprised that I am able to write. But the truth is that my latest picture, "A Night in Casablanca," is so fraught with international intrigue that I have become an expert in that field. Thus, I decided I must write this vital article which every man, woman and child in the nation can afford to overlook.

Let me lead you step by step from elementary code work right up to the firing squad. In the first place, you must understand that there is more than one kind of secret agent. There is, first, the General Spy, whose activities are unlimited. Then there is the man who specializes in bargain-counter and lunch-counter cases, and he is, of course, the Counter-Spy. Finally there is the Northern Spy, which hasn't anything to do with the subject except that it's good eating if you like apples.

But I am getting away from my theme. I always say an article is like a lady's stocking—it's important to keep the theme straight. I knew we'd get around to women sooner or later. Aren't you glad?

On becoming a spy, you will have to learn to deal with feminine wiles. The temptation of a beautiful woman can be your downfall—if you're lucky. Of course, Marx, the Master Spy, is proof against blandishments of the sveltest brunettes and the most ravishing blondes on earth. On the other hand, a redhead can get anything out of me in two minutes flat.

Let me tell you about my first *femme fatale*, that suave, bejeweled agent of Hungroslavia. Her name was Mandolin, and I shall always remember that evening in her scented boudoir on the Rue de la Strapontin-Casace. My mission was to wrest from her the blueprints of the fearsome Gatling gun . . .

But I am getting ahead of my story. Let me tell you how the mission first started. Our spy outfit was stationed on a secret island off the French coast. We had all been through a terrifying period: We had run out of paper clips, and we could no longer file reports in sextuplicate. We had to have clips! One panic-stricken soul among us suggested we try a clip joint, but that would have been tantamount to dealing in the black market. I was running feverishly all over the island. I was ready to drop in my tracks, except that I don't run on tracks.

Then the General approached me. "Marx," he said, "you must go to the mainland in a small, unseaworthy craft and then proceed to Paris on a small, ungroundworthy motorcycle. Once there you must wrest the blueprints of the fearsome Gatling gun from the beauteous Mandolin. May you wrest in peace."

I set out at midnight in a dory. The waves were so high that they broke over the gunwales (pronounced gunnels). All I could find to bail with was a funwale (pronounced funnel). To make matters worse, the night was black as a tunwale (pronounced tunnel). This kind of humor is known as beating a dead horse, so let's drop it.

Suffice to say, I eventually reached Paris and burst in upon the beauteous Mandolin. "Dear lady," I said as I took her in my arms, "I am not hemmed to fit the touch of your skirt!" (This is the way spies always talk to each other—code language.)

"Mandolin," I continued, "I have come to curry favor." I ran my fingers through her hair. "Sorry I forgot my currycomb." Then I prostrated myself before her. "Mandolin," I slavered. "I swear that your beauty has crazed me. Your eyes, how they shine! They shine like the pants of a blue serge suit!"

At that moment the plans of the Gatling gun dropped from her bodice—I snatched them.

"Monster!" she shrieked "For this night's work you shall reap dismay!"

"You've got it all wrong," I said. "I shall plow dismay—I won't be reaping till dis-august."

At that point Mandolin's lover, the Count de la Défense d'Afficher rushed into the room. I had to swallow the blueprints quick, and I must say they were the worst I've ever tasted.

"*Cochon!*" cried the Count. "What are you doing in my fiancée's apartment?"

"Well, right now I'm trying to find a bicarbonate of soda."

He advanced and slapped me across the cheek with his gloves. I could not let this challenge go unheeded. I produced my card-case. "Take one, Monsieur," I snapped.

He did.

"What is it?" I said.

"Queen of spades."

"Pay me—I drew the ace."

This did not satisfy him, however, so I stalked away to my motorcycle and drove off in low dudgeon—I couldn't make high on the gasoline we were getting in those days.

This whole episode goes to prove an important point: A good spy must be able to take insults and hardships in his stride. He must keep constantly gruntled—the moment a spy becomes disgruntled he is of no use to anyone. For instance, let me tell of another important case of mine. This one happened right in New Jersey.

As I sat one night swatting mosquitoes, I received three mysterious telephone calls. The first two were wrong numbers; the third was an acquaintance of mine, J. J. Fusty, who runs a large penwiper factory in Hoboken. "Come to me quick, Inspector," he pleaded.

I rushed right over. A butler ushered me into the drawing room where Mr. and Mrs. Fusty were waiting to greet me.

"Thank heaven you are here, Inspector," said Fusty. "Sit down anywhere."

I sat down in Mrs. Fusty's lap.

"Inspector," continued Fusty, "my business is going to rack and ruin. Labor is scarce. Supply is turning my hair gray. Price is dangling a sword over my head."

"Why don't you dangle a sword over Price's head and see how *he* likes it?"

"You don't understand, Inspector. There is worse trouble—a suspicious character is writing me letters, threatening to hijack my trucks."

"That's right down my alley," I said. "Do you have an inkling as to the fellow's identity?"

"None at all, except that he poses as an Army officer."

"Hah," I said, "anyone with half an eye could clear up this case. Unfortunately, I don't happen to know anybody with half an eye, so I'll have to do the job myself."

Without further words I plunged out into the night. As luck would have it, I ran across a suspect that very evening. He was dressed in Army khaki, but my sharp eye noted that the insigne was not that of any Army outfit. I trailed him for three days, and his actions were most suspicious. Every day he would sneak out into the woods around town and meet up with a band of midgets. Then they would all go about setting fires.

I determined to bring my quarry to bay. So one evening as he trudged along the road with his midget band, I sprang from the bushes and confronted him. "I am Marx, the Master Spy," I snarled.

"Glad to meet you, Mr. Marx," he said. "I am Clarence Snood, Scoutmaster of the Beaver Troop."

Of course it was a bitter pill for me to swallow, but in a way I did not regret it—we all toasted marshmallows and became fast friends. Incidentally, J. J. Fusty's business did go to rack and ruin. It is now known as Rack & Ruin Inc., and I understand the new owners are making a go of it.

What, you may ask, is the practical use of spy work? Can it be applied to everyday life? Yes, I say. Persons with sound espionage training can overcome many social problems that would stagger ordinary householders.

Suppose, for instance, that boring Mr. and Mrs. Pratt down the street are about to call on you. If you and your wife have had spy training, you will immediately turn off all lights in the house.

While your wife prepares an eerie fire of bleached bones on the living-room hearth, you will disguise yourself as a mad butler. After quickly shaving your hair off, you will insert a dagger in your chest so that a conspicuous bloodstain will spread all over your shirt front. Then, when you welcome the Pratts at the front door, Mr. Pratt will probably laugh nervously and mumble something about not being able to stay long.

If the Pratts are difficult cases, I suggest hiding a dead Balkan minister in the coat closet (you should be able to pick one up cheap). When the Pratts are hanging up their wraps, the body will fall out at their feet. There is no need to make introductions, even though they may express some curiosity as to who he is.

The next step is to usher the Pratts into the living room where the bleached bones are crackling dismally. Your wife will have set out phials of poison on the coffee table (these should be clearly marked with skull and crossbones or you'll get into trouble with the Food and Drug Administration).

If you can get hold of a baby sitter to come over and clank some chains in the cellar, so much the better. But baby sitters are hard to get nowadays.

By all the laws of averages, the Pratts should make their adieux within 20 minutes by the clock. But if they persist in sticking around, it is considered justifiable to take them out to the garden wall and shoot them down with rifles. Fastidious hosts will, of course, remember to supply eye bandages and a last cigarette.

Well, I think that just about covers the subject of spy work. If any of you have further questions, merely drop me a letter stating your age, weight, height and sex.

I'm particularly anxious to hear from a few blondes under 30 who enjoy canoeing.

This Week
February 16, 1946

Standing Room Only

"Standing Room Only" was published during a time of professional inactivity for Groucho. Groucho and Kay's daughter Melinda had been born in August of 1946 and Groucho spent most of his time that summer at home writing, mainly working with Norman Krasna on revisions of their play, Time for Elizabeth. *In keeping with his habit of drawing material from the headlines, Groucho tackled the nation's post-war housing shortage in "Standing Room Only."*

Not so long ago, a New York news reporter discovered a woman midget living in a public phone booth. Her housekeeping equipment consisted of a Sterno stove, a folding camp chair, some baby lima beans and a "Reader's Digest." "I consider it a windfall," she stated. "Just think I not only have a home, but I have something even harder to get—a telephone!"

If Tel and Tel doesn't object to the loss of a few million nickels a year, this may be the beginning of a new way of life.

Now, I realize that there are probably more phone booths than midgets, but I think with practice taller people too can adjust themselves to such surroundings. Of course, you'd have to learn to sleep standing up, but that isn't so hard. Even horses can learn that.

There are many other possibilities for gracious living besides telephone booths.

One friend of mine has found refuge in a municipal gas tank. The family has to wear respirators, to be sure, and the man's wife won't let him smoke indoors. But at least he has a roof over his head—about 240 feet over his head, to be exact.

Another fellow keeps bachelor hall in a cement mixer. He doesn't even need an alarm clock: when the workmen start the mixer revolving in the morning, it wakes him up without fail. However, he does complain that it's hard to dress on a dead run.

Have you thought of a barn? Half the people I know were brought up in a barn, and they're making big money today.

Out in California, people have more elaborate ideas for finding homes.

They are buying streetcars and converting them into bungalows. The latter come complete with kitchenette, bathroom and a fine bell system for summoning the butler, if you have a butler. Personally, I prefer a French maid. However, my general feeling is that you'd best forget the immobile streetcar and settle down in one that is still going places. Your natural answer will be—you may not get a seat. Just as I thought—you're the kind who wants to sit down and loaf for the rest of your life. But let's not argue about it. The trick is to get to the car barns early in the morning. For a nickel—or seven cents, if you live in Cleveland—you've got a home for the day. I realize that you'll get bumped around a little, but, in exchange for that, you'll see a lot of new faces, and I might add that most of them will be an improvement over yours.

Living in a streetcar has many advantages. There is a constant change of scene; if you are too stingy to buy a paper, you can wait for a passenger to throw his on the floor. If the streetcar goes through a rich neighborhood, you may even pick up some magazines. And, who knows—if you are a woman, after a few years you may marry the motorman.

Another possible home is a cage at the zoo. I don't recommend this for married couples, since, frankly, there isn't much privacy in a cage; but for a single chap it definitely has possibilities.

The monkey house is probably your best bet. You might even be able to remain there permanently without anyone knowing the difference. In order not to look too conspicuous, I suggest you remove your clothes before entering their cage. Don't let's make a problem of it—if you are an ex-serviceman, there is a strong likelihood that you haven't got any clothes.

If you are one of those lucky persons who own a pen that writes under water, you might try living in a swimming pool. You could bathe and handle your correspondence simultaneously. You will find a pool in almost any back yard in Hollywood. These pools come complete with springboard, rubber raft for story conferences and three bathing girls who look like Jane Russell.

If you are fortunate enough to live outside California, and can't find a swimming pool, you might follow the example of a fellow I know who lives in a well. The only equipment required is a pair of hip boots and a large supply of carrots so you can read in the dark. My friend says the commutation service is fine—he leaves home by the 8 a.m. bucket and returns by the five-forty-five. He says the only drawback to living in a well is that the neighbors keep dropping in.

If you aren't a coward, you might solve your housing problem by renting a haunted house. The back streets of America's towns are lined with fine haunted houses that are empty simply because cravens are afraid to live in them. A homeless young couple won't hesitate a moment to move in on the wife's parents but if you suggest a haunted house to them (a far safer place in my opinion) they turn pale and chatter lame excuses.

However, if you are the yellow-streak type, I recommend a tree. A tree is absolutely safe unless you walk in your sleep, and from the top limbs you get a lovely view of the surrounding country. I would suggest a nut tree—preferably a walnut. Walnuts are large and chock-full of vitamins and the empty shells can later be used for ashtrays.

By this time, you will probably agree with me that the housing shortage can be solved. The trouble with us is that we have been allowing ourselves to get soft—our thinking is wrong; we still cling to the old-fashioned notion that man can only be happy in a house.

How ridiculous! In the rural sections, chicken coops are getting increasingly popular. The fancier coops are equipped with oil stoves, sun lamps and mash troughs, and the addition of a few pictures and some dotted swiss will make them even homier. In order to avert suspicion, it is a good idea to start crowing promptly at sunrise. However, if the farmer is one of those trigger-happy rustics who enjoy blazing away with a shotgun, you'll just have to use your wits and outfox him. Listen for his footsteps and if you think he is approaching the coop, drop whatever you are doing, hop on a few eggs and just sit tight until he goes away.

There are many other substitutes for homes. There are Quonset huts, drain pipes, tents, sleeping bags and even large doll's houses. I don't recommend the latter, however, since I once had an unhappy experience in a doll's house. The doll's old man chased me out with a baseball bat.

Many people are living in the balconies of movie theaters. The loges are ideal for sleeping and so are most of the pictures. In the lobby, you can purchase pop corn, Sen-Sen, chocolate bars and peanuts. In the rest rooms, you will find ice water, weighing machines and poetry.

In conclusion, I say to America: "Keep your chin up—remember, we're a nation of producers—a home is what you make it."

If I had the time, I could show you many other ways to beat the housing shortage, but I have to go now and look for a furnished room. The Great Dane whose house I rented is returning from Florida and, as I always say, no house is big enough for two families.

This Week
November 17, 1946

Many Happy Returns

"Many Happy Returns" was a preview of Groucho's second book, which was published in January of 1942 by Simon & Schuster.

March used to mean the beginning of spring; now it's the end of your bankroll.

That is when you have to answer the government's quiz program—a costly little game played by mail. You answer thirty-two questions concerning your public life—such as how much money you earn and where the hell is it? The only difference between this and other quiz programs is that you don't get paid for giving the right answer.

But, somewhat like the program called True or False, you do take the consequences for giving the wrong replies.

Having answered all the questions on the quiz, you run madly through office buildings looking for a notary public. This is a gnome with a green eyeshade and a rubber-stamp who will testify to practically anything for two bits. Although he has never seen you before, he'll swear on anything from a stack of Bibles to flapjacks that you are the man you say you are, although secretly you know you're not half the man you used to be.

You're probably saying to yourself, "Why do I have to pay an income tax? What does the government do with my money?"

This is a pretty dull routine and I'd advise you to change it if you expect to get anywhere with yourself. What do you *think* the government does with your money? Spends it on a woman? Gets drunk? Or plays the ponies? That's what *you* might do with the money, or, if you have to get personal, what *I* do;

but I can assure you that the government is not just out for a good time. It has a job to do in Europe and Asia.

Why does the government need money? Well, a steam engine will run only if you throw coal into it. Wouldn't *you* run if someone was going to throw coal into you?

Here is a picture* of the governmental train shooting down the track.

It has a fully equipped dining car with a full crew on board. The President is the engineer. Members of Congress, the cabinet, the FBI, and a lot of other swell fellows are the crew. The revenue collector is the fireman who pours your coal into the engine; the Secretary of Agriculture is the dining-room steward; the Vice-President is the Vice-President; and Wendell Willkie is the fellow who missed the train, but is going right along with it anyhow.

You will notice the smile on Mr. Willkie's face. He is in a position to throw things at the engineer, but he doesn't because this is a democracy, which is you and I and the farmer in the Iowa cornfields, and the George Washington Bridge. Mr. Willkie merely comments constructively on the track. Is it muddy? Fast? Clear?

That is why the government needs money. And I haven't begun to list the incidental expenses, such as two Thanksgiving days, which means a double order of turkey at forty-six cents a pound, not to mention the extra cranberries.

There are two methods a government can use to get money. One is by taxes; the other is printing. To print money requires very expensive paper (otherwise you can't use cheap post-office ink) and to buy expensive paper you have to have money. That, again, means taxes.

Besides, the printing of money means inflation, which I shall explain very briefly.

Suppose you take a gallon of whiskey and pour three gallons of water into it. Or perhaps it would be better to pour three gallons of whiskey into a quart of water. Any kind of water will do, but be sure to use 100-proof whisky.

Perhaps this is an even clearer explanation. Take a small glass; pour in a hooker of rye whiskey; drop in a piece of ice (unless you have your skates on), a lump of sugar, a dash of bitters, a cherry, and a slice of pineapple.

---

*Publisher's Note: What picture?

G.M.: The one I gave you.

P.N.: That one? You should be ashamed of yourself.

This isn't much of a drink, and you would have to drink an awful lot of them to get crocked, but it makes a wonderful fruit salad. And even this is better than inflation.

Now, to go a step further, I want to explain what happens to your tax dollar. Your tax dollar goes right to Washington, where, contrary to popular impression, it is not thrown across the Potomac River and caught by a dollar-a-year man who bites it to see if it is counterfeit. Nobody bites your dollar. The bite is put on you.

I have prepared a chart showing what happens to this dollar of yours. Technically it is known as a pie chart, the dollar pie chart. The fifty-cent pie is apple, peach, or coconut custard. Just as the dollar pie shows what happens to your money, the fifty-cent pie shows what happens to your stomach.

Obviously there are a few governmental expenses I had to omit—the cost of the war, for example—because the pie was so small. Even as it is, it comes to $1.08.*

You can see, though, that the government is not making a nickel on you. The government is not out to make money. If it were, would it be owing $60,000,000 to every Tom, Dick, and Harry?

I have no hesitation in saying that every government nickel is accounted for. Can you say as much for your own nickel?

Saturday Review
January 24, 1942

---

*Publisher's Note: Who's counting?
Treasury Department: We are!

PART FOUR

Jamison, Take a Letter

A Lift from Groucho Marx

When the Marx Brothers arrived on Broadway they immediately became the darlings of the New York critics. One particular critic, however, found them considerably less enjoyable than did the others. Percy Hammond had been a critic for the Chicago Tribune *during the Marxes' vaudeville days. In his 1972 concert performances Groucho fondly recalled one of Hammond's early diatribes: "The Marx Brothers and their various relatives ran around the stage for almost an hour yesterday afternoon. Why, I'll never know." Hammond's bad reviews weren't reserved just for the Marx Brothers. His reputation once resulted in the Shubert organization barring him from their shows' Chicago openings. Hammond called* The Cocoanuts *"a routine Marx Brothers show," adding that it was "not so funny as its predecessor." He didn't like the script or the music, but didn't mind Groucho's performance. Of* Animal Crackers, *Hammond wrote, "the 'book' is a lame goose and the tunes are spiritless." While virtually every other critic reported gales of laughter on opening night, Hammond wrote, "Seldom have I heard so many sure-fire musical comedy wise cracks fall as silently as they did last night." On a few occasions, Groucho wrote to Hammond at the* New York Herald-Tribune. *This playfully sarcastic letter, written shortly after the opening of* The Cocoanuts, *appeared in Hammond's column, "Oddments and Remainders."*

A Lift from Groucho Marx.

ANYTHING that Groucho Marx says is funny, I think, and so the following note is passed on to you as containing, probably, a whim or two:

Sir: Fourteen of my friends called me up yesterday to tell me that Percy Hammond had taken a slam at the Marx Brothers, and what was I going to do about it?

I immediately got dressed, ran to the newsstand and swapped my copy of "The Graphic" for a Herald Tribune, and, sure enough, at the bottom of your review of another show (name on application), I did see something about the Marx Brothers.

Now comes the problem: How can I avenge an insult unless I am sure it was an insult? If anybody but you had written it, I would have instantly written to all the department stores and ordered them to withdraw all advertising until that so and so learns to temper his pen. But, Mr. Hammond, your language is always so elegant, expensive and etiological that I am never sure when you are praising or razzing us.

Anything you can do to clear up this mystery will be greatly appreciated by one of your most ardent admirers—namely,   GROUCHO MARX.

Sir:

Fourteen of my friends called me up yesterday to tell me that Percy Hammond had taken a slam at the Marx Brothers, and what was I going to do about it?

I immediately got dressed, ran to the newsstand and swapped my copy of the "The Graphic" for a "Herald-Tribune," and, sure enough, at the bottom of your review of another show (name on application) I did see something about the Marx Brothers.*

---

*[In his review of *The Merchant of Venice*, Hammond had quoted the two biggest laugh lines in the show, adding that "both of these will probably be snapped up by the Marx brothers before the end of the week."]

Now comes the problem: How can I avenge an insult unless I am sure it was an insult? If anybody but you had written it, I would have instantly written to all the department stores and ordered them to withdraw all advertising until that so and so learns to temper his pen. But, Mr. Hammond, your language is always so elegant, expensive and etiological that I am never sure when you are praising or razzing us.

Anything you can do to clear up this mystery will be greatly appreciated by one of your most ardent admirers—namely,

Groucho Marx

New York Herald Tribune
January 6, 1926

That Marx Guy, Again

During a period of inactivity for the Marx Brothers in 1934, Groucho appeared in a summer stock production of the Ben Hecht–Charles MacArthur play Twentieth Century *in Skowhegan, Maine.* Time *magazine gave Groucho a favorable review, adding that, "this was one of the rare times when any of the four Marx Brothers has been seen onstage without the others."* Variety, *however, failed to review the show. This did not escape Groucho's notice and his letter to the editor quickly followed.*

Aug. 23, 1934
Editor, 'Variety':

There are only two things that ever make the front page in Maine papers. One is a forest fire and the other is when a New Yorker shoots a moose instead of the game warden. Last week, however, they not only had a story that made the front page, but overlapped right into the sporting section.

The story was that Groucho Marx had entered the legitimate, and sans moustache, black eyebrows, and insults to a dowager, had stepped into the Oscar Jaffe role in 'Twentieth Century,' and created a furore that hadn't been equalled since Mansfield played 'King Lear' in Portland.

When Variety arrived at the grocery store in Skowhegan, I quickly snatched it out of the grocer's hand (he was looking through the routes for the address of a fan dancer who had promised him one of her fans as soon as the season was over) and hastily thumbed it for the review. Well sir, you could have knocked me over with a copy of Harrison's Reports. There wasn't a line about it. To be sure there were many items of interest. There was a little gem that someone was optimistic and would try burlesque in Pittsburgh, there was a piece about a girl trapeze artist that had sprained her elbow in Kansas City, and a back page telling the world that Joan Blondell always uses Lux after she has removed her cosmetic. But the important fact that I was keeping the drama alive in the Maine woods wasn't even in the obit column.

I realize that you boys are busy making book, but if you want to keep the theatre breathing it might be advisable for you to occasionally get up out of those barber chairs and inject some theatrical news into that so called trade paper of yours.

Don't forget, gentlemen, Groucho Marx in the legit is an important theatrical event and certainly rates as much space as the review you gave to the opening of a cafeteria in Cedar Rapids.

In conclusion I want to say that on my opening night in 'Twentieth Century' the audience cheered for 20 minutes at the end of the first act, but for some reason or other never returned for the next two acts.

Respectfully Yours,
Groucho Marx

Variety
August 28, 1934

Groucho Marx Insists 'Variety' Plug His Book

Shortly after the publication of Many Happy Returns, *Groucho began a brief (and futile) publicity campaign for his doomed second book, of which this letter to* Variety *was a part.*

Beverly Hills
Editor, 'Variety':

If the financial position of your paper has been as precarious as that of most of the other theatrical journals of recent years, you probably have never had any traffic with the Internal Revenue Department. If, however, you are one of the fortunate few Lindy Hoppers whose weekly-envelopes have been stuffed with heavy money, you undoubtedly have had to dig down for Uncle Sam, and it seems to me that a copy of my book, 'Many Happy Returns,' should be your constant companion.

I have had considerable experience with the income tax department since they first began operating and when I say operating, I am not kidding. I am a professional delinquent of many years' standing—at the moment I am being hounded for 1933–34–35, so you can see that the tax information I dish out is right from the feed box.

The whole purpose of this letter, if you can call it that, is to persuade you to run it in your shifty sheet with a good, big heading—say, five-point Gothic, whatever that means. Briefly, I have been plugging for your throwaway for many years and it's about time you turned around and helped boot this book of mine into a best seller.

Lovingly yours,
Groucho Marx

Variety
February 4, 1942

Groucho Marx Rebuttals

Reacting to the less than favorable reviews of Many Happy Returns, *Groucho again wrote to* Variety.

Beverly Hills
Editor, 'Variety':

It seems to me I spend most of my time defending myself against attacks by trade-paper Pulitizers, journeyman hacks and fly-bitten critics. I had no idea when first I embarked on a shady literary career that there were so many posts to defend. I imagined that once having written a classic ('Many Happy Returns'; Simon & Schuster, $1) it was done with and I could then rest on my literary oars and gracefully float into the harbor of the 10 best sellers. How do you like my metaphors? Perhaps I was wrong in abandoning the theatre and vice versa. I used to do eight shows a week, no one bothered me once the opening night reviews were over and, if the show was a success, I had plenty of time and money for Lindy's, the Polo Grounds and an occasional canter in the park—and I don't mean Eddie. I used to be a big Broadway star with a fur-lined coat, three Benham suits and a full line of Sulka underwear.

If this sniping doesn't cease, I warn all these puny Hunekers I'll abandon literature and go back to the theatre. I was born in the theatre and I can die in the theatre and, if next season turns out anything like this present one, it won't be any trick at all to die in the theatre.

Groucho Marx

Variety
March 11, 1942

Dear Simon & Schuster

By the fall of 1942, Groucho had accepted the failure of Many Happy Returns, *and made light of its fate in a letter to Irving Hoffman's column. This letter provides some explanation for the seventeen-year gap between the publication of* Many Happy Returns *and Groucho's next book,* Groucho and Me.

Dear Simon & Schuster:

I received the Royalty Statement today on 'Many Happy Returns,' and whose idea was it to do a comedy book on income taxes? There I was, sitting in the Warwick Hotel, and somebody from the S & S fox-hole contacted me (repulsive expression) and, in syrupy tones, pleaded with me to dash off a comic classic that would not only stupefy the critics but sell at least 100,000 copies. As a matter of fact, I'm glad I did the book—it proved conclusively that there's no interest whatever in this country in income taxes or Groucho Marx. I think, in the future, it might be wise to confine my literary efforts to the cheaper and more gullible magazines. The pay is good, the work is dignified and I get Thursdays and Sundays to myself.

Groucho

Hollywood Reporter
September 24, 1942

Groucho Marx's Back-to-the-Soil Movement Flivs

While he was starring on Pabst Blue Ribbon Town, *Groucho found time to entertain the troops at nearby army bases and hospitals and generally supported the war effort at home. President Roosevelt's idea of the Victory Garden and growing one's own vegetables, however, was too much for citizen Groucho, who, incidentally, spent the next twenty-five years trying in vain to grow fruit trees.*

Beverly Hills, April 27
Editor, 'Variety':

When you don't hear from me, it isn't because I love 'Variety' less, but because I love radio (the squirrel cage of show business) more. Most of my working hours and a good deal of my sleeping ones are now consumed huddling in badly ventilated cubby holes with my sextette of itinerant Shakespeares. Here we sit and debate just what vintage jokes to perpetrate on the public from week to week.

The balance of my time is spent trying to coax a group of reluctant vegetables to raise their ugly heads out of the ground so that they can be eaten by your correspondent.

I have always been opposed to the Farm Bloc. In my opinion this was just another pressure group with a high-sounding name. I have always believed that the granting of higher prices to the farmers would be a long step towards uncontrolled inflation, resulting eventually in the collapse of the banks and insurance companies and a ruinous weakening of our entire financial structure.

In recent weeks, however, I have been wielding a hoe in the backyard and these few jousts with the soil have radically changed my political and economic attitude toward the farmer and his problems. I am now convinced that a farmer cannot be paid too much for his products.

Mark you, mine is merely a miniature farm—I don't scramble out of bed a little past midnight in zero weather to wheedle milk from a swishing and erratic female. I don't spend hours hosing out smelly pig sties, nor are my meadows alive with crows, red rust and boll-weevils. I have a minimum of gophers and I have more moles on my back than I have in my fields—in short, I do none of the hundred and one odd chores that the honest yeoman has to do to keep his acres flourishing and his family alive; however, the past few weeks have convinced me that farming is certainly no profession for a creaking vaudevillian.

Don't think I haven't tried; I have fertilized my crops with a variety of stimulants. I have scattered Hitler's speeches and most of Dupont's more expensive chemicals over their stunted growths, but so far all I have to show for my trouble is a small bed of wild marijuana, a sprig of mint and a dislocation of the trunk muscles that has an excellent chance of developing into a full-blown rupture.

My neighbors, a friendly group of burghers who idolize me because of my mongrel dog that keeps them awake most of the night, barking at the moon and stray birds, have dubbed my land "Marx's Dust Bowl," and I only hope that Uncle Sam isn't relying too heavily on my Victory Crop to sustain the nation through the coming winter.

The late afternoons are when I am at my saddest. It is then that I peer over my fences and discover that I am surrounded by a group of horticulturists who, apparently, majored with Burbank.* They haul cabbages out of the ground that, for size, would even have won the approval of Paul Bunyan. The rest of their vegetables match the cabbages. Then I turn back and look at my mangy half acre—a half acre that has all the fertility of a railroad yard in the coal mining regions—and black despair grips me.

I am beginning to realize that I have no talent for squeezing nourishment out of the good earth. The weary ploughman stuff is obviously not for me. It's

---

*[Luther Burbank, pioneering botanist and agricultural scientist.]

probably because I was born in New York City, in the shadow of a brewery, just a dill pickle's throw from a delicatessen. The rumble of the subway is more familiar to me than the sound of thunder on the prairie.

Well, my conscience is clear. I've tried. The Victory Garden was a sincere, patriotic attempt to contribute my mite to the war effort but, as they say in tennis, every man to his own racket.

Fortunately, I can get along without vegetables. My theory is, when you have eaten one vegetable you have eaten them all and, frankly, the smell of a corned-beef sandwich on rye bread excites me much more than the fanciest bowl of succotash.

So, you real farmers of America, get in there and pitch. Just don't rely on me. I'm not the type. I'm not sturdy enough for the meadows. I'm just an old dead-end kid. My beat is the hot pavements. Tonight I am having my back untaped and then, farewell soil, I am turning my ploughshare into a sword and my sword into a can opener!

Groucho Marx

Variety
May 5, 1943

Groucho's New Idea

While never needing an excuse to write to his favorite show-business journal, Groucho found one when his comments about radio were inaccurately reported in Variety.

Hollywood, Nov. 1
Editor, 'Variety':

I received the Broadway column (columnist shall be nameless, for his sake) and it's about as inaccurate as most columnar reporting. He said that my comments were the 'talk of the town.' This is far from true. I queried the butcher, the bootblack and three movie producers—none of them had heard the radio discussion and, on further investigation, three of them had never heard of me. So I guess I'm pretty safe here for awhile.

The radio racket seems to be progressing in the proper Crossley direction and, who knows, maybe some day I'll be as well known as 'Breakfast at Sardi's.' I have been toying with the idea of putting on a similar type program. The background would be a kosher restaurant and it would be called 'Goulash at Groucho's.' Please let me know how this idea strikes you and where.

Groucho Marx

Variety
November 10, 1943

Letterature

With the breakup of the Marx Brothers still relatively recent news in the fall of 1942, several show business writers assumed that the Marxes had fallen on hard times. Some speculated (correctly, it would turn out—at least for Chico) that their financial misfortune would force them to work together again. Groucho used Irving Hoffman's column to dispel rumors of his financial ruin.

Dear Irving:

It was extremely interesting to read the capsule life of the Marx Brothers as reported by one of the coast columnists. It was not only interesting, it was pretty inaccurate. My dear fellow, where did that pillar-penner gather the information that Harpo, Chico and Groucho were virtually paupers and just a stone's throw from the County Poor Farm?

Why, Irving, we are all immensely wealthy men. I, for example, wear silk underwear, eat T-bone steaks three times a day and brush my teeth with imported gin. Why, it costs me fourteen dollars a month just to feed my Great Dane. Yesterday in a fit of sheer extravagance, I casually flung thirty dollars' worth of fertilizer on my fruit trees. Last year when I was in New York, I saw the World Series from a field box, ate frankfurters all through the game, and, in the evening, dined at 21. This takes real money—no indigent could possibly live in this manner.

I have eight suits of clothes, all with two pairs of pants; my shoes all have Adler built-in heels. I have my own stable of horses and when not too tired, frequently run with the hounds. I have five good tires, a yacht, six lumps of sugar, three gold teeth and a two-year subscription to *Fortune* magazine. Last year my income tax was so big that the government couldn't absorb it and I had to pay it in quarterly installments.

So I wish that colyumner would stop telling people that I am a penniless bum. I wish he'd tell them, if he must, that I have no talent, that I am a wife-beater, or was, tell them that I am a secret agent for the Gestapo—but not that I have no money. This sort of publicity can't possibly do me any good, and if the local finance companies get wind of it, there's a strong likelihood that they'll stop lending me money on my furniture.

Groucho Marx

Hollywood Reporter
October 29, 1942

And That's Why Groucho Is Not Going Into Vaude

During times when the Marx Brothers weren't working together, there were often rumors of either their regrouping or of single acts being worked up by any or all of them. Groucho wrote such funny letters denying these stories it is tempting to conclude that they were planted just to provoke his rebuttal.

Beverly Hills, Aug. 25
Editor, 'Variety':

Some fly-by-night press agent, obviously desperately in need of an item, sent out a story announcing that I was shortly to appear in a Paul Small vaudeville show.* This story, like most stories that emanate from press agents, is completely without foundation and I would appreciate your printing this denial.

There are many reasons why I don't intend to appear in vaudeville again. To begin with, the black greasepaint that I once used to convert my upper lip into a mustache is all gone. When shoeshines rocketed to 20¢, the black greasepaint came in very handy. The wardrobe trunk that once carried my frock coat and penciled trousers over the Orpheum and Pantages circuits now lies open and rusted in my backyard. My dog, the Errol Flynn of Airedales, is at present using it as a love nest. In addition to the loss of these

---

*[Chico had appeared in the Paul Small production *Curtain Time* with Connee Boswell in 1943.]

semi-essentials, there is the small matter of an act. I just can't walk out on the stage and say, "A funny thing happened to me on my way to the theatre." The audience, having been soaked three bucks a ticket, might be curious and want to know what it was.

The announcement of my reappearance in vaudeville has already aroused a tremendous amount of interest throughout the civilized world and an avalanche of mail is pouring in from all quarters of the globe. This morning, for example, I received 33 threatening letters, an automatic shotgun and a Japanese hara-kari sword. So, for the sake of the postal department and for my own health, please announce that the report of my reappearance in vaudeville is greatly exaggerated.

Groucho Marx

Variety
August 30, 1944

Groucho Clears It Up

In its March 4, 1946, issue, Time *magazine reported that MGM producer Sam Marx was "no relation to Karl, Groucho, Harpo, Chico [or] Zeppo." The April 1 issue contained letters from both Gummo and Groucho's son Arthur confirming that Sam was indeed a second cousin of the Marx Brothers. As usual, Groucho got the last word.*

Sirs:

I see where numerous relatives of mine have written TIME, frantically yelping that they are cousins of Sam Marx of M-G-M. The Marx fortunes have certainly sunk to a low ebb when members of the family find it necessary to rush into print to claim relationship to anyone.

I don't know about the rest of them, but I was born during a volcanic eruption in one of the banana countries in Central America. I don't remember which one—I don't even remember the bananas; I hardly remember the stalk.

At the age of three, an utter stranger apprenticed me to a basket weaver in Guatemala. I soon learned to weave with such dexterousness that, by the time my second teeth arrived, I was known throughout the village as the basket child of Guatemala.

After I was run out of Guatemala, I met two other fellows, named, I believe, Harpo and Chico. After considerable bickering, they convinced me that America, softened up by an excess of rationing, could be persuaded to swallow another dose of Casablanca—this one to be called *A Night in Casablanca.*

Well, we made the picture and that's that. The point is that Harpo and Chico are brothers but they are both strangers to me. And, as for Sam Marx of M-G-M who reluctantly confesses to being their cousin—well, he's slightly mistaken. The fact of the matter is he happens to be their joint child by a former marriage.

Groucho Marx
Beverly Hills, Calif.

Time
May 13, 1946

And That's Why I Won't Imitate the Four Hawaiians

As Groucho was preparing to film Copacabana, *his first film without his brothers, he again had occasion to straighten out the editors of* Variety, *this time concerning a report about the Marx Brothers.*

Hollywood
Editor, 'Variety':

Am I to assume that all the items in VARIETY are as inaccurate as the ones that I know something about? For example, this week you state that the Marx Bros. can get $20,000 a week working as a unit, that this is much more than they are earning at present, and why don't they work together again? Apparently you are under the impression that the only thing that matters in this world is money. This is quite true and since we are all enormously wealthy we enjoy the luxury of not having to look at each other.

You say that Harpo is going to Detroit to play there. If you were as familiar with the automobile situation as you are unfamiliar with the Marx Bros., you would know that Harpo's reason for going to Detroit is not to garner a few paltry dollars, but to buy a Ford vegetable truck which he plans to present to his wife for Christmas.

Chico was in Boston because he is crazy about Harvard and baked beans. Besides, he had a lot of money bet on the Red Sox and he wanted to be sure that Ted Williams would hit to left field in the World Series.

As for me, I have no desire to ever again see the middle west, except from an airplane that is on its way to New York, or vice versa. Plus this, I am doing a picture called "Copacabana" in which I make love to Carmen Miranda and perhaps even Andy Russell. They have quite a cast lined up. Earl Wilson, the biggest front man in America; Louis Sobel, the syndicated midget; and a shabby character from VARIETY, who at times masquerades as an editor. The picture opens with a character called Monte Proser making a play for Gloria Jean. In the third reel Gloria's mother enters and Monte, having memorized the Mann Act, switches from Gloria to her mother. In the fifth reel Glenn Billingsley has Monte arrested for stealing his doorman's whiskey flask—and, in the sixth reel (if we ever get that far), Monte has Billingsley arrested for harboring Winchell in the ladies' locker. The whole thing closes with a big girly number in which I get Miranda, Monte gets Proser, Andy Russell gets his contract cancelled, and Gloria Jean elopes with a picket who has been casing the joint under the impression that it was the White House.

Groucho Marx

Variety
October 30, 1946

A "RIOT" ON THE PANTAGE'S CIRCUIT

(Special to THE SHOW WORLD.) Spokane, Wash., Aug. 6.—The Three Marx Brothers & Co., in "Fun in a Schoolroom," made the biggest hit at Pantages' last week that has been registered in that house in more than a year. The applause was wonderful and the act from first to last caught on tremendously. "The General," manager of the act, is more than pleased and the Marx Brothers are coming in for wide praise from the critics.

From the vaudeville trade publication *Show World*, Gummo, Groucho and Harpo during their first tour of the Pantages circuit in August 1911. *Collection of Bill Marx*

Gus Sun—real name Auguste Klotz—ran one of the numerous small-time vaudeville circuits that offered the Marx Brothers employment in their early days. When the Four Nightingales first played the circuit in 1909, it consisted of fewer than a dozen theaters in Ohio, upstate New York and western Pennsylvania. *Collection of Robert S. Bader*

Julius Schickler—also known as "Uncle Julius"—surrounded by his nephews Gummo, Groucho and Harpo, during the period when they were touring the country in "Fun in Hi Skule." *Collection of Bill Marx*

Jack Johnson, the heavyweight champion of the world, around the time he caught the act of the Six Mascots at Chicago's Pekin Theater in March 1910. *Library of Congress*

In "Press Agents I Have Known" Groucho wrote, "I'm still looking for a press agent who will get me some publicity without making me roller-skate down Broadway." But he neglected to mention the real-life incident in which the Four Marx Brothers did precisely that to promote their hit Broadway show *I'll Say She Is* in October 1924. *Collection of Paul Wesolowski*

Harpo has the last word on the often-tackled subject, "Why Harpo Doesn't Talk." *Collection of Matt Hickey*

Groucho, Ruth and their nine-year-old son Arthur sail for England on December 29, 1930—nine days after the publication of "My Poor Wife." *Collection of Miriam Marx Allen*

Our Father and Us: Ruth, Frenchy, Chico's daughter Maxine, Harpo, Groucho and Arthur in 1924 at Minnie and Frenchy's home in the Richmond Hill section of Queens. The family purchased the home when they moved back to New York in the summer of 1920 after being based in Chicago for a decade. *Collection of Maxine Marx*

Chico, Groucho and Harpo engage in a favorite vaudeville pastime at Groucho's house in 1938. *Photo by Ernest A. Bachrach*

Harpo, Groucho and Chico ride down Hollywood Boulevard in the Santa Claus Lane Parade, December 17, 1940. Four months later they announced their breakup and Groucho turned his attention to radio and writing. *Collection of Maxine Marx*

Forward Marx: Veronica Lake, Groucho and his *Blue Ribbon Town* co-star Fay McKenzie entertain the troops at Camp Haan in Riverside, California, on September 11, 1943. *Collection of Miriam Marx Allen*

A rare color photograph shot for the June 16, 1940, issue of *This Week*, where it appeared with "What This Country Needs." *Whitney Communications Company*

Another rare color shot for *This Week*, this one for the February 17, 1946, edition and "How to Be a Spy." *Whitney Communications Company*

This late-forties publicity photo captures Groucho in between movie stardom and the career resurgence that came with *You Bet Your Life*. He occasionally used it as an author photo, and it was featured on the *Reader's Digest Condensed Books* jacket along with "How to Entertain a Guest." *Collection of Robert S. Bader*

Groucho Marx

October 23, 1956

Dear Max:

      Sorry I didn't see more of you in New York. We were both ill, and I must say that the outcome of the World Series didn't help any.

      I'm enclosing a speech I was obliged to make for a friend of mine who has made some money for me over the years. Thought you might enjoy reading it.

              Regards,

              Groucho

Mr. Max Gordon
55 West 42nd Street
New York 36, N.Y.

GM:db
encl.

The letter Groucho sent to theatrical producer Max Gordon, along with a copy of his manuscript of "The Odyssey of the Goats." The comment about the World Series refers to baseball fan Groucho's long-time disdain for the New York Yankees, who had just defeated the Brooklyn Dodgers in the fall classic. *Collection of Robert S. Bader*

Left: A publicity photo for the final broadcast of *You Bet Your Life* in 1961. *Collection of Paul Wesolowski*

Right: The *Minnie's Boys* playbill from March 1970—signed by the less-than-enthusiastic production consultant. *Collection of Robert S. Bader*

This photo of Groucho at age eighty-three appeared alongside "Whenever I Think of Scotch, I Recall the Immortal Words of My Brother Harpo." *Courtesy of Hiram Walker & Sons, Inc.*

An Apology

The first full-length biography of the Marx Brothers was published in June of 1950. The Marx Brothers by Kyle Crichton was reviewed in the July 1, 1950, issue of the Nation. *The August 19 issue contained a letter from a Mr. E. O. Joynes of New Llano, Louisiana. Mr. Joynes complained that the town of Nacogdoches was in Texas, not Louisiana, as was stated in the review. Once again it took a letter from Groucho to set the record straight.*

Dear Sirs:

In answer to Mr. Joynes's complaint in your issue of August 19 [that Nacogdoches—which Groucho Marx once said was "full of roaches"—is in Texas, not Louisiana], it was Kyle Crichton's error, not mine. I clearly told him Nacogdoches, Texas. Or perhaps not too clearly, for at the moment I was gnawing away at cut plug, and it's difficult to be a silver-tongued orator with a mouth full of Mail Pouch.

At any rate, I want to apologize to everyone in Louisiana for pushing Nacogdoches over into their state. I assure you it will never happen again,

unless Crichton writes another book about the Marx Brothers and I happen to have a mouth full of chewing tobacco.

Groucho Marx
Los Angeles, August 24

Nation
September 9, 1950

My 2¢ Worth

It must have seemed to Groucho that he would spend his old age writing letters to various newspapers and magazines correcting erroneous Marx Brothers reports. This letter was a response to columnist Al Capp, well known as the creator of the L'il Abner comic strip, who had written that the Marx Brothers lost their audience and had to bow out of pictures when they changed their style of humor from "anarchistic" to "semi-lovable."

To The Mirror:

Herewith a copy of a letter I have written your columnist, Al Capp:

"If I were not an ardent admirer of your works I wouldn't go to all this trouble to explain a few things about the facts of life to you.

"I am in complete accord with what you wrote about Mr. Nixon's lack of lovability contributing to his defeat. However, when you write about the Marx Brothers, like most other columnists, you don't know what the hell you are talking about.

"The reason we switched from being anarchistic in our humor, to being semi-lovable, was simply a matter of money. In our early pictures we were, as you said, hilariously funny fellows, knocking over the social mores and customs of our times, but with each succeeding picture the receipts slipped just a bit.

"Our last anarchistic (to use your description) picture was 'Duck Soup.' We then signed with Irving Thalberg, who said, 'Of course, I want you fellows to continue to be funny, but if somewhere in the story you occasionally help someone, the audiences will like you better and your pictures will be financially more successful.' 'Duck Soup' grossed $1,250,000 while 'A Night at The Opera,' our first picture for Thalberg (made under the sign of lovability), grossed close to $5,000,000.

"In conclusion, our audience didn't drop us. We dropped them. The pictures just became physically too tough to do and we decided to retire to greener and more comfortable pastures."

Groucho Marx

NBC Studios
Sunset and Vine,
Hollywood.

Los Angeles Mirror
February 15, 1961

PART FIVE

Marx Remarks

My Life in Art

Around the time that the Marx Brothers brought I'll Say She Is *to Broadway, Constantin Stanislavski, the great Russian actor, published his autobiography. The book was called* My Life in Art. *Shortly after the opening of* The Cocoanuts, *the* New York World *asked several prominent New Yorkers associated with the theater to write an essay about their own lives in art. Groucho's essay appeared alongside contributions from George S. Kaufman, Marc Connelly, Dorothy Parker and several other members of New York's literary and theatrical elite.*

I was sitting in my dressing room making a very funny joke about Lord Craven being an appropriate name for a coward, and that if I had my choice I would rather be on Ellis Island than Coney Island. I had just gone to the mirror to rehearse the expression so that it would look good and extemporaneous for the evening performance when a window was thrown open, a piece of paper fell through to the floor and a hush stole over the room.

The note said "Will you please write a 200-word essay explaining your views on the American stage in connection with yourself, and whether you think the auto will ever take the place of the horse for saddle riding? Be sure you don't write over 200 words, and don't write less, as the space allotted would look awfully silly with only thirty or forty words in it, and if you wrote over 200 words they wouldn't be able to use any of it."

You ask me what are my views on the American stage in connection with my own work. Up till now I have been so busy dodging book agents, real estate men, stage-struck girls, solicitors for benefits, benefits for solicitors, street cars, taxis, candies, pop corn and chewing gum that I haven't had time to give it any thought, and now that I think of it there is so much to be said on both sides, particularly mine, that I don't believe it would be said in less than 300 pages.

New York World
March 7, 1926

What Is Wrong with the Theater

As both a writer and a performer, Groucho could count 1929 as one of the busiest years of his life. While Animal Crackers *continued to fill the Forty-fourth Street Theater every night, the Marx Brothers were making their first film. Groucho was also having his writing published in magazines and newspapers at an increasing rate. Broadway stars who could write were rare and Groucho was often asked to share his thoughts and opinions in print. "What Is Wrong with the Theater" was Groucho's take on what was a very hot topic at the time.*

I am all agog at having been asked, or rather implored, by the editor of The Telegraph to write an article on conditions in the theater. I am excited because I have been for years a consistent reader of the *Telegraph*, especially when my travels led me to such world capitals as Tijuana, Havre de Grace and Churchill Downs.

But let that go. I have been asked to throw some light on a moot subject—"What Is Wrong with the Theater?" This subject may be hard for some writers but it is moot for me. Let that go, too.

There are many things wrong with the theater—there is a draught backstage, the stage creaks and it takes me five minutes to walk from my dressing room to the prima donna's. I'm speaking of course of the Forty-fourth Street Theater, where "Animal Crackers" is, to put it mildly, panicking them.

Some people think traffic conditions hurt theater conditions. This is wrong. The only traffic regulation that could hurt business would be one decreeing that autos move sidewise on Forty-fourth street. I spoke to

Whalen* only the other day, suggesting he divert traffic so that it would have to pass through the lobby of our theater. I am sure this would help conditions in the theater, but he couldn't see it that way.

Another good feature of our theater is the fact that even if the roof leaks we wouldn't get wet. We have protection above us in the form of the Bayes Theater, which is the highest theater in town—in altitude not prices. It helps us a lot because we get their overflow. Their overflow to date consisted of a boy and his sister who went to the Bayes Theater thinking "The Red Robe" was playing there. When they found their mistake they passed through our lobby and were promptly collared and brought to me, the tears streaming down their cheeks. I happened to be the local agent for the Travelers' Aid Society, the head of the Missing Persons' Bureau and the local secretary for the Uplift of Fallen Women.

I immediately took them under my wing because I was sorry for the little tots. I have children of my own; my heart bled for the youngsters. I would hate to have my little lambs running around the dark streets these parlous times looking for "The Red Robe."

They needed someone to look after them—and I didn't turn them away. Still babbling about wanting to see "The Red Robe," they turned over $17.60 to me and saw "Animal Crackers" from G24, 26 in the balcony and liked it. Well, maybe they didn't, but at least they saw some good clean fun. Nothing to corrupt their morals like cardinals and duels and plots and God knows what else such as feature all these sexy shows on the French Revolution.

Some of the main things that are wrong with the theater are the abolitionists, the carpetbaggers, the Louisiana Purchase, the clipper ships, the Boston Tea Party, the Stamp Act, the Continental Congress and Ol' Man River.

Any one deploring present conditions in the theater can do his bit toward helping a worthy cause by enrolling in the Theater Relief Association. Send all checks to the executive secretary, headquarters, Theater Relief Association, Forty-fourth Street Theater. The secretary's name?

G. Marx, Esq.

New York Morning Telegraph
February 17, 1929

---

*[Grover Whalen was New York City's police commissioner from 1928 to 1930. Prior to that he had supervised the city's transit systems as commissioner of Plant and Structures.]

This Theatrical Business

With the advent of talking pictures, a common thought in the late twenties was that the legitimate theater was doomed. Newspapers ran many articles and editorials detailing how the theater could be saved. Groucho tackled this subject on several occasions. "This Theatrical Business" ran just a few weeks before "What Is Wrong with the Theater." Having two pieces so similar in subject published in such a short span of time was possible only because New York boasted as many as a dozen daily newspapers during the twenties.

Some people may well ask "What's wrong with the theatre?" I myself prefer to ask "Wass ist los mit der Untergrabengesellschaftinstspielhaus?"—but that's a matter of taste. The Mayo Brothers say it's virulent contraction of the sartorius muscle coming to a head at the box office. The Smith Brothers say it's too much menthol in the matzoth, and the Brown Brothers—five, count 'em—say it's the bad crop of saxophone reeds this year. But the Marx Brothers of "Animal Crackers"—well, gather round, children, and gather in the lowdown. That's more than most theatre treasurers have been gathering in lately, anyway—except maybe in the way of wool and such.

It's the prices. Walk up to a box office and get insulted by a smooth guy who only wants six-sixty apiece for seats in W. Go to an agency and watch 'em smile sheepishly while they ask you four times box office for a piece of cardboard one inch by four. That's only $3 a square inch. Why, even a fill-in show that's probably funnier than anything on Broadway since the Cherry

Sisters lowers itself by letting you in for three bucks—unless you want to walk downstairs and save the difference. Nobody's going to buy seats at low prices.

Managers have got to learn as much. The public pays so much for everything nowadays that it gets all puzzled and scared when it figures that good shows are only up 100 percent since the war. That's psychology—or maybe it's Pelmanism.

Class is what the theater needs these days. Five-fifty a whack for something good? You have to pay as much as that for a pair of gloves. Look at the ermine coats going in a lobby door at 8:45 and try to think of a shrinking little five-spot with a four-bit piece beside it—if you can. Fifty-five would be more like it—and think of the strain it would take off the income tax. Use that for a slogan, "Be a sucker at the box office and give your government a merry Christmas!" Don't worry about the people who still remember what a dollar bill looks like. Let 'em go to the movies. They will, anyway.

Punishment is what the people want. This is no time for compromise—everybody's talking about it—there must be something wrong with the theater. Managers of the right sort will now add another zero to the house-scale, stop worrying and go to Florida.

Well, if you don't want to play that way, how about the way the dramatic authors are falling down on the job? Sure—that's it—the Shakespeare Society's last census showed that there were fourteen reporters on metropolitan dailies who'd never written a play and never intended to. Three of them were on ship news and the rest were legmen. A thing like that hasn't happened since the last can of milk was delivered at the Astor for Anna Held* to bathe in. There are four playbrokers' offices on Broadway where the reading staff can finally see daylight through the windows. One of the them broke out in a fever the other day when she discovered they'd dug down to the level of 1882 and found the first manuscript of "Ghosts" under three inches of dust, five plays by members of Augustin Daly's stock company and a pair of rubbers.

The theater never can be itself again until more plays are written especially by the actors, who are practically forgetting their duties to civilization. Start a "buy-a-play-a-week" campaign and sell the idea to the producers. The Dramatists Guild needs the money.

Well, all right—if it is talking pictures, it is—get your finger out of my eye! The acoustics of the theaters are all off. Install a good, lively, hollow echo

---

*[Anna Held, wife of Florenz Ziegfeld, reputedly bathed daily in gallons of milk.]

in every theater so that the gangster chief will still be talking long after he's stopped. Have somebody double for the whole cast in the wings with his head down a rain-barrel and feed the cast salt-water taffy (Atlantic City—Ad) so they can't possibly let out a yip. Let the audience stay home and listen to the performance on a bad phone connection. That would save money on ushers, carpets, doormen, and the light fiction that goes into programs—now don't tell me that isn't a good idea.

Who's talking through his hat! I'm just talking the way other people do— prices, over-production, talking pictures. Now, if you asked me politely, I'd say it was over-production—but that's too simple.

New York Times
January 27, 1929

One of the Marks to Shoot At

"One of the Marks to Shoot At" was written at a critical time in the Marx Brothers' career. Duck Soup *had been released in November of 1933 to a largely indifferent critical and public response. Edwin Schallert, writing in the* Los Angeles Times *on January 1, said, "Every indication points to the Marx Brothers being through with the movies for the time being." Groucho had announced that the brothers were finished with Paramount and the movies. There were rumors, even an announcement that Sam Harris and Max Gordon would produce a revival of the Pulitzer Prize–winning musical* Of Thee I Sing, *which would bring the Marx Brothers back to Broadway. Nothing came of it. In March of 1934, Groucho and Chico tried radio again, this time on CBS with a show called* The Marx of Time. *It ran for only eight weeks. On March 30, after much speculation, Groucho finally made public Zeppo's letter of resignation from the act. For Groucho and his brothers, 1934 was a year of uncertainty and unemployment.*

The Drama Editor of The Times, who has not panned one of our shows since we last played on Broadway, called me up this morning and asked me if I would write a few words for his paper. At first I refused, and then realizing what this would mean to THE TIMES in the way of canceled subscriptions, I asked him how much was in it. After he told me I hung up and decided to move to a cheaper hotel. He then called back and told me they would raise this $5, so here I am at the typewriter, carving out history.

I asked him if there was any particular subject he would like me to touch upon. I was hoping he would say spiritualism, but strangely enough he never even mentioned it. This left me in a funk. Spiritualism would have been right up my alley. I have a departed grandfather who could tip a table (never the waiter) with the best of them, and he had been after me for a long time to let him be my ghost writer. Well, we wise-cracked back and forth, with me (you may be sure) having all the best of it, and finally he told me that a thousand funny words on Hollywood would suit him fine. I told him that a hundred funny words on any subject would satisfy me and he hung up a beaten man.

Today, while the whole world is suffering from an economic depression, unprecedented in its severity, while Cabinets and Ministers are tottering and troops are goose-stepping up and down Saar Basin and probably getting their feet soaked, the news flashes out of Hollywood that another couple are getting a divorce, another fine old cinema marriage has foundered off the matrimonial rocks and the tabloids again are oiling up their presses for the grimy details.

This particular divorce fills me with a feeling of ineffable sadness. It seems only yesterday that they were married. As a matter of fact, it wasn't much longer than that, it was only last year. Ah, they looked so happy marching down the aisle, throwing rice and innuendos at each other. I turned to the best man, who had been married to the bride a year previous and was absent-mindedly making a play for her all over again. I turned to him and said, "Here is a marriage that will last; this will be none of your Hollywood brief moments, but a real union of two people filled with stern resolves to let neither snow nor rain nor wind—no, that's not right, that's got something to do with the post office; just what, I can't recall—but it certainly has nothing to do with marriage and this fine young couple's determination to live as one."

And now, a year later, they are getting a divorce, and I, as a loyal Californian, attribute it solely to the climate. In the East there is only one spring, just as there is only one Babe Ruth. This spring runs for about twelve weeks and then goes on the road until the following year. In California, however, it is always spring. Orange blossoms are always hanging from the trees, dripping with honey and incense; birds are always singing their full-throated songs, and as has always been the case since time immemorial—in the spring, my friends, a young man's fancy lightly turns to thoughts of—well, etcetera.

The result is that people are always falling in love and writing poetry to each other. To avoid reading the poetry, most of the inhabitants get married, and eventually the headlines have another field day. I doubt if there is any surefire solution. Certainly, people that live in California shouldn't get married. This also goes for Colorado, Texas and Ohio. If they insist on getting that certain feeling that leads to the altar and they can't control it, the best thing to do is to call up THE TIMES and offer to write a funny piece. This supreme effort will kill any marriage. In fact, if my wife runs across this, it will kill mine.

New York Times
January 7, 1934

Movie Glossary

Initially, the Marx Brothers' move to Hollywood resulted in fewer published writings for Groucho. Perhaps this was a result of being away from New York and its dozen daily newspapers. In the fall of 1932, Groucho had been in Hollywood for over a year. Horse Feathers, *the Marx Brothers' fourth film (and second to be made in California), had been released that summer. "Movie Glossary" is one of the first things that Groucho published after moving west.*

NEWS REEL
King George laying a cornerstone

LAP DISSOLVE
The Casting Office

AUTOGRAPH HUNTER
A broken down stamp collector

CLOSE-UP
What you say to the wife
in the morning

SNICKER
What the collaborator
contributes to the script

BELLY LAUGH
Your own gag

CUTTER
The executioner

OFFICE BOY
The fellow who used to be President

TRAILER

A warning to next week's patrons

CONFERENCE

A clearing house for golf scores

FADE OUT

A Shubert blackout that's gone

Hollywood

VINE STREET

The Broadway of Cedar Rapids

RUSHES

A Wassermann test in the dark

PREVIEW

The beginning of a studio shake-up

CROONER

A fellow that uses his mouth
to sing through his nose

TWO-REELER

A five-reeler that's been previewed
twice

CHARACTER ACTRESS

An ingenue's comeback to the
movies

LONG SHOT

Any scene without sex

LOCATION

A box lunch in the hot sun

Hollywood Reporter
September 19, 1932

M O V I E   G L O S S A R Y

By GROUCHO MARX

NEWS REEL
King George laying a cornerstone.

LAP DISSOLVE
The Casting Office

AUTOGRAPH HUNTER
A broken down stamp collector

CLOSE UP
What you say to the wife in the morning

SNICKER
What the collaborator contributes to the script

BELLY LAUGH
Your own gag

OFFICE BOY
The fellow who used to be President

TRAILER
A warning to next week's patrons.

CONFERENCE
A clearing house for golf scores.

FADE OUT
A Shubert blackout that's gone Hollywood.

VINE STREET
The Broadway of Cedar Rapids.

RUSHES
A Wassermann test in the dark.

PREVIEW
The beginning of a studio shake-up.

CROONER
A fellow that uses his mouth to sing through his nose.

TWO-REELER
A five-reeler that's been previewed twice.

CHARACTER ACTRESS
An ingenue's comeback to the movies.

LONG SHOT
Any scene without sex.

CUTTER
The executioner

**The Maddest Marx Creates
The First Pictures That
This Gigantic Industry
Ever Colossaled At And
It's All True — Too Vrai**

LOCATION
A box lunch in the hot sun.

Night Life of the Gods

At the Circus, the Marx Brothers' ninth film, was released in the fall of 1939 to mixed reviews. Graham Greene wrote in the Spectator, *"We must regretfully accept the fact that, thanks to the Metro millions, the Marx Brothers are finally imprisoned in the Hollywood world." It was an odd criticism considering that* A Night at the Opera *and* A Day at the Races *were both made with a far greater share of the "Metro millions" than was* At the Circus *and were hailed by critics as their best films. The problem with At the Circus was, in fact, just the opposite. The film was hampered by its small budget. By 1939 the Marx Brothers had become a low priority at MGM. The claim that they had become "imprisoned in the Hollywood world," however, was true. They were a part of the studio system of the time and sadly were no longer a prominent part. "Night Life of the Gods" was Groucho's look at Hollywood social mores in the days of the studio system. The title was originally used by Thorne Smith for his 1934 novel concerning gods of the Greek, as opposed to Hollywood, variety.*

When one considers the setup, it seems to me that this local bull pit called Hollywood has considerably less scandal than it is entitled to. Here is a town teeming with beautiful ingenues, marble-chiseled juveniles, low-priced vintage wines and half-priced bedroom suites; it has a desert moon, a neighboring ocean and dozens of lovely, lonely mountain tops, yet, despite all this, its Sodom and Gomorrah Crossley is lower than any hinterland cowtown.

What is the reason for all this? Is sex going the way of the horse and buggy? Is a well-turned ankle less important than a well-turned phrase? Not that it matters—but where is the next generation coming from? Be calm, my friend, love is still alive and kicking, but Hollywood is too wrapped up in its groups and sets, its cliques and intrigues to bother about that little thing called love.

To begin with, there is the young whippersnapper group. This is the 16–21 crowd. The studios pair them up like horses at a state fair and they are instructed weekly with whom they are to go and when to announce their engagements. They are usually snapped with their current fiances, holding hands at a night club, sharing a nutburger at a drive-in, or gingerly holding a tennis racket at El Mirador. The fact that they have never played tennis has nothing to do with it. It gives them a chance to pose in shorts, and besides, there's a sort of unwritten publicity law that all young starlets (as they are revoltingly called) must be photographed at some time in their young careers brandishing a tennis racket. If the lenser is particularly ingenuous, he poses them peering coyly through the gut. This is tops in photography, as it combines both sex appeal and sport! This crowd also goes in for mass bowling, serenading each other on roller skates and officially greeting visiting Washington Congressmen who look as though they might vote for the Neely bill.*

Then there is the gambling group! They bet on anything—a card game, a roulette wheel, whether their next kid will be a boy or a girl, local and national prize fights, the horses, African golf, the market, baseball, and most of all, football. The football chatter usually starts around July in the studio commissaries and ends up the following January at the Rose Bowl. They bet on punch boards, lotteries, high and low scores and have even been known to make book on how many collective pounds a team will shed in one afternoon. These boys go in for plenty of check-kiting and financial legerdemain and their mornings are usually spent in a bank trying to square things with a brace of vice-presidents.

---

*[The Neely bill (proposed by Senator Matthew M. Neely of West Virginia) forbade film producers and distributors from controlling movie theaters. The eventual passing of a similar bill led to the decline of Hollywood's studio system.]

Then there is the cultural or white-tie-and-tail crowd. They spend half of their lives running to the Philharmonic to hear lectures, concerts, symphonies, to see dancers from Bali and Monte Carlo, and, in fact, anything that promises a high-hat opening. They take French and Spanish courses at the local universities; they specialize in first editions and Old English plate; they rush over to Pasadena for Maxwell Anderson and Shaw and will entertain any visiting lecturer who can be induced to stop over for dinner or cocktails. They won't attend a preview unless there is a canopied awning in front of the theatre, a red-carpeted sidewalk of at least 400 feet from their limousines to the main entrance and a grandstand of not less than 3,000 admiring yokels. In addition to this, the theatre manager has to guarantee in writing that when the show is over the carriage starter will bellow their names in an English accent for not less than five minutes.

The busiest and most voluble group, however, are the social-conscious kids. They go to a meeting every night—any kind of a meeting will do. If it's a cause that they agree with, so much the better; but their theory is, any cause is better than none. At the drop of a hat, they'll boycott anything. It's a night lost when they don't issue an official white paper, denouncing something. They have you slaphappy signing papers, petitions and protests. It's all very confusing and frequently you find yourself sending money to both sides of a great cause. Unless you are exceptionally strong-minded, you eventually belong to more organizations than an insurance agent soliciting the Sons and Daughters of I Will Arise.

And now we come to the final crowd—the old guard! Somebody once said: "The old guard dies, but never surrenders!" Well, this crowd has done both. They are known as the low blood pressure group. They all have minus thyroid, leaping arthritis and droopy eyelids. Their idea of a ducky evening is to sit around and discuss their symptoms. Insomnia is their favorite topic and, at the slightest provocation, they will reel off hours of evidence to prove they haven't slept a wink in weeks. They subsist largely on a diet of aspirin, vitamins and shots in the arm. They swallow tablets all night to put them to sleep and chew benzedrine all day to keep them awake! They are easily recognized on the street—they all walk with a little jerk and a slight toss of the head like Lionel Barrymore in his last five pictures. They see their dentist twice a year and their doctor twice a day; they take daily massages and scalp treatments and spend more money on X-rays than they do on jewelry.

So you see, love staggers along out here under many handicaps. It's doubt-ful if even Tommy Manville* would thrive under these conditions, and that, gentlemen, is the acid test!

So if you think the scandal from the Western Front is a bit on the dull side, don't blame it all on Vine Street.

Variety
January 3, 1940

---

*[Tommy Manville, heir to the Johns-Manville asbestos fortune, was well known for marrying thirteen times.]

Just Another Anniversary

Groucho and Variety *had a long history. His first notice in the so-called "Bible of Show Business" came on February 2, 1906, with the review of a singing act called Lily Seville and Master Marx. Over the years,* Variety *chronicled the career of the Marx Brothers more thoroughly than any other publication and Groucho and editor Abel Green became friends. Although no formal arrangement was ever made, Green regularly printed Groucho's articles and letters in the paper. "Just Another Anniversary" appeared in the thirty-eighth anniversary issue.*

I used to have an aunt in Long Island—in fact, I still have—who was always having an anniversary. It didn't have to commemorate a wedding or a birth or anything important. It was just that she was crazy about anniversaries and would throw one at the slightest provocation. If, for example, her cocker-spaniel broke his leg on the 10th of April, the following year on the 10th of April she would hold a party and hand out sandwiches, cake and coffee.

The 9th of October, as she remembered it, was the date she picked up her current husband in the subway kiosk at New Lots, Brooklyn. A year later she invited people in to celebrate the day she first met the loafer she eventually proposed to. I don't think she gave a darn about her husband—as a matter of fact, I don't think she even cared much for the cocker spaniel—all she really cared about were anniversaries and she would use any excuse to celebrate one.

So why does 'Variety' always have to be having anniversaries? It proudly announces that it is 38 years old. So what? Lots of things are 38 years old. My bedroom slippers are 38 years old. I was once 38 years old myself.

As I recall it, the day passed uneventfully. It was quite some time ago. I received many gifts. My son presented me with a bag of jelly beans; my daughter gave me a furtive peck on the cheek, and an unknown admirer stuck a live mouse in my overcoat pocket. The birthday dinner was memorable. We had kidney stew, coleslaw and a bread pudding with 38 plumber's candles stuck in it.

After dinner we all went to the movies. Since it was my birthday they insisted I pay for the tickets. While I was getting the stubs back from the doorman they all raced ahead and got themselves good seats. By the time I got inside there was nothing left but the front row. This meant looking up at the screen for three and a half hours. Try that sometime with a stiff collar and bifocals. I don't remember the name of the movie but all the characters looked like Basil Rathbone in one of his thinner roles. I was pretty tired by the time we got home and in no time I was fast asleep.

When I awoke the next morning I discovered that during the night someone had stolen the jelly beans. Well, anyway, happy anniversary fast asleep.

Variety
January 5, 1944

Grouchoisms

When Pabst Blue Ribbon Town *chose not to retain him as its host, Groucho had few prospects for employment. His career was in a tail-spin until* You Bet Your Life *resurrected it, first on radio in 1947 and then on television in 1950. The years between* Blue Ribbon Town *and* You Bet Your Life *would see the Marx Brothers briefly reunite in 1946 to make* A Night in Casablanca. *Groucho would also make his first film on his own. Of* Copacabana, *Groucho once remarked, "I played second banana to the fruit on Carmen Miranda's head." One scene in the film featured cameo appearances by several show business columnists, among them Abel Green and Earl Wilson. The day that* Copacabana *premiered in New York, Wilson's New York* Post *column was written by guest columnist Groucho Marx.*

Variety, which calls itself the Bible of show business—actually it's the babel of show business—or if you want to whip a pun to death, the Abel of show business—recently printed a news story to the effect that in The Jolson Story Al Jolson's cut, despite the fact that he didn't appear in the picture except for a brief moment, would amount to three and a half million dollars.

I have appeared in many pictures through the years (at the moment I can be seen in all my pristine loveliness in "Copacabana") and I would swear on a stack of Bob Stacks that I have never pulled down any dough that has even remotely touched this figure.

Perhaps this is the signpost that show business has been waiting for. If, for example, a Jolson picture can roll up a $10,000,000 gross without Jolson, how much more could it have done without Evelyn Keyes and William Demarest? Maybe the studios have been going at it the wrong way. Perhaps they should stop the present custom of bunching seven or eight stars in one movie, and eliminate all the feature names in a picture.

I can just see the marquee at the local theater. As a matter of fact, I can't see it—in fact, I can hardly see the typewriter keys, but let's skip that. Coming next week—"I Wonder Who's Kissing Her Now," without Olivia de Crawford and Clark Power.

It can't miss. I am sure that millions of people stay away from the movies because they dislike the stars that are appearing at the local Bijou, but if they were assured that so and so wouldn't show his or her ugly kisser on the screen, my guess is they would tear the doors down to get in.

I am speaking from personal experience. In my time I have met hundreds of people who have said, "Hey, jerk, when are you going to quit the movies and get a job?" And if it's true of me, it certainly must be true of dozens of other cinema incompetents, many of whose talents are even less than mine.

This system could also be applied to other fields of endeavor. I am sure that many political candidates are defeated because the public has been given an opportunity to see what they look like. The next great political victory will be achieved by the party that is smart enough to have nobody heading the ticket.

I'll admit that there have been political parties that have had nobody heading their ticket, but even these have always had some spavined schmoe on the rostrum endlessly babbling the same old nothings.

The first party that announces that as of today they are going to get along without any candidate will, I think, sweep into office.

My theory is that there are too many people and too many things. Suppose you got that semi-annual card from your dentist notifying you that most of your fangs are about to drop out and you had better get up to his abattoir before you spend the rest of your life gumming your fodder. Wouldn't you rush up there with much more alacrity if you were certain that this white-coated assassin, who calls himself a doctor, wasn't there to greet you with his chisel in one hand and his pliers in the other? Imagine if horse racing had no horses, thousands of people could go to the track each day and save millions of dollars.

I don't know what my theory could be called. There was one years ago called Technocracy. Perhaps this could be called the Theory of Scarcity. Take the actors out of the movies; take squash and rutabagas out of restaurant menus; take Slaughter and Musial out of the Cardinals; and take Gromyko out of the U.N.

Take the wives out of marriage. I know hundreds of husbands who would gladly go home if there weren't any wives waiting for them. Eliminate women from marriage and there wouldn't be any divorces. But, someone might say, "If there are no women, what about the next generation?"

Look, I've seen some of the next generation—perhaps it's just as well if the whole thing ended right here.

New York Post
July 12, 1947

Run for Your Career, Boys

Just as talking pictures had threatened the business of the theater, the advent of television had the entertainment world thoroughly spooked in the late forties. The conventional wisdom of the day held that no one with a television set would pay to be entertained outside of the home. Groucho's editorial on the subject appeared in Arthur Engel's "On the Air" column in the Hollywood Reporter.

Run for your career, boys. A new monster has arrived scaring the daylights out of actors, producers, theatre owners, sports promoters and sponsors. According to some of the prophets, within six months most of the theaters, night clubs and sports arenas will be dismantled and converted into parking lots. We may not even need the parking lots because no American with a television set is ever going to go outdoors again.

To hear them tell it, we will soon be a nation of squint-eyed hermits huddling around wooden boxes with glass fronts. Only a lower-case cretin will ever go to a movie again. Who in his right mind is going to look at *Johnny Belinda* or *Hamlet* when he has the choice of sitting home and watching a twenty-year old western with the same story, plot and cast that he saw—not only the night before, the month before, but the year before. Can you conceive of anyone journeying to a ball park, sitting in that awful fresh air eating hot dogs and drinking beer when, by just flicking a switch, he can remain at home and see the catcher's left shoulder, the first baseman's right ear, the third finger on the left hand of the right fielder and, if he keeps his eye peeled, some time during the evening he may even see the baseball.

What young lover is going to take his girl out for an evening of dancing, and whatever the current equivalent is for necking, when he can watch a chorus of six girls without faces dancing hazily on Kinescope.

As for the poor old theatre, it's dead again. This happens every ten years. It was killed long ago by the movies, then by radio and now, the *coup de grâce*, by television. It is sad but it's true. Who wants to see *Death of a Salesman*, *South Pacific* or any of the great plays when that same time can be consumed in watching a seal juggling a rubber ball, puppets with dialogue out of the first reader by Joe Miller, and second-rate plays with stock company actors in papier-mâché sets.

I am sure television will grow bigger and more professional each year, but people will still want action. They will still want to smell the turf at Santa Anita, the rush to the betting window, the fun of personally cursing the umpire and the drama and crowd of the fight arena.

This is America, my fine calamity howlers. This is still the land of the pioneer and the adventurer; of Daniel Boone and Lewis and Clark; of the jet plane test pilot; of Johnny Appleseed and Errol Flynn. Basically we are a gregarious and crowd-loving nation and no mechanical invention will ever plant us permanently in front of a fireplace. Home is unquestionably where the heart is, but it is also the place where you bathe, change your clothes and get the hell out of as quickly as possible.

Hollywood Reporter
April 28, 1949

I Never Could Grow a Moustache

By the mid-1950s, Groucho was one of the biggest stars on television, with You Bet Your Life *consistently among the top rated programs. Although initially asked to appear on the show with his familiar greasepaint moustache, Groucho refused to do so. He'd already appeared on the screen without the greasepaint in* Copacabana. *After making a brief appearance (with his real moustache) in the Marx Brothers' thirteenth and final film,* Love Happy, *in 1950, Groucho made several more films with his real moustache. He had a small cameo role in* Mr. Music, *a Bing Crosby film, in 1950 and he starred in two films for RKO (*Double Dynamite *with Frank Sinatra in 1951 and* A Girl in Every Port *with William Bendix in 1952) before deciding that he'd had enough of the daily grind of movie making. He'd make an unbilled walk-on in* Will Success Spoil Rock Hunter? *in 1957 and later that year he'd appear in one scene in* The Story of Mankind, *but most of Groucho's time off from* You Bet Your Life *during that period would be spent working on his third book,* Groucho and Me. *"I Never Could Grow a Moustache" is one of his few published short pieces from this period*

I know there's been a lot of whispering going on in high places about me; there always is about great men. My usual way of handling such whispering in high places is to whisper right back—in low places. I have found four of the lowest places in the world to whisper in and if any of you girls want to join me in a nice quiet whisper, please get in line. Or contact my agent, Miss Ducky Lucky.

My whispering fee is quite nominal in certain cases if you don't mind my cigar. For Miss Universe of 1954, for example, I am quoting one of the lowest whispering fees in the history of the universe.

I suppose you're already wondering why people are wondering about me. Well, I simply dread telling it right out like this but all the fellers are saying that I can't grow a moustache. I mean they're coming right out and saying that hair shuns my upper lip like grass avoids the desert, or original ideas shun my competitors or even those who offer me no competition—Hope, Benny, Thurber, Twain, Farouk, to mention a mere handful. And a *merer* handful you never heard of.

Let me give you an example of how they're talking. I was walking along Fifth Avenue the other day and passed a cluster of small bearded jerks (a political group related to the Bedouins).

"Look at him," one of the hairiest said, smirking in my direction. "Look at that bald upper lip. It looks like a peeled egg. The dread Japanese chestnut blight doubtless holds him in thrall."

"Let's thrash him on general principles," another moustached villain said. "No, let's thrash him right here on Fifth," said a moronic looking third, twirling the waxed ends of his schnurrbart.

Clamping my tiny fisto in rage I walked over to the group and holding them with my cold blue eyes, I said: "Gentlemen, the truth is that I have one of the most fertile upper lips in history; hair grows so fast on my upper lip that it makes the Five o'Clock Shadow of your normal male look like High Noon. Without Gary Cooper. My battery-powered razor must be kept in almost constant service to keep me the clean-faced man my audience and I have come to love. Now skat. All of you!"

They slunk off properly chastened. But all the same the fact is that I never *could* grow a moustache. And, while I want you to keep this in strictest confidence, there is a tragic reason behind it. It has to do with women. Oh, you've already guessed it; my, you *are* quick!

Yes, the truth is that if I grew a moustache, the carnage among my feminine admirers, already historic in proportion, would get completely out of hand. Not to mention what would happen to me.

The dangers to myself and to my public if I grow a real moustache were pointed up by what historians are now calling the Stork Club Incident of

1936. This horrifying event was due to the oversight of my barber, a purblind ex-jockey lent to me by Bing Crosby's son.

It seems that the barber had omitted the usual examination of my upper lip by a high-powered microscopic lens, specially ground for me at the Corning Glass Works (adv.). So, all unwittingly, I appeared for my luncheon engagement with the fuzz breaking out all over my lip. Well, sir, when I was unveiled at my table by Mr. Club, the owner of the Stork, a small group of 100 women who had been crowding around Gable's table, admiring *his* poor excuse for a moustache, rushed me.

Unprepared as I was, I saw I could put up a very poor defense and I yielded at once. Yielding turned out to be a masterly gesture, though after half an hour of yielding I was tiring rapidly.

In desperation I mounted my chair. "Ladies," I said. "Ladies! I appeal to your reason."

"Down with reason!" cried a statuesque blonde whom I later found came from 32 Highland Avenue, Upper Sandusky, a really charming little rose-covered cottage.

"I'm only a man," I protested simply, casting my eyes down and dimpling.

"Get that dimple!" screamed a statuesque brunette from 10-02 Queens Boulevard. "No, get that moustache!" the others yelled.

I can say with certainty and gratitude that, on this occasion, I owe my life to the quick thinking of Mr. Club. Throwing a damask veil over my face (a not unflattering piece of apparel itself if you have fine brooding gray eyes like mine), he whisked me away from the inflamed group by breaking down a secret door to a secret street. Thrusting me into the arms of my expensively garbed chauffeur, he muttered: "And stay out!"

Some of my more bitter competitors have said that the Stork Club incident was pure publicity. They point to the fact that shortly afterwards, the selfsame incident occurred to me at The Mocambo, The Twenty-One, The Troc, The Twenty-Two, Jack Dempsey's, and The Twenty-Three Skiddoo. And they say that the feminine admirers who rushed me were on my payroll and that the idea originated in my office.

Envy is a bitter thing to witness and I need only point out to these detractors that my office is in my hat and my payroll is in my office. And they're not going to get *any* of it. So there! What else a man can say is beyond me.

But I do have a further answer to my detractors. (The fact is I can go on like this till you scream.) Few know, for example, that a beautiful filmed version of *Hamlet*, in which I play that great prince, and which was made some years ago, had to be withdrawn from circulation at once and now lies musting in a vault. Why? Because the glaring lights magnified a minute line of hirsute loveliness on my upper lip.

The melancholy fates of the women who viewed the preview of my *Hamlet* forced me to withdraw the masterpiece from public sight.

At the first glimpse of me in the opening scene, fifty lovelies, led by a maddened Powers model, rushed the stage. "Get pieces of the screen for souvenirs!" screamed the leader.

"Pluck down benches, forms, anything!" screamed an old Shakespearean actress.

In a matter of moments the place was a shambles; twelve were hurt, two seriously.

When the reports of the riot came in, I was with the producer. "Box office be darned," I said, gravely concerned. "Women and children first. Particularly the women. Bury the film where it can never be seen again."

The producer begged me to reconsider. But I stood firm. It shattered him and he has never recovered. I sometimes help him out now. In little ways. A nickel now. A nickel then. Only last month I had him on my NBC television program—"You Bet Your Life." But nobody wanted him. To cheer him up I gave him a simple question which even a child could answer. He stood to receive money for the correct answer. But he failed. The man's simply broken beyond repair. Why, *everybody* knows the names of my first six movies.

And that's how it goes. But if you hear any more whispering about me in high places, please feel free to write. I'll be right down here waiting for your letter. And don't forget to enclose a photograph. You know the chances for stardom in Hollywood are ENDLESS. After all, you *know* what I look like.

Coronet
March 1955

Whenever I Think of Scotch, I Recall the Immortal Words of My Brother Harpo

Like many celebrities, Groucho endorsed many products during his career. He advertised a wide assortment including Old Gold cigarettes, Personna precision razor blades, Bulova watches, GE light bulbs and television tubes, Kellogg's Frosted Flakes, Skippy peanut butter, Blatz and Rheingold beers and Smirnoff vodka, not to mention the products of the companies that sponsored his radio and television shows. In 1973 Groucho participated in a rather unique advertising campaign for Teacher's Scotch Whisky. A series of two-page ads ran in several national magazines. Each ad featured an essay by a famous comedian or actor extolling the virtues of Teacher's. The facing page carried a full color photograph of the essayist. Other participants in the campaign included George Burns, Redd Foxx, Mel Brooks and Zero Mostel. Groucho's contribution, which ran in Playboy *and* Esquire *in the fall of 1973, was called "Whenever I Think of Scotch, I Recall the Immortal Words of My Brother Harpo." It was among the last things that Groucho wrote for publication.*

Harpo was a man of very few words, except when it came to scotch, horses and ladies.

Actually, scotch ran a poor third. Which wasn't easy considering the way his horses ran.

And the way his horses ran could be summed up in a word.

Last.

Whenever I think of Scotch, I recall the immortal words of my brother Harpo.

BY GROUCHO MARX

HARPO WAS a man of very few words, except when it came to scotch, horses and ladies.

Actually, scotch ran a poor third. Which wasn't easy considering the way his horses ran.

And the way his horses ran could be summed up in a word.

Last.

He once had a horse who finished ahead of the winner of the 1942 Kentucky Derby.

Unfortunately, the horse started running in the 1941 Derby.

And as far as the ladies go, Harpo's ladies always went.

As a matter of fact, they went a lot faster than his horses. Although his horses were a lot prettier.

But that's a horse of a different color.

Anyway, back to the subject at hand. What was it again? Oh, yeah, scotch.

When it came to scotch, Harpo's words were memorable.

Unfortunately, I forget them.

I remember the thought behind them, however.

The thought was that Harpo appreciated good scotch. Especially one kind of scotch. I know this because one morning I found my liquor cabinet broken into. All the scotch was opened and apparently samples were taken of each bottle. Except in the case of Teacher's Scotch where the case was taken.

I immediately put on my Sherlock Holmes hat, replaced my cigar with a pipe and looked for my thinking cap, but I couldn't find it.

"The Case of the Missing Case," I called it.

Harpo was my number one suspect. He was also my number two and my number three suspect.

The night before I had heard a honking sound in my living room. At first I thought it was a car looking for a parking space in my apartment. (That used to happen a lot until I had parking meters installed.) Little did I know, however, that it was my brother committing one of the most unbrotherly acts since the Andrews Sisters.

So I threw a mackinaw over my Dr. Denton's and dashed off to Harpo's. I must have cut quite a dashing figure.

When I arrived at Harpo's house, there, big as life, were my bottles of Teacher's.

"Why, Harpo?" I asked, lighting my cigar and putting it out on the rug, the one on the floor.

Harpo answered with a honk that was worth a thousand words.

I understood them immediately.

What it boiled down to was that Teacher's tasted better to him than any of the other scotches I had.

I agreed with that. It also tasted better to me. That's probably why we're brothers. After all, scotch is thicker than water.

And, on the subject of brothers, Harpo said he knew enough about scotch to know that Teacher's wasn't one of those scotches everybody and his brother drinks.

I told him he was doing his best to change that.

Then I asked him how he knew that anyway.

Well, to make a long story longer, it seems that he had gone through Gummo's liquor cabinet, too. As well as Zeppo's and Chico's. Before he went through mine. And he said that I had the best taste.

I said, "That's all very interesting, Harpo, but now it's time to play 'You Bet Your Life.' And give me a finger of my own scotch while you're at it."

To show me how generous he was he poured some scotch into a glass and put his whole hand into it. I'd had scotch and water, scotch and soda, but never scotch and hand. But then, Harpo's an old hand at serving scotch. At the risk of beating a hand to death, let me continue. Where was I...

At this point I told Harpo I didn't want to hear any more horns.

He honked.

I said, "Say it with strings."

So he grabbed his harp and proceeded to play me to sleep. I snored in accompaniment.

It was while I was sleeping that he uttered those now immortal words. You know the words I mean. At least I hope you do. Cause you couldn't expect me to remember the words somebody said to me while I was sleeping.

But, after all, why harp on that.

86 Proof Scotch Whisky Blended and Bottled in Scotland by Wm. Teacher & Sons, Ltd. © Schieffelin & Co., N.Y., Importers

He once had a horse who finished ahead of the winner of the 1942 Kentucky Derby.

Unfortunately, the horse started running in the 1941 Derby.

And as far as the ladies go, Harpo's ladies always went.

As a matter of fact, they went a lot faster than his horses. Although his horses were a lot prettier.

But that's a horse of a different color.

Anyway, back to the subject at hand. What was it again? Oh, yeah, scotch.

When it came to scotch, Harpo's words were memorable.

Unfortunately, I forget them.

I remember the thought behind them, however.

The thought was that Harpo appreciated good scotch. Especially one kind of scotch. I know this because one morning I found my liquor cabinet broken into. All the scotch was opened and apparently samples were taken of each bottle. Except in the case of Teacher's Scotch where the case was taken.

I immediately put on my Sherlock Holmes hat, replaced my cigar with a pipe and looked for my thinking cap, but I couldn't find it.

"The Case of the Missing Case," I called it.

Harpo was my number one suspect. He was also my number two and my number three suspect.

The night before I had heard a honking sound in my living room. At first I thought it was a car looking for a parking space in my apartment. (That used to happen a lot until I had parking meters installed.) Little did I know, however, that it was my brother committing one of the most unbrotherly acts since the Andrews Sisters.

So I threw a mackinaw over my Dr. Denton's and dashed off to Harpo's. I must have cut quite a dashing figure.

When I arrived at Harpo's house, there, big as life, were my bottles of Teacher's.

"Why, Harpo?" I asked, lighting my cigar and putting it out on the rug, the one on the floor.

Harpo answered with a honk that was worth a thousand words. I understood them immediately.

What it boiled down to was that Teacher's tasted better to him than any of the other scotches I had.

I agreed with that. It also tasted better to me. That's probably why we're brothers. After all, scotch is thicker than water.

And, on the subject of brothers, Harpo said he knew enough about scotch to know that Teacher's wasn't one of those scotches everybody and his brother drinks.

I told him he was doing his best to change that.

Then I asked him how he knew that anyway.

Well, to make a long story longer, it seems that he had gone through Gummo's liquor cabinet, too. As well as Zeppo's and Chico's. Before he went through mine. And he said that I had the best taste.

I said, "That's all very interesting, Harpo, but now it's time to play 'You Bet Your Life.' And give me a finger of my own scotch while you're at it."

To show me how generous he was he poured some scotch into a glass and put his whole hand into it. I'd had scotch and water, scotch and soda, but never scotch and hand. But then, Harpo's an old hand at serving scotch. At the risk of beating a hand to death, let me continue. Where was I . . .

At this point I told Harpo I didn't want to hear any more horns.

He honked.

I said, "Say it with strings."

So he grabbed his harp and proceeded to play me to sleep. I snored in accompaniment.

It was while I was sleeping that he uttered those now immortal words. You know the words I mean. At least I hope you do. Cause you couldn't expect me to remember the words somebody said to me while I was sleeping.

But, after all, why harp on that.

Fall 1973

PART SIX

The Schweinerei

When an Act's Successful
and
The Small Time's Season

For the 1919–1920 vaudeville season, the Marx Brothers found themselves in the enviable position of being booked solid with their new show, N'Everything, *which was an updated version of their hit,* Home Again. *They'd been through every part of the country several times with* Home Again, *which debuted in 1914. It was with that show that the Marxes made the leap from struggling small-timers to big-time stars of vaudeville. Groucho's whimsical verses about life in small-time vaudeville appeared in* Variety *as* N'Everything *enjoyed a lengthy northeastern tour on the big-time circuit.*

By this time he could joke about people like notoriously thrifty vaudeville booker Jule Delmar and the awful conditions on circuits like Pantages, Poli and Ackerman & Harris—which performers nick-named "The Death Trail"—because he wouldn't need them again.

WHEN AN ACT'S SUCCESSFUL
By JULIUS H. MARX

It's easy enough to be pleasant, when you've played a year 'round New York,
When your act's going great, and your agent of late, is full of that soft
    pleasant talk;
The manager's fine, he takes you to dine, why, he even grabs for the bill—
But you wave him away, it's your turn to pay—you'll show him you're no pill.

At the theater, a pipe, your act is just ripe, and the audience clamors for
more;

They holler and scream, you know what they mean—they want you to do
your encore.

While out there they screech, you pull a neat speech, you know the old
Eddie Len;

Then you smile and you smirk, like a terrible Turk, and you stagger down
to your pen.

Remember when you played the wine halls 'round Cripple Creek, Denver,
and Chi.?

You sure were a hick and you often were sick from living on sinkers and pie.

WHEN AN ACT'S SUCCESSFUL

By JULIUS H. MARX

It's easy enough to be pleasant, when you've played a year 'round New York.
When you're act's going great, and your agent of late, is full of that soft pleasant
The manager's fine, he takes you to dine, why, he even grabs for the bill—
But you wave him away, it's your turn to pay—you'll show him you're no pill.

At the theatre, a pipe, your act is just ripe, and the audience clamors for more;
They holler and scream, you know what they mean—they want you to do your en
While out there they screech, you pull a neat speech, you know the old Eddie Len.
Then you smile and you smirk, like a terrible Turk, and you stagger down to your p

Remember when you played the wine halls 'round Cripple Creek, Denver, and Chi.?
You sure were a hick and you often were sick from living on sinkers and pie.
Remember the Jane in the dance hall, the one with the hair down her back?—
She was wild over you and you knew it, too; that is, while you had the jack.

Remember when you joined the Minstrels, twenty per week and your cakes,
How the show lasted five weeks and you rode back to Chi. on the brakes?
Food wasn't scarce in Chicago, not if you had the old kale,
But to you 'twas as much of a mystery as Houdini busting a jail.

And then came a year with a Rep. show, "East Lynn" always for a run;
You played Sir Francis Levinson and then did three songs in "one";
And then you branched out as a single, some parodies, hoofing and gags,
Parodies, then, used to kill 'em; that was before they sang rags.

A year for Ackerman & Harris, a season for Pan. and for Loew;
A season for Delmar and Poli, and a year with a No. 2 show—
Your act grew as smooth as molasses, your clothes had just the right fit,
You started to kick at your billing—and that's the first signs of a hit.

You now were a big time single with a drop and a car and a wife;
You spent your Summers in Freeport, and learned not to eat with your knife.
The actors on Broadway all know you, but you're getting up stage and cold,
'Cause some of them cop all your riddles and others they borrow your gold.

But don't get too cold and distant, remember the wine halls round Chi.?
It's a short life at best and a sweet one, and some day we all have to die.
So try and help those who are struggling, help those who try to be true,
You won't always be next to closing, some day you'll be back No. 2.

No 2 up with St. Peter, up where the good Actors go,
Vaudeville up at its highest, where no one opens the show;
Where every act gets the same billing, and each gets the same time.
It's Heaven, you know, for your Agents below,
And so I will close up my rhyme.

Remember the Jane in the dance hall, the one with the hair down her
   back?—
She was wild over you and you knew it, too; that is, while you had the jack.

Remember when you joined the Minstrels, twenty per week and your cakes,
How the show lasted five weeks and you rode back to Chi. on the brakes?
Food wasn't scarce in Chicago, not if you had the old kale,
But to you 'twas as much of a mystery as Houdini busting a jail.

And then came a year with a Rep. show, "East Lynn" always for a run;
You played Sir Francis Levinson and then did three songs in "one";
And then you branched out as a single, some parodies, hoofing and gags,
Parodies, then, used to kill 'em; that was before they sang rags.

A year for Ackerman & Harris, a season for Pan. and for Loew;
A season for Delmar and Poli, and a year with a No. 2 show—
Your act grew as smooth as molasses, your clothes had just the right fit,
You started to kick at your billing—and that's the first signs of a hit.

You now were a big time single with a drop and a car and a wife;
You spent your Summers in Freeport, and learned not to eat with your knife.
The actors on Broadway all know you, but you're getting up stage and cold
'Cause some of them cop all your riddles and others they borrow your gold.

But don't get too cold and distant, remember the wine halls round Chi.?
It's a short life at best and a sweet one, and some day we all have to die.
So try and help those who are struggling, help those who try to be true,
You won't always be next to closing, some day you'll be back No. 2.

No. 2 up with St. Peter, up where the good Actors go;
Vaudeville up at its highest, where no one opens the show;
Where every act gets the same billing, and each gets the same time.
It's Heaven, you know, for your Agents below,
And so I will close up my rhyme.

Variety
October 3, 1919

THE SMALL TIME'S SEASON
By JULIUS H. MARX

Tell me not in mournful numbers, we have but two weeks to go,
Every time I save two hundred, two weeks layoff makes it blow;
When they route me in September, I get contracts by the score,
But the first six weeks they give me nearly always shrinks to four.

Through October's golden autumn, when the leaves are turning red,
I buy costumes for the Wifey, silver spangles made of lead.
When November rushes on us, with its thankfulness and cheer,
I pay eighty-five for photos, and the other ten is clear.

By the time it gets to Xmas, I am laying up some jack,
Then I'm two weeks minus labor, and I'm once more on my back.
Then comes eight long weeks of winter, four of them I'm laying off:
When March comes I've got two hundred, and the Wife has got a cough.

April showers bring May flowers and they also bring the flu—
And the whole three towns I'm booked in are closed up as tight as glue.
How my bank account is fading, like the early morning mist,
And the time I lost in April makes of me a pessimist.

Gee! How hot the days are growing, shows are closing everywhere;
Palm Beach suits will soon be showing, summer's smell is in the air—
Actors running thick on Broadway, giving all the girls a treat;
Hoofers crowding into lunch rooms, giving rest to weary feet.

Think I'll hie me to the country, out to where it's cool and nice;
I played fifteen weeks in fifty, three of them without a slice—
I know where the fishing's nifty, where the streams run smooth and clear,
Where the fish will bite on cardboard, and old Mother Nature's near.

For I'm tired of wigs and greasepaint, songs and dances make me ill,
Five-piece bands and sawing fiddlers, of them all I've had my fill;
Maybe next year I'll be lucky, maybe I will grab a show—
Maybe I will change my agent, maybe I will save some dough.

But right now I'm going fishing, where the brook comes tumbling down,
No more props and no more spotlights, no more muggin', no more clown;
In September I'll be ready, from my agent I'll expect—
"Akron next week, wire answer" dollar eighty-five, collect.

Variety
January 2, 1920

THE SMALL TIME'S SEASON

By JULIUS H. MARX

Tell me not in mournful numbers. we have but two weeks to go,
Every time I save two hundred. two weeks layoff makes it blow;
When they route me in September. I get contracts by the score,
But the first six weeks they give me nearly always shrinks to four.

Through October's golden Autumn, when the leaves are turning red,
I buy costumes for the Wifey, silver spangles made of lead.
When November rushes on us. with its thankfulness and cheer,
I pay eighty-five for photos, and the other ten is clear.

By the time it gets to Xmas. I am laying up some jack,
Then I'm two weeks minus labor, and I'm once more on my back.
Then comes eight long weeks of winter. four of them I'm laying off;
When March comes I've got two hundred, and the Wife has got a cough.

April showers bring May flowers and they also bring the flu—
And the whole three towns I'm booked in are closed up as tight as glue.
How my bank account is fading, like the early morning mist,
And the time I lost in April makes of me a pessimist.

Gee! How hot the days are growing, shows are closing everywhere;
Palm beach suits will soon be showing. Summer's smell is in the air—
Actors running thick on Broadway. giving all the girls a treat;
Hoofers crowding into lunch rooms, giving rest to weary feet.

Think I'll hie me to the country, out to where its cool and nice;
I played fifteen weeks in fifty, three of them without a slice—
I know where the fishings nifty. where the streams run smooth and clear,
Where the fish will bite on cardboard, and old Mother Nature's near.

For I'm tired of wigs and greasepaint, songs and dances make me ill,
Five-piece bands and sawing fiddlers. of them all I've had my fill;
Maybe next year I'll be lucky. maybe I will grab a show—
Maybe I will change my agent, maybe I will save some dough.

But right now I'm going fishing. where the brook comes tumbling down,
No more props and no more spotlights. no more muggin, no more clown;
In September I'll be ready. from my agent I'll expect—
"Akron next week, wire answer" dollar eighty-five, collect.

Alibis

By the fall of 1927 the Marx Brothers had graduated from vaudeville and were the toast of Broadway. Their first show, I'll Say She Is, *spent a year on the road before debuting on Broadway. Their second show,* The Cocoanuts, *toured from September 1926 until February 1928 after 276 performances on Broadway. Two Broadway hits provided Groucho with enough expertise to pen a guide to the excuses for failed theatrical enterprises. "Alibis" appeared in* Variety *as the Marx Brothers performed* The Cocoanuts *in Denver, Colorado.*

In compiling this memo of everready alibis, also known as tried and true squawks, I willingly release them to the show business at large. In our march across the map with "Cocoanuts," we have heard them all, as other shows have before and others shows will after.

Some are geographically placed and others cover the country if not the world. Permission is granted for rewrites, replacements and revisions, along with adaptations.

For the more intelligent reader, the squawks are divided into months, in case anyone wishes to send them out as Xmas cards:

September—Too early in the season. People not back from country. Those returning busy preparing the children for school.

October—First part of month World Series killing business. Second half of month, unseasonable weather.

November—Political and business uneasiness due to elections. Last half of month, football games draining locals.

December—Cinch. Always bad. Xmas shopping.

January—Bankrolls depleted after Xmas shopping. Thousands of department store clerks in sanitariums from overwork.

February—Huge blizzards paralyze railroads. Suburban towns hemmed in by gigantic snowdrifts. Oldest inhabitant calls it biggest blizzard since '88.

March—Income tax filings.

April—Lent.

May—Unseasonable weather. Daylight saving. People out in cars.

(If now playing New England, substitute—mills on half time. Silk stockings killed cotton industry.)

Western Pennsylvania—Steel business in record slump. Mills fighting unions. Workers in ugly mood.

Detroit—Business either bad because Ford's new car isn't out or bad because Ford's new car is out.

Mississippi Valley—Floods ruined farmers. Theatrical business will be bad until bills are passed giving farmers wheat guarantee and federal flood relief.

Southern Territory—Everything south attributed to cotton situation. Show may be 1,000 miles from cotton fields but this is the standard alibi. Used from Wilmington to Phoenix, to New Orleans, via any road.

Variety
November 30, 1927

When I Was Young and Charming

It seems odd that Groucho wrote a piece looking back on his long career before the Marx Brothers had even made their first film, but by 1929 he had spent nearly a quarter of a century on the stage. The mild deception of knocking five years from his age had already begun, and he refers to his stage debut as having occurred in 1909 with the Three Nightingales. In fact, Groucho made his debut a few months before his fifteenth birthday in 1905 and he worked without any of his brothers for almost two years. The Three Nightingales— with Groucho and Gummo—debuted in 1907 and the addition of Harpo in 1908 made them a quartet. The act performed for the last time in 1909 and none of the various fourth Nightingales was ever named Marx. The Four Marx Brothers first came together when Chico joined the cast of "Fun in Hi Skule" in 1912.

Some of Groucho's other recollections might confound researchers were they to use "When I Was Young and Charming" as a reference source. Dates were never important to Groucho. Charlie Chaplin toured the Sullivan–Considine vaudeville circuit while the Marx Brothers worked the Pantages in the same territory in 1913. Chaplin had yet to perform in the United States in 1909. But Groucho's fondness for a bygone era is obvious, if not historically accurate.

Twenty years ago, when I first took to the stage, the Four Marx Brothers were the Three Nightingales, and Matty* was the greatest pitcher in the world.

Theme songs were unheard of, and cornetists wore their derbies instead of blowing through them. Stage hands got twenty-five dollars a week, and Will Rogers was roping steers instead of steering ropes.

A young comedian, Charles Chaplin by name, was getting forty dollars a week, playing the Sullivan–Considine circuit. He used to watch our act every day and confided that he had been offered $100 a week to play in Keystone Comedy motion pictures. He was undecided whether to accept the offer, as he didn't have much confidence in moving pictures and said that no comedian in the world was worth $100 a week.

Vaudeville was at the height of its popularity, and three performances a day, with four on Saturday and five on Sunday, was considered a vacation. A week which only called for one split engagement was a rest cure. Every parlor and church had an organ, and people used to go to the movies to get away from organs, not to get near them. On amateur nights one would see real amateurs, and the Cherry Sisters played all their engagements behind a wire screen.

A great mechanical feat was to have songs illustrated by slides and people shook their heads and said, "What are they going to do next?" The lyrics were written for the slides, instead of the slides being made for the lyrics. There was always a couple by a lagoon, by a park bench and in a parlor. Sweet Marie by a cherry tree and Sweet Estelle by a moss-covered well.

The Three Nightingales became the Four Marx Brothers when Brother Arthur joined the act. When he spoke his first lines we realized he was born to be a pantomimist. We laughed indulgently when he said he'd like to take lessons on a harp and our act was called Fun in Hi Skule. This spelling was considered to be very comical in those days and, in fact, was the biggest laugh in the act. As I recall it now, it was the only laugh. In those days, when a man was a failure in another line of vaudeville he usually ended up in a school act. George Jessel, Eddie Cantor, Georgie Price, Herman Timberg and Lila Lee were a few failures who were also appearing in school acts.

Curtains were rolled on a log, and to be hit by one was sure death. Stage hands changed the sets in full lights and their shirt sleeves, and the proprietor's daughter always played the piano. That's how he came to be the proprietor. William Faversham was the reigning matinée idol and John Barrymore was just another juvenile hanging around booking offices. There were three

---

*[Christy Mathewson, Hall of Fame pitcher for the New York Giants.]

companies of The Merry Widow on tour, and the Shubert youngsters, Sam and Lee, actually had an interest in nine different productions. The standard vaudeville wage was forty dollars for a single and sixty dollars for a double; quartets were paid $150 and headliners $200.

Railroad fare was two cents a mile, and hotels had a standard rate of six dollars a week, including a midnight supper after the show.

Paul Whiteman was driving a taxi in Denver, and a jazz band was a jazz band, not a symphony orchestra. It was considered quite the thing to have the saxophone player stretch out across the piano, and the violinist was a bust unless he could fiddle behind his back. All good drummers threw their sticks in the air, and the member of the orchestra who played the loudest was made the leader.

David Warfield was wringing their hearts in The Music Master, and Barney Oldfield and Ralph DePalma actually drove their cars faster than seventy miles and hour. Jack Johnson knocked out Ketchell with nonchalance and a right hook, and "skidoo" was considered a pretty smart crack. Beer was a nickel a glass, and "Frankie and Johnnie" was only sung on Mississippi levees. Twenty-eighth Street was the center of the New York theater district, and bad breath was called bad breath. A two-dollar top meant a two-dollar top, and by cut rates people meant twenty-five cents for a haircut.

The Wright brothers were considered a couple of daredevils who would break their necks any day now, and Bleriot flew across the English Channel, although a lot of people thought it was a hoax. Maurice McLoughlin and Melville Long went to Australia after the Davis Cup and came back without it. George Cohan could have been mayor of New York, and dinners with candles were unknown except in homes of plumbers. Mrs. Fiske was considered winsome in Salvation Nell, and the only time an actor could get his picture in the paper was when he died. St. Louis was still hoping for a pennant, and Eva Tanguay kept telling the world she didn't care.

What the country needed was a good three-cent cigar, and guns still were a novelty in Chicago. It was a swell house that had more than one bathroom, and the Hippodrome was New York's greatest theatrical attraction, with Messrs. Shubert and Anderson's "World-Famous Babel-Tongued, Universally Praised, Epoch-Making and All-Conquering Productions." Sothern and Marlowe opened the sumptuous New Theater—now the Century—in which nothing was omitted except acoustics.

Art Fisher, a monologist, disturbed our poker game in Champaign, Illinois, by calling Arthur "Harpo"; Leo "Chico"; Herbert "Zeppo"; and me "Groucho."* He was the only kibitzer on record who ever said anything of value. Our Uncle Al Shean wrote an act for us called *Home Again*, and hadn't as yet met a fellow named Gallagher.** Uncle Al told us he could probably get us a New York booking, but we were afraid the Big Town wouldn't like our stuff. Our booking agent was one Minnie Palmer and so was our mother.

Harvard still won football championships and Maxine Elliot, Elsie Janis, Frances Starr, Blanche Bates, Grace George, Carlotta Nillson, Mrs. Leslie Carter and Anna Held were the toasts of the town, and dry toast was unknown then. People were saying that Fannie Ward was getting pretty old, and yokels were constantly being fooled by the wax policemen in the Eden Musée. Robert Hilliard was a sensation in A Fool There Was, and men who played golf were considered effeminate.

Any President could win if he came out against Wall Street. Anybody who spoke French was thought affected, and you hadn't seen anything unless you'd seen Forbes-Robertson in The Passing of the Third Floor Back. There were very few two-car families, but there was always meat on the table.

An eighteen-week engagement was considered a good run on Broadway— and still is. There were wild reports that Marconi would soon fix it so that people could talk through the air, and WJZ were only letters of the alphabet. Every well-dressed man wore an elk's tooth for a watch charm, and Maude Adams was breaking their hearts in *What Every Woman Knows*. Bernard Shaw had never appeared in the Talkies, and that bad little Dempsey boy was knocked out of the third grade of school and never returned.

Only lowbrows read detective stories, and the Sunday paper could still be lifted with one hand. Everybody agreed that there never would be another slugger like Delehanty, and the name of the fourteen-year-old catcher on the baseball team of the St. Mary's Industrial School in Baltimore was George Herman Ruth. Tetrazzini was standing them up at the Metropolitan, and John

---

*[This actually happened in Galesburg, Illinois, and Fisher named Milton "Gummo." Herbert was named "Zeppo" at a later date, since he was only thirteen years old and not yet in the act when this incident occurred in May 1914.]

**[Actually, Gallagher and Shean teamed up in 1910, well in advance of the fall 1914 debut of *Home Again*.]

Drew was always hanging around the Lambs. Liver was given away with each purchase of meat, and you could still buy drugs in a drug store.

President Roosevelt would have scorned to ride a mechanical horse, and steerage was called steerage and not Students' Third. Young Ty Cobb and Honus Wagner led the American and National leagues in batting, and the best burlesque shows in town were at Joe Weber's, Twenty-ninth and Broadway. Annapolis, University of Virginia and Georgetown failed to finish their football seasons because of injuries, and everyone agree the game was doomed as a sport. A trip to Europe was an event, and a bulldog was considered pretty classy.

Henry Mencken was a columnist on the *Baltimore Sun*, and Lew Dockstader was considered some cut-up. Nobody smoked cigarettes to cure anything, and blindfolds were only used in children's games. Zangwill's Melting Pot was a sensation, and word "bootleg" hadn't been heard since the Civil War. William Winter retired after forty years as a critic on the *Tribune*, and Walter Winchell was singing songs with Eddie Cantor at the Regent Movie Palace on One Hundred and Sixteenth Street.

Peary reached the North Pole, and one-tenth of the automobiles were run by steam or electricity. Ford was unheard of, and street cleaners still had plenty to do. DeWolf Hopper married his third wife and was still two behind Nat Goodwin.

Coney Island had no boardwalk, and the German flag was seen in Yorkville. Regal created a sensation by charging $3.50 for a pair of shoes, and the mention of Yonkers on a vaudeville stage was always good for a laugh.

Klaw and Erlanger were czars of the legitimate stage, and there never were more than two benefits on a Sunday night. Sutton Place was a group of livery stables, and Great Neck was a farming center. Full-dress parlors supplied clothes for almost everybody, and everyone changed his underwear in April. A gentleman by the name of Merkle neglected to touch second base, and the word "bonehead" came into its own.

Bernhardt, at sixty-five, made positively her final farewell tour, and no college was considered first class unless it broke up at least four musical shows a season. Half the population had stiff necks from looking at Halley's Comet, and you could park as long as you liked in Times Square.

An actor was not considered a trouper unless he had been stranded on the road four times, and the suffragettes were forgetting their manners in London. Vitamins and Vitaphones were unheard of, but the Vitagraph films were the last word in motion pictures. Girls blushed when a wise-cracker would say, "Oh you chicken!" and Alice Joyce was much better known than Peggy. H. B. Warner was appearing in *Alias Jimmy Valentine*, and an unknown juvenile named Douglas Fairbanks was offered a part in *The Cub*.

Eugene Walter's *The Wolf* was considered the pinnacle of drama, and "Love Me and the World Is Mine" was the song hit of the day. Tabloids hadn't appeared yet and Bernarr MacFadden's muscles were being displayed in every drug-store window. The burlesque stars of the day were Fannie Brice, Jim Barton, "Beef Trust" Billy Watson, Bobby Clark, Al Reeves and the Watson Sisters, and only rich people played the stock market.

Irving Berlin wrote "Alexander's Ragtime Band," and Clarence H. Mackay was elected president of the Postal Telegraph Company. The musical saw had not made its appearance on the vaudeville stage, and every burlesque show had an Irish and a Jew comedian, as well as a rich widow. James O'Neill was a headliner, but no one had heard of his scapegrace son, Eugene, who was working as a sailor. The Marx Brothers played every milk depot in the United States, and their father was in New York measuring people for suits. No trip to New York was complete without a view of the Flatiron Building, and a fellow who could blow smoke rings was a social success.

Marilyn Miller, as one-fifth of the Five Columbians, was knocking them dead as a child wonder, and Moran and Mack were getting the princely salary of $200 a week. Eddie Foy threatened to play Hamlet, and Buster Keaton was still bouncing on vaudeville stages. Joan Lowell was a tot on a Pacific freighter and the Book-of-the-Month Club was still to be formed. Only farmers wore galoshes, and all vaudeville theaters had green rooms. Asquith was Prime Minister of England, and the Jones Act was a couple of acrobats playing Pantages's time.

Cutler of the Fort Wayne Register declared that the Marx Brothers were the worst comedians he had ever seen, and New York hadn't been honored by a visit from St. John Ervine. Songs about trolley rides were still being sung, and Cleveland had a three-cent fare. Chorus girls were picked for weight, not speed, and shop girls wore silk stockings only on Sundays.

No hot dog was complete without sauerkraut, and only millionaires had two-car garages. Jokes about farmers blowing out the gas light appeared in every comic weekly, and Ed Walsh won forty games in a single season. Movie critics were unknowns, and B.L.T. on the Chicago Tribune was showing the boys how to write a column. Jeffries and Johnson agreed to fight in Reno for the unbelievable purse of $101,000, and the Dolly Sisters were playing in Jacksonville, Florida, for sixty dollars a week. Strawberries did not appear in New York until April, and only in a terrific windstorm were a girl's knees visible.

Actors spent their spare time in pool rooms, and if anybody had told me that a magazine would pay me to write articles I would have sneered derisively—if I had known what that meant.

Saturday Evening Post
June 22, 1929

Ahead of the Times

The Marx Brothers opened a ten week engagement in Animal Crackers *at Chicago's Grand Theater on December 22, 1929. Early in the run, Groucho met* Chicago Daily Times *columnist Arthur Sheekman. Their lifelong friendship got off to an amusing start when Groucho wrote a guest column for Sheekman.*

Sheekman introduced Groucho to his readers: "Mr. Groucho Marx, the noted author, poker player and co-star of Animal Crackers, *is this column's guest conductor today. Groucho is, to my notion, the most comical fellow on the American stage."*

The Curtain Rises

Dressing room No. 3—Grand Opera House, January 7—this column, gentle, kindly, wholesome reader, is being dictated to a battery (A and B) of stenographers while Art Sheekman stands by, making sour faces when the lines get off-colorful. Maybe he isn't making faces. Maybe he looks like that. Anyway—

The Mildly Low-Down

Dorothy Parker can out-curse any man in New York. And, what's more, any woman . . . . Whenever there's a party at Heywood Broun's house, Heywood's 10-year-old son, Junior, is awakened at midnight for a cocktail . . . . Alex Woollcott, the critic, wouldn't think of going across the street without his galoshes . . . . Since Arnold Rothstein left this world, Nick the Greek is New York's foremost gambler, and it's almost impossible to nick the Greek. One fine

autumn day he won $200,000 in a crap game. Yes, Phil baker contributed . . . .
George Kaufman, the playwright, keeps his job as drama editor of the *New
York Times* so he'll have a place to write . . . . George gets more phone calls
from women than any other married man in New York.

The same Heywood Broun mentioned above has the biggest feet west of
the Ohio River . . . . Harold Ross, editor of the *New Yorker*, is the unfunniest
practical joker in America. One night, in a playful mood, he locked his wife
out of the house . . . . George M. Cohan doesn't smoke, and when George
Jessel's cigar gets down to seven inches in length he throws it away—and
then picks it up again . . . . Robert Benchley has a passion for quartet singing
and he always carries a tenor around with him . . . . Rueben, the sandwich
magnate, has an oil painting of a corned beef sandwich in his living room . . . .
If you buy your copy of *College Humor* right away you might be able to avoid
the February issue, which has a piece (adv.) by me called "Holy Smoke." . . . .
Mayor Jimmy Walker of New York hasn't missed a party in seven years and
six months, except the parties given by the alderman in the city hall.

Ed Wynn likes to rub ketchup on the doorknob of his house, which always
starts the parties out swell . . . . Herbert Bayard Swope, the former editor,
never uses a telephone. When he whispers in New York he can be heard in
Philadelphia . . . . Neysa McMein, the artist, won't buy the *Saturday Evening
Post* for fear she'll see one of her covers on it; and she can't bear looking at
her own stuff . . . . Harpo Marx once hit a croquet ball that killed a sheep in
Central Park, and G. Kaufman said that he had heard of chicken croquet, but
not sheep . . . . David Warfield has given up acting because it takes his mind
off pinochle playing . . . . FPA (Franklin P. Adams, the columnist who used to
be a Chicagoan) wears the loudest ties in the world . . . . When Eddie Cantor
plays ball in Long Island he wears baseball pants, a silk hat and dinner jacket,
and his game is in keeping with the costume . . . . So what?

Some Recollections

I can remember those days in Tacoma and Seattle, Washington, when we'd
meet Charlie Chaplin after the show and shoot craps on the floor for pennies. Charlie was getting $35 a week in the variety act called "A Night at the
Club," and was always about three weeks behind—or maybe I should say
ahead—on his salary. And we were getting I won't say what for playing in
"Fun in Hi Skule."

Charlie would always refuse to shoot craps with anyone who was smoking a cigarette. He was afraid his celluloid collar would catch fire.

Club Note

Although originally an actors' club, the Friars' (in New York) now has four pants salesmen for every actor. And it's disconcerting, because when you tell a fellow member what a hit you were in Milwaukee he'll immediately recall that he sold 658 pairs of pants to a hard-boiled buyer there.

Why I Like the Movies

I am what is known as a screen slumberer. Give me a good movie and a comfortable deluxe chair and I can sleep happily. I slept best at a picture called *The Cocoanuts*, even though it was terribly loud. But so was my sleeping.

Chicago Daily Times
January 7, 1930

Heywood Broun

While the Marx Brothers were camped in New York with three hit Broadway shows, Groucho became a regular contributor to many of his favorite newspaper columns and forged friendships with several New York literary figures. During this period, Heywood Broun began running amusing letters from Groucho in his New York World *column, "It Seems to Me."*

A typical example from the February 28, 1926, edition:

It was a great shock to my brothers and myself to learn that you were addicted to pajamas. It was a little discouraging too. We have always told everyone that you wore nightgowns. It was just a natural inference on our part. Why, we never dreamed that you were such a flossy dresser. Pajamas we had always thought of in connection with slick Stacomb* sheiks, slim-hipped spotted devils.

You, we always looked upon as a sort of ascetic. Whenever we spoke of you (which was often) we always fancied you lumbering around a bare unadorned bedroom in nightgown, sleeping cap and woolen slippers, prim and austere, maybe even a candle in your right hand. In my family Broun and nightgown were practi-

---

*[Stacomb was a popular hair cream.]

cally synonymous. It was just like Weber and Fields, Mellon and aluminum, bacon and eggs.

I don't know whether you have ever worn a nightgown, but some-day you will. They all do. For freedom, grace, comfort and ven-tilation, yes and even looks, they are superior to those boudoir Prince Alberts.

I will concede that a nightgown wearer looks awkward crawling out of, or even into, bed, but this can easily be overcome by wearing pajamas underneath. Yours for flowing robes.

To this Broun would respond with something like, "Groucho and the other Marxes have no right to talk about me, often or infrequently, if they are simply disseminating fallacies. Why don't they brush up on the subject of Broun. Lumbering indeed!"

Broun claimed to have attended more than twenty performances of The Cocoanuts on Broadway and joked that his tombstone would read, "Killed by getting in the way of some scene shifters at a Marx Brothers show." When he wasn't having fun with the Marx Brothers, Broun was a champion of social causes and became the most con-troversial journalist of his time. In 1930 he waged an unsuccessful campaign for congress on the Socialist ticket, garnering endorse-ments from friends like Irving Berlin, Helen Hayes, Robert Benchley, Fred Astaire and, of course, Groucho Marx, who introduced Broun at a campaign rally at the Broadhurst Theater that was broadcast over WABC radio in New York. The New York Herald-Tribune and several other newspapers around the country printed Groucho's remarks shortly after the broadcast. No recording is known to exist.

Man and boy, I have known Heywood Broun for thirty years. He has also known me for thirty years. This makes a total of sixty years and brings us down to the fiscal year of 1861, when conditions were much the same as they are now. My fa-ther was out of a job at the time, the farmers were complaining about the prices, and the Prices, who lived right next door, were complaining about my father.

While the other boys in our neighborhood were out stealing apples, Broun was home stealing bananas and reading the Congressional Records. This was quite a feat, as the printing press had not yet been invented, and a $10 overcoat was considered a way uptown.

Two weeks later, troops were massed at the border, plowshares were being bitten into plows, and in a little garden a boy who was later to become the Archduke Ferdinand was playing with his tin soldiers, little recking that an assassin's pistol was lying in wait for him. That little assassin, ladies and gentlemen, was Heywood Broun.

Heywood Broun, the Great White Father of Heywood the Third, first saw the light of day in the sleepy little village of Centerville, New York.

Three days after he was born he took his carpetbag in hand, stuffed it with marked cards and Marc Connelly, and boarded the steam cars for the big city. At the depot the train went wild with joy as the crowd pulled out, and twenty minutes later a tiny dot appeared in the sky, broke through the clouds and brought the plane down for one of the prettiest little accidents ever seen on the fields of Mineola. That little accident, ladies and gentlemen, was Heywood Broun.

When we next clap eyes on Heywood Broun the horse had disappeared. Up and down the Mississippi went the word; from Natchez to Vicksburg, from Cairo to Shreveport, and from Tinker to Evers to Chance sounded the tocsin. A new five-cent cigar had made its appearance. Little buzzing knots in the cigar made it almost impossible to smoke. "Broun's Folly," sneered his opponents. Came the day of the great experiment, clear and windless. On its windlass, Broun is hoisted into the cockpit of the cigar while a thousand throats are hushed. "Will it fly?" is the unspoken query in the hearts of the multitude.

Look. Look! Slowly it strains at a gnat, swallows a camel and rises. It is off, to the roar of a million throats!

But in a far off corner of the field, with tears in her great brown eyes and a lump in her throat, a horse is watching. That horse, ladies and gentlemen, is Heywood Broun.

And so, pupils of the Pratt Street Grammar School, we have come together today to observe Ann Arbor Day and plant a tree in honor of that great Polish explorer, Heywood Broun.

Let us hope that one day the frozen Yukon wastes will give him up. Let us hope that something, at least, will give him up. Perhaps he will give himself up. I gave him up a long time ago.

WABC Radio, New York
December 12, 1930

The Psychology of Psocks

One fact of Hollywood life that disappeared along with the studio system of the 1930s and 1940s was that movie stars endorsed products. Lots of products. Somehow Groucho came to write an endorsement for Real Silk, a company that sold socks door to door. (Their slogan was, "Sold only in office and home.") The advertisement ran in the Saturday Evening Post *with this note from the advertiser: "We engaged Groucho Marx to write this advertisement, reimbursing him at his regular rate. The result is a hilarious burlesque of the Realsilk Representative calling on Mr. Marx on his Hollywood set and making the sale."*

This is a true pstory, which I have translated from the Russian, first, however, putting on a neat Russian blouse to get the "feel" of that difficult language. It concerns the sox-life of the former Grand Duke Grouchidor ("Tiger Rose") Marxisoxsky.

One day a commoner came to my castle in Hollywoodograd. He caught the Grand Duke with a hole in his sock. Imagine catching the Grand Duke with a hole in his sock. Imagine catching anyone with a hole in his sock. I felt chagrin creeping all over me. I blushed through my tunic.

The commoner took one look at the rosy ducal toes and playfully said, "This little pig went to market; this little pig stayed home."

The *Psychology* of *Psocks*

by GROUCHO MARX

ADVERTISER'S NOTE—We engaged Groucho Marx to write this advertisement, reimbursing him at his regular rate. The result is a hilarious burlesque of the Realsilk Representative calling on Mr. Marx on his Hollywood set and making the sale.

This is a true pstory, which I have translated from the Russian, first, however, putting on a neat Russian blouse to get the "feel" of that difficult language. It concerns the sox-life of the former Grand Duke Grouchidor ("Tiger Rose") Marxisoxsky.

ONE DAY a commoner came to my castle in Hollywoodograd. He caught the Grand Duke with a hole in his sock. Imagine catching anyone with a hole in his sock. I felt chagrin creeping all over me. I blushed through my tunic.

The commoner took one look at the rosy ducal toes and playfully said, "This little pig went to market; this little pig stayed home."

"Enough," I cried, "quit profaning the Grand Duke's toes and come to the point." Hastily I threw my *mantilla* over the offending members.

"Don't let the hole in the sock get your goatsky," he said. "You'd be surprised how many holes in socks, or stockings for that matter, go on under cover. In fact, I just came from the exclusive Malibu Beachsky section, where I found three leading men and an ingenue with holes in their hosiery. I helped them, and I can help you, too."

"You have moved me strangely," said the Grand Duke. "Who are you?"

"The Realsilk Man—come to bring you the glad tidings of wonderful socks—wholly without holes—and of such quality that Grand Dukes, and even people with regular jobs, are proud to sheathe their feet within them."

He started firing questions at me rapid-fire.

"Is your sox-life a happy one?

"Can a Grand Duke do first-class duking in socks like those you now wear?

"Do you feel at ease when you take off your shoes in company?"

By this time we were both in tears. I dried his and vice versa.

"Shako," I said at last, doffing my own with a bow, "but why are you taking so much trouble just for a poor old broken-down Grand Dukeovitch?"

"You look good for at least a dozen pairs of these non-rippable, extra quality, superguarded toed, double-decked soled, handsomely patterned, longer-wearing famous Realsilk socks. I feel sure that I have shown you the error of your previous sox-life. Shall I put you down for two or four dozen pairs?"

Of course, a Marxisoxsky never takes the first figure offered, so I got him down to one dozen pairs before I bought. And I can truthfully say, it was the turning point in the Grand Duke's life.

Now, on the set, when the boys and girls have recess from the hurly-burly of lights, cameras, sound mixers, directors and gagmen, and have gathered together for a moment's relaxation, instead of importuning me to do my card tricks, bird calls, or ocarina solos, they say:

"Grouchidor, show us your socks,"

—and I'm proud to say that I do!

To Women: If you have read this sock ad please know that the Realsilk Representative who calls at the home also brings a complete line of women's fine hosiery and lingerie, as well as wearables for all members of the family.

THE SOCKS WITH SEVEN EXCLUSIVE FEATURES

(1) **Six-Ply Toe**—which is the best wearing sock toe in the world (patent pending). (2) **High-Spliced Heel**—to prevent those exasperating holes where the shoe rubs. (3) **Double-Layer Sole**—longer wear. (4) **More Compact Weave**—more actual fabric—more actual wear—and better looks for the money. (5) **Longest Silk Leg Found in Any Socks**—the bigger the foot size, the longer the leg. (6) **Double-Thick Garter Bonds**—non-rippable—comfortable. (7) **Triple-Fast Hygienic Dyes**—fast to light, washing and perspiration. Color cannot harm the feet. Realsilk Hosiery Mills, Inc., Indianapolis, U. S. A. World's largest manufacturers of silk hosiery. Branches in 250 cities.

REALSILK

SOLD ONLY IN OFFICE AND HOME

"Enough," I cried, "quit profaning the Grand Duke's toes and come to the point." Hastily I threw my *mantilla* over the offending members.

"Don't let the hole in the sock get your goatsky," he said. "You'd be surprised how many holes in socks, or stockings for that matter, go on under cover. In fact, I just came from the exclusive Malibu Beachsky section, where I found three leading men and an ingenue with holes in their hosiery. I helped them, and I can help you, too."

"You have moved me strangely," said the Grand Duke. "Who are you?"

"The Realsilk Man—come to bring you the glad tidings of wonderful socks—wholly without holes—and of such quality that Grand Dukes, and even people with regular jobs, are proud to sheathe their feet within them."

He started firing questions at me rapid-fire.

"Is your sox-life a happy one?

"Can a Grand Duke do first-class duking in socks like those you now wear?

"Do you feel at ease when you take off your shoes in company?"

By this time we were both in tears. I dried his and vice versa.

"Shako," I said at last, doffing my own with a bow, "but why are you taking so much trouble for just a poor old broken-down Grand Dukeovitch?"

"You look good for at least a dozen pairs of these non-rippable, extra quality, super-guarded toed, doubled-decked soled, handsomely patterned, longer-wearing famous Realsilk socks. I feel sure that I have shown you the error of your previous sox-life. Shall I put you down for two or four dozen pairs?"

Of course, a Marxisoxsky never takes the first figure offered, so I got him down to one dozen pairs before I bought. And I can truthfully say, it was the turning point in the Grand Duke's life.

Now, on the set, when the boys and girls have recess from the hurly-burly of lights, cameras, sound mixers, directors and gag-men, and have gathered together for a moment's relaxation, instead of importuning me to do my card tricks, bird calls, or ocarina solos, they say:

"Grouchidor, show us your socks,"—and I'm proud to say that I do!

Saturday Evening Post
January 23, 1932

Author in Search of Characters

For many years before he became a Sunday night television fixture, Ed Sullivan was a newspaper columnist. In the era when New York had more than a dozen daily newspapers, Sullivan worked for the Evening Mail, *the* Morning World, *the* Morning Telegraph, *the* Bulletin *and the* Leader *before landing at the* Evening Graphic, *where he replaced Walter Winchell as the Broadway columnist in June 1929 when Winchell jumped to the* Daily Mirror. *By the time of Sullivan's ascent to the Broadway beat, the Marx Brothers had recently completed their run in* Animal Crackers, *their third and final Broadway show, so Groucho was not featured in his column to any significant degree. Ten years later Groucho made up for this, at least for one day, by filling in for the vacationing Sullivan and writing his nationally syndicated* Chicago Daily Tribune *column.*

When the phone rang, I had a premonition that hard luck was coming my way, and when I put the receiver to my ear, I was sure of it. "Look, Groucho, if I can get 28 fellers who can write (not an easy task in Hollywood), I can go to Florida and toast my body on the warm sands of Miami."

Well, I've seen Sullivan's body and although I don't know whether toasting would help it any, it certainly couldn't hurt it. This is, indeed, the toasting age: they do it to bread, cigarettes, after-dinner speakers and cornflakes, and now, how wonderful, a writer is going to Florida and toast his carcass on the hot sands! (Is that a thousand words yet? What—only a hundred!)

Why was I sucker enough to tell Sullivan I would do this? How can anyone do this every day? What is there happening in the world important enough to fill up this much white space every 24 hours! Why don't they just leave it blank and say Harpo wrote it? (I suppose that's a bad idea.) Let's see, what does Sullivan write about? Not so loud, Groucho, the editor's liable to hear you.) Oh, yes, names make news!

Who was at the Clover Club last night? No, that won't do—that place has been closed for two months. I'll try it again. Wrapped in ermine and mink, the Cinema's brightest lights gathered at the Troc for the opening dance of the winter season. (Groucho, the Troc has been closed for two months.) Is every place closed for two months? What a fool, looking for news around abandoned night clubs!

Of course—the race track! Personally, I can take it or leave it—but the names do gather out there and ye old reporter—plenty old by this time with 600 words yet to go—tweed suit, checkered cap, and field glasses slung carelessly over left breast (must be authentic; that's the way Rosenbloom wears them) is off to the races. Hey, I'll grab enough gossip in 15 minutes in the paddock to fill three encyclopedias! Reporting isn't so tough! You just have to know where to go, that's all! What a dope I was, fiddling around deserted night clubs! Well, enough of this recrimination.

Here we are at the track. What a day! Not a cloud in the sky, and now that I look, not a sucker in the grandstand! What's the matter with me—has racing been repealed? Is the Sport of Kings dead in California? I read the papers every day—why didn't I see this item? What—this is the wrong track! This is Inglewood! So what? Don't they race at Inglewood? Man alive! I've seen them race at Inglewood! Didn't I lose two bucks last August on a dog that I got hot out of the feed box! Of course they race at Inglewood, but this happens to be February, vacuum head, and the ponies are slithering through the mud at Santa Anita.

Say, maybe there's more to writing a column than meets the eye. You not only have to know what to write but you have to know where to go. (You mean to say that I have written only 600 words and that I have 400 to go?) Listen, Sullivan, how about a short column for a change? People are getting awfully tired of these long columns. They haven't time to read a thousand words, day after day. Socrates wrote only one paragraph a day and he did all right! Let's see, there must be 400 words that I can think of. How about cat? That's a good word. It's a little short but every little bit helps. Constantinople! There, gents, is a word! It doesn't take many Constantinoples to fill up a column. I'm crazy about that town. Had a great history, too. Let's see, wasn't that where the Turks fought the Moors at the battle of Waterloo?

Why does Sullivan have to go to Florida to lie in the sun? What's the matter with the California sun? Isn't it hot enough for him? Doesn't it have just as much violet ray? What's the matter with California? I've lived here eight years and it's treated me pretty well. Doesn't the gentle Pacific (gentle Pacific! Did you ever get your head bashed in by a comber at Malibu?) roll its tiny wavelets on our warm sands? Aren't our bathing beauties just as seductive as the Floridian eye-fillers? Why don't you forget about your body, Sullivan, and give your mind a chance to develop? Who was it—oh, yes, James Russell Lowell—who said, "There are few brains that wouldn't be better for living on their own fat for a little while." You know what that means, Sullivan that means you should sit down and think once in a while! Toast your mind for a change—forget about your body! Don't forget, the body disintegrates: the only substance that remains is the pure, crystal thought of your mind. Say, that's not a bad philosophy! Maybe I should have been a philosopher. It's not a bad racket—at least you don't have to write a thousand words every day!

That reminds me: I must have a thousand by this time, haven't I? What—I need two more! Okay, Ed, Merry Christmas!

Yours,
GROUCHO

Chicago Daily Tribune
March 1, 1939

Tales of Hoffman: Letter to Chico

Groucho didn't write many letters to his brothers, since they spoke either in person or on the phone on a fairly regular basis. When a letter from Groucho to another Marx Brother found its way into print, it was usually a gag.

The January 15, 1952, issue of Look *contained a feature article called "The Secret Letters of Julius Marx." One of these "secret" letters was to Chico Marx:*

> *Ravelli, I have never told you this, but as a pianist, I am no great admirer of yours. You are a handy man with a deck of cards, and I understand there have been times when you were facile with the galloping cubes, but as a musician, you leave a great deal to be desired. After sitting on the stage for 25 years, listening to you grope your way through the ivories, I realize that there is a wide margin between your piano playing and that of, say, Vladimir Horowitz. You have many other qualities I admire, but as a pianist, as they say in Paris, "Pouf."*

Groucho's frequent contributions to Irving Hoffman's Hollywood Reporter *column also included a letter to Chico. Groucho wrote Hoffman, "I'm enclosing the letter I sent to Chico, and if you care for it, print it in your column—only don't run it with the prison stuff."*

Dear Chico:

Our correspondence is becoming increasingly strained and I can only attribute it to the curious and mystifying ways you have of answering your mail. In the past three weeks I have written you three times. In return you have sent me a package of cheese, a small barrel of herring and a smoked tongue. These are eloquent answers—much stronger than words—but you must admit they are difficult to decode unless one has spent his early years as a delicatessen apprentice. What is this unholy terror you have for the written word? Were you once scared by a vowel or a consonant?

Words, in case you don't know, are beautiful. Keats, Shelley and Conrad enriched and gladdened the whole world with words. Is it possible that your odd method of correspondence is more effective? Have you stumbled on something that will replace all the beautiful poems and love sonnets of the centuries? I only ask you this because I've heard it told that you conduct your romances in the same manner. It is well known that for years you left a trail of broken hearts and sawed-off shotguns from the Orpheum Theatre in Bangor to the Pantages Theatre in San Diego. Is delicatessen your secret weapon? Do you sent pot cheese where others send orchids? When a love-sick girl sends you a perfume-scented note pleading for your kisses, I understand your answer is three slices of pumpernickel. I don't say that this last present may not be just what she needs, but you must concede it's a novel slant on a subject that has bewildered experts since Adam and Eve. Romeo was considered quite a lover in his day but I'm sure Juliet's love for him would have wavered had it reeked so strongly of the pickle barrel. But then your views on love and life have always been unique and bizarre and I guess on you, it looks good.

Unless you answer this letter and I don't mean with delicatessen, groceries or alphabet soup, but with plain words (the dictionary, by the way, is full of them) it will be necessary for me to reduce my correspondence to the same level and my answers in the future will consist of shoe-string potatoes, salamis and apple strudel.

Love and garlic from the Hebrew National, Woloshin's, Levitoff's, Isaac Gellis's, Greenblatt's and Rubin's.

Yours,
Groucho.

Hollywood Reporter
August 29, 1942

How to Crank a Horse

Groucho was a prolific contributor to This Week *during the early 1940s, with seven pieces in the magazine between 1940 and 1943. But "How to Crank a Horse" was published as Groucho was a couple of weeks into his sixty-two week run as the host of* Pabst Blue Ribbon Town. *A regular job on radio cut into his writing time and* This Week *waited until 1946 before Groucho returned to their pages. Like much of Groucho's written work of the World War II period, "How to Crank a Horse" deals with sacrifices on the home front.*

Once, when I was a lad, I came home from school with an A card clutched in my chubby fist. My family was so delighted and surprised that they presented me with a dollar. Yesterday, I came home from the gas-rationing board with an A card and my family threw me out of the house. An A card, according to optimistic government statisticians, is ample for the needs of the average motorist. They've been pretty lenient, too, for though they don't allow you much mileage, they give you a wide choice of directions—north, south, east or west.

Now, dear reader, I realize that there is nothing as cheap as advice, particularly the advice that I dish out, but if you will just sit quietly and wipe that brooding, paranoiac look off your face, I believe I can offer some suggestions that will help to alleviate your transportation problems.

To begin with, I suggest that for the duration you forget about the car (I only wish the finance company would forget about mine). Drive it in the garage, jack it up, place in on blocks and let it rot slowly and thoroughly.

Now then, let us look around and see what can possibly take the place of the automobile. The first thing that comes to my mind is Betty Grable. The second thing that comes to my mind is Betty Grable and the third thing that comes to my mind is the horse—just a plain, old-fashioned, everyday horse. It is well known that a horse requires no gas, doesn't have to be greased and, what is more important, doesn't have to have air blown into his shoes every few days. He is content with a daily apple, a few wild oats and an occasional pat on the rump. And, after all, for practical purposes there isn't much difference between a horse and an auto. However, if you're going to the beach, I wouldn't advise you change into your bathing suit on a horse.

If you are one of the lucky ones who live in the cold country, you're sitting pretty. All you need is a sled, eight Eskimo dogs and a reasonable amount of snow. Unfortunately, I live in Hollywood where snow falls only in the studios and is, confidentially, cornflakes or oatmeal. Doused with cream and sugar, these are delicious cereals—they give boundless energy and are excellent substitutes for snow, but it would cost a fortune to sprinkle all the highways in California with breakfast food and I don't think the taxpayers are in any mood for this sort of hanky-panky.

When the rainy season arrives—and at this point I want to say that our rainy season isn't any worse than the monsoon season in Burma—when the rainy season arrives and the gutters are swollen with dew, if you are lucky enough to have an outboard motor left over from your summer at the lake, you can get yourself a few weeks of cheap transportation by hitching the motor to a washtub or an unoccupied sofa.

The Chinese must be laughing up their sleeves at us and our gas problem. The wise Orientals, ever inscrutable, saw this coming centuries ago and prepared for it by quickly inventing the rickshaw. For those of you who don't read the National Geographic, I might explain that a rickshaw is a blown-up baby buggy with horse shafts and no horse. It is pulled by a Chinese coolie, togged out in slacks, bedroom slippers and a beret. It is a surprisingly pleasant way to travel and quite inexpensive. You see, a rickshaw puller in good condition will get about eight miles—or eight Japs—to a rice pudding.

There are still many other ways of getting around. One is the pogo stick. This blunt instrument, once regarded as a toy and used condescendingly at fashionable watering places, has now taken its rightful place on the highways.

Veteran pogo fanciers say it is far more practical than kangaroo riding, a sport that is quite popular in Australia. Nevertheless, it is not a perfect vehicle—even its friends concede that it has its shortcomings. For example, if you are going to the grocery store for a quart of milk, I wouldn't advise using the pogo stick or you are apt to arrive back at the house with cottage cheese.

In Arabia where the sands are hot and the Arabs are hotter, the camel is used much as we use the streetcar. This doesn't mean that they resemble each other—no, indeed, there's quite a difference between a camel and a streetcar. The streetcar, for example, doesn't eat peanuts and the camel, on the other hand, doesn't have a slot machine for nickels up front. Perhaps I'd better describe just what a camel does look like. It has four legs, two humps and a goatee. I have an uncle who also answers this description: the only difference is, he has only two legs and won't kneel in a sandstorm. The Arab and his camel are inseparable. It's been said that an Arab would give up his wife rather than give up his camel. Personally I haven't got a camel, but I think it's a great idea.

Camels would thrive in our climate and inasmuch as they multiply rapidly, they would quickly help to solve our transportation problem. Of course, they don't multiply as rapidly as guinea pigs, but then who does? The up-keep of a camel is negligible—all he eats is tree tops and sand. His clothing requirements are extremely modest. In the summer, he runs naked; in the winter, if the snow is heavy, you might have to buy him a camel's-hair coat. Unfortunately, the camel, despite his many fine qualities as a desert taxi, is a blue-nosed fanatic. He goes for eight days without a drink and it's question-able whether the average American would want to associate with anyone as dull as that.

If you are lucky enough to get a dinner invitation and the dinner is being thrown in a neighboring village, you might try a scheme that I have been using recently with considerable success. The day before the dinner, have someone in your family wrap you up in heavy manila paper, cart you to the post office and ship you off parcel post to your host. Be sure they put enough stamps on your carcass to insure your arrival. Once when I was be-ing shipped to a dinner engagement, my family understamped me and I not only missed the dinner but I spent two weeks trussed up in a cubbyhole at the dead-letter office.

One sure way to get a free ride is to disguise yourself as a woman or, even better, as a young girl. Just tog yourself out in silk stockings, high-heeled shoes, a peekaboo waist, a blond wig and some nail polish, and you'll be surprised how many pickups you'll get. Try to select a busy intersection; wait for a car with a lone occupant—preferably a fat man with glasses. As his car draws near, roll your eyes violently and wiggle your hips just a trifle. It will astonish you to see how susceptible the average man is to a maiden's wiles. Don't, under any circumstances, allow yourself to be picked up by a gent in an open car. Open-car drivers are usually college students, full of the joy of life, and in the ensuing struggle, your blond wig might fall off, embarrassing both of you to no end.

All these methods failing, there is still a way of getting around. I'll admit it's a little old-fashioned and you may not even remember it. It's called walking. It's not hard to do—you just put both feet together, raise the right foot and bring it forward about one yard, then bring the left one forward, then the right and left and right and left and there you go down the street, happy as a lark, free as the air, no troubles, no cares.

Who said, "The automobile's here to stay"?

This Week
April 4, 1943

S. J. Perelman and Al Hirschfeld

S. J. Perelman and Al Hirschfeld were closer to each other than either was to Groucho, but both men had long friendships with him. The Groucho–Perelman relationship is well documented. (And, even in these very pages.) But Groucho's friendship with Hirschfeld is less so. Hirschfeld's images of the Marx Brothers from the posters and publicity material for their MGM films have become as iconic as the films themselves. Hirschfeld once said that he knew this work was successful "when the Marx Brothers looked like my drawings rather than the other way around." Writing in Hirschfeld's Hollywood, *Hirschfeld archivist David Leopold stated, "There were many satiric portraits of the team before Hirschfeld's, but so complete was his rendition that all future drawings merely reinterpreted his. Even MGM's makeup department tried to get the Marx Brothers to conform to Hirschfeld's image of them. In* A Day at the Races, *their second MGM effort, Groucho's coiffure began to resemble the two triangles Hirschfeld gave him in his drawings." Groucho had been an admirer of Hirschfeld's work prior to their MGM association and he liked him personally.*

Advertisements for Hirschfeld's 1951 book, Show Business Is No Business—*which incidentally includes a caricature of Groucho—stated, "You don't have to buy copies of Al Hirschfeld's* Show Business Is No Business *from Groucho Marx even though Marx is setting himself up in competition with legitimate booksellers. Who knows what he's charging?" Groucho added his own footnote: "I am personally responsible for selling 11 copies of* Show Business Is No Business. *This is by far the funniest book of the year. I never thought a cartoonist, especially one encumbered with a beard, could write with such charming bitterness."*

Hirschfeld illustrated several of Perelman's books, including Westward Ha!, *the chronicle of their 1947 trip around the world. Prior to their departure, Groucho delivered a speech in their honor at a dinner at Chasen's restaurant in Hollywood. Groucho ribbed Hirschfeld by deliberately confusing him with radio comedian and cartoonist Harry Hershfield. This mistake was once so common that when Groucho's publisher asked him who should illustrate his book,* Memoirs of a Mangy Lover, *Groucho simply replied "Hirschfeld." He was later surprised to see that the book was not illustrated by Al Hirschfeld or Harry Hershfield, but by Leo Herschfield, whose name does not appear in the text of Groucho's Perelman–Hirschfeld speech. (But Groucho did eventually get his man. An Al Hirschfeld caricature adorned the cover of* The Secret Word Is Groucho *in 1976.)*

As a rule I don't waste my valuable time attending banquets. The only dinners I attended last year were the Academy Award dinner, the dinner that Basil Rathbone gave for Mrs. Rathbone, the dinner the railroad men gave for Chu Chu Johnson honoring Chu Chu Martinez, and the dinner that Mrs. Rathbone gave for Basil Rathbone.

Other than getting a meal on the cuff I don't much see the point to a public banquet. I assure you that there are more edifying sights than a group of elderly men stuffing themselves with free food tossed at them by an obscure magazine of doubtful literary distinction.

So Hirschfeld and Perelman are leaving the country. I can just imagine the furor this will cause throughout the civilized world. After all, other men have scrammed for parts unknown. Abe Hummel left the country, Judge Crater has never been found and Dore Schary finally landed at R.K.O.

I don't know Mr. Hirschfeld except by reputation. The last time I heard him he appeared with Lee Francis on "Can You Top This."

But Sid and I go back a long ways. I remember him when he started with Judge magazine. He was an instant success for he was the first writer they had that stole all his jokes from Whiz Bang. I remember Sid as a farmer, when he was too poor to buy fertilizer and kept his crops healthy by using the New York Daily News instead.

A boat trip can be tragic if two people aren't compatible, but I am sure that Sid and Al will get along swimmingly. Sid is a lovable companion and a born diplomat. I might say he's as comfortable to be with as an old glove, and just about as interesting. I remember once, years ago, he and I went to Jersey City by ferry and by the time the boat got to Canal Street he had kicked the bootblack in the groin because he had charged him ten cents for a shine.

There will be times in far off places, Mr. Hirschfeld, when you will be unable to get porters for your baggage. But with Sid at your side you can rest easy. Sid is a thumping big fellow and a work horse to boot and he gets a kick out of lifting heavy things. I remember the time he was arrested for lifting a fur coat at Saks Fifth Avenue.

I am sure that Sid and General MacArthur will have some high old times together in Tokyo. I can see them at night—warming themselves over a Geisha girl and chuckling over the old days when MacArthur used to shoot at Sid's relatives from the White House steps.

This trip will do President Truman a lot of good, for you must remember it is under his administration that the boys are leaving the country. This is one thing the Republicans won't be able to take credit for.

I want to wish you two a successful and happy journey. Come back to America safe and strong, for America needs you. A country is only as strong as its weakest link and it is only lads like you that can supply that.

So I say to you two bold adventurers—stretch out your hands for the fruits of the world. Bring back Tales of African Veldt, of the Snows of Kilimanjaro, of the Roumanian peasants plowing the furrows and chanting the songs of Boris Morros. Tell us more of the Dutch boy with his finger in the dike and, if possible, bring back a dike to each of us.

Live dangerously my young friends. Have yourselves a brawl in Singapore and go on a bust in Bali. Nab the world by the tail—there is plenty of it around if you keep your eyes peeled.

As for your book, I'm sure it will be a huge success. I know that I, for one, will be standing in line to grab a copy as soon as it reaches the lending library.

I know that predictions can be dangerous, but I want to go on record as saying that some day the book of Perelman and Hirschfeld will take its place alongside *Dombey & Son*, John Drinkwater's *Life of Carl Laemmle* and *Mexican Hayride*.

Chasen's Restaurant
Unpublished
January 15, 1947

Light and Airy

Jack Hellman, the radio (and later television) editor of Daily Variety, *was known for exuding clouds of cigar smoke and lunching at the Brown Derby restaurant in Hollywood—both of which he occasionally did with Groucho. His long tenure at* Daily Variety *began in 1933 and his column, "Light and Airy," was an important and influential one for the broadcast business until his retirement in 1977. Hellman, a San Francisco native, first met Groucho when both were new to Hollywood. Hellman worked briefly as a film salesman at Paramount when the Marx Brothers were at the studio. By the time he wrote a guest column for Hellman in 1945, Groucho had made something of a pastime of filling in for his columnist friends.*

Somewhere on a flat-bottomed scow on a mountain lake sits a hungry, cadaverous, grim-looking columnist. It is late afternoon and the western sun is beginning to redden and set over the giant firs. The air is cool and piney and is a tonic to tired souls. In one corner of the boat a catch of glistening lake trout are piled high; from the other end of the boat dangle three bottles of cool, imported beer.

Five hundred miles from this mountain paradise in a Westwood slum sits the writer of this gruel. He is bent low over a smoking hot desk, a cheap cigar droops from his tired kisser and, at the moment, he is scratching the remnants of a magnificent head of hair for an idea that will give that Daily Variety hack ten days away from Vine Street.

It's my own fault—I should have stayed away from Vine Street—everything happens to me on Vine Street. I was sitting in the Derby one noon, trying to convince a bored waiter that there was bacon in the kitchen. I had forgotten it was Friday and that the kitchen contained nothing but fish. I then sparred for hamburger, then down to braised turkey legs and, as happens to all men, I finally settled for rainbow trout. In the midst of this discussion, I was clipped by Hellman. He said, "Groucho," accepting one of my cigars with a minimum of hesitation, "I'm going to the mountains for ten days and I would like you to knock off a column." He really meant write a column but you're not allowed to use the word "write" in the Brown Derby because it's full of radio people. With my cigar in his mouth and my watch in his hand, he continued, "I'd like a thousand words—something good and funny about radio." I couldn't say "no" because at the time I had a mouth full of pumpernickel. By the time I could say "no," the waiter had appeared with the rainbow trout, which, despite his vehement denial, was obviously river carp. While the fish and I were engaged in sizing up each other, Hellman quickly disappeared toward his table, but not forgetting to take another cigar before he left. Good old Vine Street! Here I am stuck for a thousand funny words on radio, a fish lunch, and minus two cigars. Why do columnists have to go on vacations? They have the softest racket in America. All they do is drink, look through keyholes and disseminate millions of inaccuracies. How can a man get tired doing that? I could look through a keyhole all night. I say this with conviction—I've looked through keyholes all night. Why do you think I wear these unbreakable glasses? Why don't columnists stay home and let the people who write their columns go on vacations. Maybe I'll be lucky enough to get sick. A good contagious disease would do the trick. He certainly wouldn't expect a dying man to write a thousand funny words. Well, I'll worry about that later. First I'll eat my lunch. I wish that fish would stop staring at me. What a morbid-looking head! It's probably my imagination but with a cigar in its mouth, that fish would bear a remarkable resemblance to Hellman.

Well, enough of this day-dreaming—you'd better get that thinking cap on and pound out that column—you ought to be able to think of a thousand funny words about radio. I thought you were a humorist—what about those jokes you overheard the other night in the Turkish bath? No, Groucho, you couldn't use those in a trade paper, you couldn't even use them in a house unless it's the kind of a house that you're not allowed to mention in a trade paper. Remember, old boy, this paper is read by women and children in addition to men.

If Chasen's served lunch, this never would have happened. I would never have gone to Vine Street and Hellman once told me he has never been above La Brea. I could be at the beach, lying in the sun. It's lovely at the beach this time of year—you just have to look out for the broken bottles. There's no finer spot in the world than Santa Monica Beach—if you keep your shoes on. That's where Hellman should have gone. He could have bathed all day and written his column at night. How did he ever get up to that lake—where did he get the gas? Maybe I ought to report him to the OPA.* This is no time to be taking a vacation—the war is only half won—MacArthur said it may continue for another year. A lot of blood goes into a piece like this. I could have given it to a blood bank—it's the only place I'm not overdrawn. I'm busy, too, I'm making a picture, "A Night in Casablanca." (It's about time I got that in.) And I'm going on the air for Corwin.** Going on the air for Corwin is not child's play (unless he does "Little Red Riding Hood")—it's hard work. He sits in his air-cooled control room, pushing the actors around as though they were actors. I wonder where Hellman got that gas? Maybe I could go up to that lake where he is—perhaps we could sit together in the same boat—maybe I could hold the line for him, then he'd have both hands free. Say, if Hellman had both hands free and a paper and pencil, which I'm sure I'd have with me, he could knock off a thousand funny words on radio in no time at all.

Variety
July 23, 1945

How to Entertain a Guest

In 1950, Reader's Digest *began publishing a series of books anthologizing current best sellers in abridged form. Available only through subscription, the* Reader's Digest Condensed Books *series initially published four volumes each year, increasing the number in later years. The spring 1954 edition featured a testimonial by Groucho on the back of the dust jacket.*

Groucho's tribute to Reader's Digest Condensed Books *apparently didn't impress the editorial staff much. Although* Groucho and Me, Memoirs of a Mangy Lover *and* The Groucho Letters *would all become best sellers, none were anthologized in the* Reader's Digest *series.*

A slightly longer version of Groucho's testimonial appeared in an advertisement for the books in the May 1954 issue of Reader's Digest, *so even Groucho's testimonial was condensed for* Reader's Digest Condensed Books.

In my penniless youth I longed for two things: a guest room and an introduction to the President's wife. By the time I had saved up a little money Dolly Madison was no longer the reigning beauty she had been in 1810, so I settled for the guest room. I decided to do it up brown. I stocked it with tropical fish, a picture of Whistler's father and a pair of fur-lined bedroom slippers. On the night stand I laid the latest volume of Reader's Digest Condensed Books. Then I waited for the guests.

They came, fed the fish, admired Whistler's pater, wore the bedroom slippers and also read the Condensed Books.

If they had liked the Condensed Books less all might have been well. But having read one volume they decided to stick around and read the rest. What had I done? After all, Reader's Digest Condensed Books are issued three months apart. I am no misanthrope, but no guest can stay in my house three months unless he is dead or I owe him money. Besides, I wanted to read the books myself.

Obviously something had to be done. I replaced Reader's Digest Condensed Books with titles more specialized. At the bedside I placed *The Koran Explained, The Economics of the Minnesota Lumber Industry from 1908 to 1914, A Guide to English Dog Cemeteries* and *Railroad Statistics*. This system worked very well. I stopped losing my books. On the other hand, I began losing my guests.

It was my housekeeper who provided the solution. "Do you mean to say," she demanded (in addition to three months' back pay), "that a man who can afford a spare bedroom cannot also afford a spare set of Reader's Digest Condensed Books? For a paltry $2 would you give up your remaining friends?" If you have ever seen my few dwindling friends you will realize this was not a difficult decision to make.

Relenting, I decided to go whole hog. I ordered a second membership in Reader's Digest Condensed Books. I put the extra set of books on the night stand in my guest room. My guests slowly returned. Now every night at nine I yawn, shake hands with my current guest and retire to my room. He retires to his. Each of us lies in his separate cocoon, happily reading Reader's Digest Condensed Books. Neither of us gets much sleep, but boy, are we well read!

And about that last, believe it or not, I am serious. Apart from Dolly Madison, who was as witty as she was pretty, Reader's Digest Condensed Books are the most compact bundles of worthwhile entertainment and information I know. And, like me, a volume of Condensed Books stays young and fresh forever.

Reader's Digest
May 1954

TV or Not TV

In the early 1950s being the star of a popular television program brought with it certain privileges. Groucho's success on You Bet Your Life *also brought the attention of the House Un-American Activities Committee and the Federal Bureau of Investigation. The FBI's file on Groucho from this period connects him to several Communist and leftist organizations dating back to the 1930s, but the FBI ultimately drew the conclusion that Groucho Marx was not a member of the Communist party. Many stars with less "damaging" material in their files were blacklisted. The committee certainly had an interest in Groucho.* You Bet Your Life *bandleader Jerry Fielding was called before the committee in 1953, but he would not name Groucho as a Communist. Fielding was blacklisted and fired from* You Bet Your Life. *Groucho wrote in* The Secret Word Is Groucho *that bowing to the sponsors' demand that he fire Fielding "is one of the greatest regrets of my life."*

For Groucho to have written a guest column for Fred Rayfield, the television reporter for the Daily Compass, *in 1951 at the height of the "red scare" was at the very least a bold move. The* Daily Compass *was a leftist newspaper published in New York between May 1949 and November 1952. It was the successor to the earlier leftist paper* PM. *Tom O'Connor, the managing editor of the* Daily Compass, *testified before the House Un-American Activities Committee in May 1952 and, like many others, refused to answer questions regarding his possible membership in the Communist Party.*

*O'Connor had previously been named as a party member by two
other witnesses. Two months later O'Connor died of a heart attack
in the* Daily Compass *office.*

*How the FBI file on Groucho managed not to include any refer-
ence to his affiliation with the* Daily Compass *is mystifying. A year
after the Rayfield guest column, Groucho filled in for Rayfield's
successor, Saul Carson, with a similar piece—just in case the FBI
missed the first one.*

Fred Rayfield is off shooting pool some place, probably with the Village
Idiot. So I'm taking over. My attorney will call on him the first of the month
to collect the fee.

As long as he has ordered me to fill this space today, I'll take advantage
of the opportunity to answer some mail. Maybe the answers will settle some
questions in your mind.

1: "How do you pick contestants for your radio and TV show?"

We pick all of our contestants from the audience, except those with interesting occupations. The latter are invited in groups and the studio audience
picks one to be on the show, by applause. And, if the applause isn't delivered,
don't come running to me: see your postman.

2: "Do you chat with your contestants before you go on the air?"

I never talk to the contestants until I meet them for the first time on the
show. In most cases, they are chosen five minutes before air time. Remember,
they're picked in the first place because they have something to say. All I ask
is that they say it, and the interview develops swimmingly. This is especially
true with swimmers on the show.

3: "Why don't you pay your gas bill?"

I'll thank that person to mind his own business.

4: "Is your program censored?"

The NBC censor actually has very little to do. But since our show is on
film for TV and recorded for radio, the editor uses his scissors frequently. We
make a 35-to-40 minute program, then the editor clips out any dull stuff or
doubtful material, and reassembles the best parts. This method has proved
of great value to us, since we don't worry how the show is going on at the
time we do it. We can explore many things with our contestants, and if they

don't produce results, we junk that part of it. By mistake they junked me one week and the program was voted the best of the year by a number of people.

5: "Who are your own favorite contestants?"

We've had 840 contestants on "You Bet Your Life" since we started four years ago and an amazing number of them have been wonderful. My own favorites were: Mrs. Cordelia Russell, an Indiana housewife, who talked without stopping for 25 minutes. All is said was: "I give up." Another favorite of mine is Harry MacDermott, an Irish Catholic maintenance supervisor of a Los Angeles synagogue. A great man!

Then there was Hannus Von Yannah, a 102-year-old Norwegian who became the subject of sermons, editorials and backyard chatter all over the country because of his philosophy: "Every morning when I get out of bed I have two choices: To be happy or unhappy. I always choose to be happy." And of course I mustn't forget the little blonde hatcheck girl at Ciro's. She wasn't on the show, but after all, I am listing my favorites.

6: "Do you enjoy television work, compared to other forms of show business?"

Yes. Of course, I'm confined and restricted beyond anything I've ever done in the theater. This is because the home television receiver screen is really very small. In order to keep all faces large on the screen, we can't have much movement. I get tired, sitting on that stool, but my producer, John Guedel, says the faces and expressions of our contestants are much more interesting than any handsprings I could offer. Guedel's theory has proved correct and sound; we've been consistently in the top 10 radio and TV shows since we started.

7: "Have any of your contestants ever been mad at you?"

Not to my knowledge. In virtually every case, they go away from the show happy, rich and dazed. I just go away dazed. But that's the way I arrive in the first place.

8: "What's the most money you ever gave away on your show?"

A Coast Guard sailor and a colonel's daughter won $6,000. Altogether, we've given away more than $100,000 in cash. People have later told us they've set themselves up in small businesses, paid for expensive operations, paid off mortgages, put their kids part way through college, and some got married on money they won on our show.

Obviously I'm on the wrong end of this thing: I haven't set myself up in business, paid for an operation, paid off my mortgage, put myself through college or got married on what they pay me.

Well, this'll give you some idea of the way we work on "You Bet Your Life." I love the show for a number of reasons: It only takes me about an hour a week to do it, what with no rehearsals or parts to learn, and as long as we keep getting good contestants, there's no reason to think we won't be around for a long time.

Very truly yours,
GROUCHO.

Daily Compass
August 28, 1951

Groucho's Zany Yule Review of Three Slap-Happy Volumes

In the spring of 1950, the authorized biography of the Marx Brothers was published. The brothers hired Kyle Crichton to write the book and the copyright for it was registered to all five of the Marxes, but interestingly, not to Crichton. The highly fictionalized and not altogether accurate book was planned as the basis for a film biography of the brothers that never materialized. Groucho plugged the book on You Bet Your Life and Chico appeared at a Los Angeles department store for a signing. The book became a best seller and in the process, many of the myths in its pages became accepted truths about the Marx Brothers.

When an article by Groucho suggesting a few books that would make good holiday gifts appeared in the New York World Telegram later that year, The Marx Brothers by Kyle Crichton was one of his recommendations. His financial and personal interest aside, it was a popular and entertaining book. Plugging the Crichton book was the likely purpose of the article, but Groucho enjoyed promoting books he liked and did so often on You Bet Your Life, where authors were always welcome guests. Groucho was also a prolific provider of blurbs on book jackets, and his quotes can be found on the covers of books by friends like S. J. Perelman, Ernie Kovacs, Eddie Cantor and Dick Cavett as well as on those by authors he admired without knowing, like William Iverson. The jacket of Iverson's book The Pious Pornographers quotes Groucho: "Iverson is one-third Perelman, one-third Thurber and one-third Benchley and

as good as any of the three." High praise from a book reviewer
filled with admiration for those particular geniuses, with whom he
also happened to be friendly.

The late George Bernard Shaw once listed in his selection of "My Ten Favorite Books" a major classic called "Beds." Since I was the author of this
masterpiece, I glowed with delight until I later discovered the old boy had
been hitting it up the night before.

All this has absolutely nothing to do with what I am about to say concerning three current books, except to establish my authority as a name to be
conjured with in the field of letters.

To begin with, I think most book reviews are too long. The last book review
I wrote was 112 pages longer than the book. In fact, I was so busy writing the
review, I never did get around to reading the book.

This is not the case with *Snobs*, an amusing little book by Russell Lynes
(Harper's, $1.00). I have read this book from cover to cover, and I can say
without fear of contradiction that it is approximately 9 inches long, 5 inches
wide and wears yellow pointed shoes. Any further information about *Snobs*
should be referred to the police department at Scranton, Pa. But keep my
name out of it. I'm in enough trouble in Scranton.

Mr. Lynes's book is really wonderful, and after reading it I'm sure you will find
an individual snob category for each of your friends. By doing this, there is a
strong likelihood that you will lose most of your friends. If they are anything
like mine, you'll be that much better off.

If you are a Charles Addams fan—and who isn't (if you're not, I'll thank
you to keep your mouth shut)?—you'll get a warm, pleasurable glow from
every ghoulish page of "Monster Rally" (Simon & Schuster, $2.95).

This little book, which resembles "Alice in Wonderland" and "Five Little
Peppers and How They Grew" in that all three of them have front and back
covers, is one of the easiest-reading books I ever ran across, particularly
since all the pages are cartoons. I've always found there's nothing easier to
read than a book without words. Unless, of course, it's a book without pages.
That, however, is another story by the same author.

There is more than mere delightful entertainment in an Addams cartoon.
I find him constructive, utilitarian and helpful. For example, who of us at

one time or another has not wondered how to silence an over-talkative wife without offending her tender sensibilities. What better way than to place her fondly in the family trailer and gently detach it at a convenient railroad crossing. And for the wife who hesitates to tell her husband about "the other man," can anything be more appropriate than a lunch pail, wired to seven sticks of dynamite.

Of course, not all of Addams's cartoons concern people like you and me. You'll also find plain, simple, lovable folk with two heads, four legs and warm, kindly, homicidal phobias.

It is a Hollywood and, I suspect, a nationwide custom at parties to dissolve into small groups and discuss Addams's work. Each of us has a favorite which, of course, we try desperately to foist onto other members of the group.

For example, one of the Addams favorites shows a housewife being grilled by the police. She is confessing that she unhooked the electric blanket from her mate's bed, put him in the freezer overnight, sliced him up the following morning in the automatic burger slicer, dropped him in the electrical disposal, washed her clothes in the Bendix, tidied up the kitchen and took off for a movie. I regret I don't remember the movie, but I'm sure it was an anticlimax.

Addams realizes full well that our future belongs to the little children and he devotes much of his book to the little tots, their dreams and toys and games and hobbies. How sweet they are as they guillotine their Betsy-Wetsy dolls, or stall their toy school buses on the model train tracks or roll huge boulders onto passing cars from the railroad overhead.

"Monster Rally" is, to my way of thinking, precisely to my way of thinking.

Until I had read Kyle Crichton's book on "The Marx Brothers" (Doubleday, $3.00), I had never heard of them. Then, after reading the book, I'm not sure whether subject matter was worth the consumption of 300 pages of expensive white paper.

This is a new and alarming trend in American letters. When I was a lad, biographers used to write about Napoleon, Dante and Byron's escapades through Italy.

I can only attribute this literary decline to the fact that there is no one left to write about. Here are five nonentities crashing into a world that formerly belonged to the brothers Karamazov. By the way, have you heard about the Karamazov Brothers' latest radio and TV show? That Groucho Karamazov (he's the one with the moustache) is a wow.

Since Christmas is right around the corner (and, oh, how I dread it!), and the shelves are going to be pretty bare of anything worth purchasing, you could do the literary world a great service by grabbing up these copies before they are all returned to the publisher and appear next year in the lending libraries as murder mysteries.

Now, enough of this kidding. I think "The Marx Brothers" by Kyle Crichton is the greatest book ever written. And that for Kinsey, Tolstoy and Mrs. Kinsey.

New York World Telegram
December 5, 1950

Humor from Silent Screen to TV

The announcement in September 1952 that Groucho would deliver a lecture at the University of Oregon received a fair amount of attention in the press. Asked what he'd be talking about by columnist Earl Wilson, Groucho said, "Almost every ad you see today, selling anything at all, has a picture of some dame in her underwear. I'm going to criticize the overemphasis on sex in a humorous way."

The lecture was a benefit for the Portland Blood Bank. The price of admission was a pint of blood and the announcement brought 559 ticket-seeking students to the blood bank well in advance of the event. The packed house ultimately donated over a thousand pints of blood, which was provided to military hospitals. Asked by columnist Hedda Hopper if he'd be giving blood, Groucho replied, "If I lost a pint of blood I wouldn't be able to speak."

Columnist Hy Gardner wrote, "Groucho tells me he's more excited about giving a lecture at the University of Oregon than he's ever been about a theatrical engagement. 'In the first place,' he gloats, 'I'm following some pretty good names—Dr. Conant of Harvard, Dr. Arnold Toynbee and Dr. Harry S. Truman. Furthermore,' he sighed, 'it'll be nice to go back to college. Not that I ever went there. The closest I came to college was when I wrote articles for College Humor!'"

I am here under false colors. Until this morning I had no idea I was invited here as a lecturer. I was under the impression that you wanted a lecherer.

Frankly, I don't know why I was asked to come here. My contacts with university life have been meager and desultory. The few college memories I have are unreal and based mostly on misconceptions. For example, I have always regarded Yale as my alma mater. I attribute this to the fact that as a youngster I feverishly followed the career of Frank Merriwell, the dime novel hero. In these stories he was pictured as a combination of Jim Thorpe, Paul Bunyan and Hercules. Intellectually he was a bust. The only Homer he had ever heard of was the victorious one he inevitably hit in the ninth inning, usually with the bases loaded. He was a one man football team. No matter what the game—hockey, rowing, track meet, it made no difference, he always emerged victorious. Oddly enough, he never emerged from Yale. I followed the Frank Merriwell stories for many years. Scholastically he never seemed to make any progress. Other students graduated and went on to become lawyers, scientists, doctors of philosophy, even college presidents. Merriwell apparently was a borderline idiot. He never left Yale. For all I know this cretin is still up at New Haven, at the age of sixty-seven, batting out homers, running the length of the field, etc. etc.

My knowledge of Princeton is based on the fact that Woodrow Wilson was once president of the university. And until I saw the movie that Twentieth Century made of his life, I wasn't aware of that.

I vividly remember the University of Michigan. I was playing at Ann Arbor with a musical show. There were twenty-four beautiful girls in the chorus and as they attempted to leave the theater at the conclusion of the performance, they were greeted by a group of potential sex fiends or, as they are sometimes called, students, who were determined to take these girls home with them. The manager of the theater, a veteran of this particular emergency, did what he always did—he sent for the fire department. A steady stream of cold water gradually cooled the students' ardor, and insured the girls' safe passage to their hotel.

At Columbia, I once spoke at the School of Journalism. I was well qualified to speak as a newspaper man for as a boy I had consistently stolen pennies from the corner newsstand.

By this time it must be pretty evident that I have no knowledge to impart that could conceivably benefit anyone in this auditorium. I am not a scientist, musician or ex-general. I have never run a haberdashery in Kansas City, or worn a coonskin cap in Tennessee. I have none of the physical assets of Marilyn Monroe. However, I have heard of the Monroe Doctrine . . . this means hands off. Whether this applies to the bouncing Marilyn I am not prepared to say.

I would like to discuss sex, but I don't think one should discuss a subject that he has only a nodding acquaintance with. When I use the word "nodding" I am referring to whoever I was out with the night before.

A pint of blood may seem like a curious admission fee but it serves a double purpose. The blood is desperately needed by the armed forces and, besides, I am hopeful it will have weakened the audience sufficiently to assure me of a quick escape at the conclusion of this talk.

I know very little about the University of Oregon. From its football record I naturally assumed it was a girls' school. However, like most of the knowledge I have acquired over the years, this too turned out to be false.

I don't want you to be alarmed by my presence here on this platform. I am well aware of the average speaker's fondness for long-winded dissertations, no matter how trivial the subject, and realize as well as you do that it's usually a smoke screen to hide the fact that he has nothing to say. You can rest easy on that score. I have no intention or desire to bore you with a long speech. What I propose to do is bore you with a short speech. In addition to brevity I deem it the better part of valor to avoid anything controversial—so my subject for today will be the man-eating shark.

As a boy I had dreams of becoming a doctor with a beard, a little black bag, and a bedside manner that would charm the most frigid female. Fortunately, someone wiser than myself was instrumental in talking me out of this ambition. This was a stroke of good fortune not only for myself, but for the medical profession as well—for I must confess that over the years my bedside manner has been remarkably unimpressive.

In the last decade great changes have taken place in our universities. Twenty years ago college boys were intellectually stimulated by the works of Sinclair Lewis, Proust and James Joyce. They wore simple clothes, sox of the same color, and had never heard of marijuana. For physical relaxation they swallowed live gold fish. In 1937 a student at Harvard established a new world's record by downing seventy-nine live fish in two hours. This, by the way, was the only athletic event that Harvard won that year.

But the world progresses. The gauche, wide-eyed naive student of the twenties has disappeared. In his place is a new type of scholar. Dressed in a pair of blue denims, straw shoes and no underwear, he too pursues the literary rainbow. But he reads the classics—Kathleen Winsor, Dashiell Hammett and Mickey Spillane. Unlike his father he isn't interested in swallowing goldfish. The only fish that interests him is the salmon. This is easy to understand for there's a biological affinity between them. Their objectives are similar. Unfortunately, the average student is not equipped to swim up the Columbia River to spawn, and even if he were he would be disinclined to do so. The modern student has discovered he can achieve the same results in the back seat of a Buick—pardon me, a De Soto.

In my frequent travels around the country I am constantly confronted by the following questions, or similar ones. What kind of a girl is Elizabeth Taylor? Will Lana Turner marry Fernando Lamas, or will she marry Mario Lanza? Or will Lana Turner marry Ava Gardner? Is Francis really a mule, and if he is why does he persist in making a jackass of himself? Is Rita Hayworth going back to Aly Khan, or will she continue to throw her can in the alley? Does Anne Baxter really smoke cigars? Yes she does, and if she doesn't quit soon I am going to start smoking cigarettes.

Actually I rarely meet any of these people, for the caste system in Hollywood is as rigid and unyielding as that of India. I have the dubious distinction of not belonging to any particular group. I'm a lone wolf in the Hollywood jungle. I am too old for the athletic crowd and too thrifty for the night club crowd.

Even the intellectual set will have none of me. Physically I look like one of them. I am greying at the temples; I walk with a slight limp and I wear thick glasses. But I have been tried and found wanting. Through a mistake that has never been explained, I was once invited to one of their dinner parties. On receipt of the invitation I rushed down to the public library and boned up on a dozen assorted subjects. I poked around Plato, scratched around Spinoza and read *Finnegan's Wake* frontwards and backwards. I understood it better backwards, but anyway I read it. By the night of the party I was sure I knew enough to muddle through the evening. I know better now. This was a writers' crowd. Most of the women had short hair and thick socks and most of the men had ulcers and no socks. Until the lights were turned on full blast for the games it wasn't easy to distinguish between the sexes.

I was still wiping the fruit-cup stains off my vest when the hostess drove us all in to the living room and quickly outfitted us with pencils and paper. They then chose sides and bombarded each other with questions that would have withered the combined brains of Senator Morse, Information Please and Professor Einstein. After a few preliminary intellectual skirmishes they let me off the hook and I slunk back to the kitchen to resume rubbing the fruit stains off my vest.

There are many other groups and sets in Hollywood. They differ in many ways but they all have one thing in common—they avoid me as though I were a Democrat in the state of Maine.

We are all prone to have curious notions about places and things we are unfamiliar with. For example, until I traveled through Europe I always thought that France was a vast house of assignation, seething with sin and decadence. Later I discovered, to my chagrin and with considerable disappointment, that the most conservative family life I encountered in Europe was in France.

Until I went to Italy I was convinced that everyone there spent their lives eating spaghetti, drinking wine and singing "O Solo Mio."

So, too, Hollywood. I have often heard it referred to as Sodom and Gomorrah. Today Hollywood is about as wicked as a cow town in Nebraska and as glamorous as a dead cat. At eleven at night they pull in the sidewalks and anyone found walking around after that hour has a good chance of being pulled in by the police. Sometimes things are so dull that the police have to arrest each other in order to stay awake. At twelve, even the police go to bed.

There was a time, many years ago, when Hollywood really was a hot spot. This was in the days of the silent movies. These were lush days for untalented people. All the equipment necessary to become a movie star was a little luck, a good profile and some hair on the chest. I am, of course, referring to the male actor. The female actress just needed the chest. Movies were made with a minimum of preparation and this left plenty of time for sin and hoopla.

Most of the movie stars were uneducated an uninhibited. Taxes were negligible. Because of this there was an enormous amount of money in circulation. The big problem was how to get rid of it. This wasn't easy for this was no fifty cent dollar, this was a dollar dollar, and it took ingenuity to dispose of that kind of money. So they went in for solid gold bathtubs, fleets of foreign cars, and a different butler with each type of wine. One actor had a home with three swimming pools—one with warm water, one with cold water, and one with no water for the days when he was too tired to swim. With the advent of the talkies, most of the silent stars disappeared. They went back to the drug stores, meat markets and gas stations.

Hollywood is a different town today. And just as the talkies changed Hollywood, national advertising is changing America. Big business has discovered sex, and its results may eventually be as far reaching as Columbus's discovery of America. Sex has replaced U.S. Steel as America's largest industry. Today it's practically impossible to look in any direction without being confronted by its attractions. Billboards, television, newspapers, magazines, no matter how high brow, are all peopled with busty looking dames with busty looking equipment hawking some gimmick or racket. Considering the amount of sexual propaganda that is tossed around these days, I am amazed that any teenager or, for that matter, any adult is able to maintain any kind of emotional equilibrium.

We talk of colonial days and the Puritans with their deep sense of morality. It was much easier then. A woman wore a poke bonnet, a long skirt, woolen stockings and a half a dozen petticoats. The men could go about their business milking cows, shoeing horses and spreading fertilizer, without the constant distraction of the semi-naked female. Oh, I don't doubt that even then there was a moderate amount of infidelity—but generally if a man hated his wife he didn't run away with his neighbor's daughter. He just gritted his teeth, grabbed a fowling piece off the wall and went out and shot a few wild turkeys. Husbands were made of sterner stuff in the eighteenth century—and besides, the neighbor's daughter, with woolen stockings, six petticoats and long underwear, didn't seem like a juicy enough dish for him to relinquish six cows, a new plough and ten acres of corn.

I go back again to the comparatively recent days of 1920. This was around the time when William Jennings Bryan was constantly running for President. Bryan, in case you have forgotten, was the Governor Dewey of his day. Women wore long skirts, their legs were called limbs and nobody knew when the word was used whether the speaker was referring to a girl or a tree.

The point I'm trying to make is that morals aren't higher or lower than they were in colonial days, but just that the charms of femininity were kept under wraps—and frequently under lock and key.

Thanks to modern advertising, today we are constantly exposed to the stimulus of the undraped female. From morning to night the average onlooker and listener is subjected to a barrage of half truths and sexy innuendos. Subjects are discussed over radio and television that certainly wouldn't be tolerated in the average American home.

As a young man I had acquired a fairly good collection of French postcards, but compared to the bra, stocking, and lingerie ads in today's papers and magazines, they seems as innocent as Peter Rabbit spending an evening with Mother Goose.

Even those of us who are not actively engaged in the glandular pursuit of the elusive nymph find it difficult to ignore its temptation. In South Pacific there is a song called "There is Nothing Like a Dame." I think most of us have been aware of this for years. In recent years big business has discovered it and is playing it to the limit. No matter what they are hawking—automobiles, dog foods, deodorants, depilatories, ice boxes—at some point during the pitch the female form will make its appearance.

The other night on television I saw a sketch where a boy and girl were about to be married. Just as the potential groom was about to slip the ring on her finger, he disappeared from the screen and in a huge close-up the bride confessed that it was hopeless, she couldn't go through with it. It seemed that the groom had suddenly, or otherwise, she didn't make this clear, acquired an odor that up to now we have always associated with a pole cat.

In the old days before TV he would not have been unceremoniously discarded. The bride would have gone to her father and hinted that the groom was a little gamey. The father would then have gone to the groom and told him that if he wanted to marry his daughter he would have to bathe more often. But that's too simple for television. Today if he wants to marry the girl he will have to wash his skull with Halo shampoo, brush his teeth with Chlorophyl, smear his carcass with Jergens lotion, and gargle with Serutan.

The gullibility of the average American is inconceivable. No one is immune. We have all been seduced by the advertiser. We will buy anything if the product is hammered at us often enough. Repetition and sex are the twin keynotes of the sponsor.

Last week I saw an ad for Strong Heart dog food. A pretty girl in a diaphanous gown was feeding this swill to a huge mutt. I quickly rushed out and bought a can of the stuff. I was halfway through eating it before I realized I didn't even have a dog. Such is the power of advertising.

I am just as susceptible to the blandishments of the huckster as you are. For example, I suffer regularly from insomnia and for years I have been hopefully reading ads that promise to cure me. The Ovaltine ad has trapped me again and again. It shows a beautiful babe in bed, deep in slumber. The ad says, "You too can sleep well. Just before retiring take a cup of Ovaltine." I know this won't work; I have tried it repeatedly. As a soporific Ovaltine is about as effective as a bowling alley on Saturday night. Nevertheless the advertisement is written so convincingly that at the moment I am the proud owner of three hundred and sixty-seven cans of Ovaltine.

For the past six months I have been eating Wheaties. I have been told over and over by the radio announcer that this is the breakfast of champions. I even began to feel like a champion. Last week I was knocked flat by an eight-year-old girl who caught me stealing her bubble gum. Actually I wasn't trying to steal it. I just wanted to use it for a while.

I frequently read editorials and letters to the editor—angry letters complaining of the paucity of educational programs on television. A few shows of this type have been successful, but they are in a vast minority. There is one in Los Angeles called "Halls of Science." Each week they present a subject by a qualified scientist. It's a well written and extremely interesting half-hour. Last week, for example, they showed how white mice can be taught to run through certain exits and entrances in a maze, and eventually find the cheese at the end of the rainbow. No matter how bright these mice are, this program will never get much of an audience. It's very difficult to attract a large audience to a program featuring live mice, when just by switching the channel the onlooker can see Faye Emerson in a low cut gown pleading with you not to be half safe. If Faye doesn't pull up that plunging neckline she's not going to be even half safe.

Today the sponsor pulls the strings and we are all his puppets. All announcers are dishonest; they have to be to survive. Many cigarettes sponsors now dress their barkers in medical outfits. They don't actually announce that he is a doctor, but the implication is obvious. From his clothes you are led to believe that he has just completed a major piece of surgery in the operating room. An hour later, on another program, this same character may be seen as a man of distinction, tearing a cigarette down the middle to prove to the audience that it may not contain any tobacco but it certainly stands up well.

Last week I saw a show where a fairly unattractive woman confessed that she had been going with a man for twenty years and couldn't get him to propose. However, she had been attracted by the exquisite workmanship in the new Bulova watch and proceeded to buy one. Three days later she said she was married. This is a new approach to advertising. A wristwatch, even if it isn't wound up, becomes an aphrodisiac.

Cigarette manufacturers have a special problem. Since most of the butts are made of the same tobacco, they have to find odd ways of fooling the smoker. The announcer on the Camel show tells you, he would walk a mile for a Camel. This announcer must be quite a jerk. If he had any sense he'd know he could buy them at the corner drug store. Philip Morris has an obnoxious midget who has spent the best part of ten years calling for Philip

Morris. I don't know who Philip Morris is, but it seems to me that this is an unhealthy relationship—Philip Morris and a midget. I'm not sure that this isn't a matter for the police. The Chesterfield salesman screams at you that their cigarette is king size. This doesn't seem like much of a recommendation when one considers what King Farouk looks like. Then there's Pet Milk; according to their announcer, Pet Milk sells milk of such purity that one is led to believe that their cows have never come in contact with a bull, except in the company of a chaperone.

Television has affected our lives in other ways. Not since Ford invented the automobile has anything had as much impact on the American home as the TV set. Today no family can hope to survive unless it has two television sets in the house. I had always suspected that there was a vast difference between men and women—I mean in addition to the fundamental differences that we all revere—but nothing has entered the American scene in the last decade that so clearly emphasizes the wide gulf that separates the two sexes.

Thousands of families are being split wide open and hurrying to Reno for a quick divorce, simply because of the inability of the mother and father to agree on what kind of programs they should look at during the evening. The late afternoon is no problem. The old man is either sweating it out in some office or brick yard—or, perhaps, hoisting a few in a saloon. The old lady, or mother, is busy cooking up a pan of gruel and a frozen vegetable for the lord and master. This leaves the TV set to the children, in front of which they sit bug-eyed watching Suspense, Dragnet, Space Patrol and Gangbusters.

Dinner over, the dishes are dumped in the sink where they remain dirty until the following morning; the children packed off to bed where they lie whimpering with fear in the darkness, thanks to the two hours of blood and lust they have just witnessed on television. The parents now square off for a few hours of entertainment. He quickly turns to channel four for an evening of wrestling, but before settling down to this edifying spectacle he goes to the ice box for a can of beer. By the time he returns with the beer, she has switched to channel eight and he now finds himself watching A Date With Judy. She then repairs to what is known in the Navy as the head, and while she is there he quickly turns the set back to the wrestling matches. However, as soon as he goes for another beer, she switches it to I Remember Mama. The husband soon realizes it's a hopeless struggle and elects to camp the rest of the evening in the kitchen near the beer. Plastered, he eventually turns in, and since they sleep together in a double bed, all hell breaks loose.

At the divorce proceedings there is no contest over who gets the children. The bitter fight is over who gets custody of the television set.

In addition to cracking up more families than adultery, television has sounded the death knell of conversation in what is loosely called our society. There was a time when a good conversationalist was considered a substantial asset to an evening's entertainment. But today he is an anachronism. He has gone the way of the garbage pail and the buggy whip. In other words, he's a nuisance and is rarely invited out unless he promises in writing to keep his trap shut. Who has time for conversation when just by remaining quiet one can hear the sparkling wit of Gabby Hayes or Ed Sullivan.

The future of television? That's in the lap of the gods and the people that watch it. In condemning the advertiser for his cupidity and irresponsibility, let us not condemn the medium itself. From morn to midnight TV grinds its way through the day. And in those twelve hours it has an opportunity to present educational shows, scientific programs and shows of special interest. Let us hope it is not eventually dragged down to its common denominator. Obviously there must be a place on it for cowboys, wrestling matches, ancient movies, vaudeville and even quiz shows. It can be a powerful force for good, or it can emulate its father, radio, and deteriorate into hopeless mediocrity. With a few exceptions radio has now reduced itself to a round-the-clock barrage of used car dealers, finance companies, oil stock promoters, and patent medicine salesmen.

Don't blame the networks. Don't blame the sponsors. They haven't deliberately set out to tear down public taste. Like most of us they are in business to make money. Many of them have tried programs of a superior quality only to see them swamped by shows inane, undistinguished, and repetitious. TV must assume the responsibility for creating programs which will attract a mass audience large enough to interest commercial sponsors, programs which will contain values of information and enlightenment calculated to help raise not only the standards of television, but also the general level of American taste. But in the last analysis it's up to you.

University of Oregon
Unpublished
December 2, 1952

Letter to Woody Allen

In his 1976 book The Groucho Phile, *Groucho called Woody Allen "the most important comic talent around." He first met him over lunch at Lindy's restaurant in New York in 1961. The lunch was arranged by Dick Cavett, who had recently met Groucho at the funeral of George S. Kaufman. Cavett had met Allen only the day before he met Groucho.*

When they discussed their friendship with Groucho on Cavett's PBS television show shortly after Groucho's death in 1977, Allen said, "He reminded me of a Jewish uncle in my family, a wisecracking Jewish uncle with a sarcastic wit. Not that different from many of the characters that turn up at a wedding or a funeral or a bar mitzvah."

Groucho became a keen observer of both Allen's and Cavett's careers and often wrote to them commenting on their various television appearances. None of these letters made it into The Groucho Letters *although one letter to Woody Allen was included in* The Groucho Phile. *Naturally Groucho didn't stop writing to his friends after the 1965 donation of his letters to the Library of Congress and the subsequent publication of the book. The letters from Groucho's later years were donated to the Smithsonian Institution along with his other papers upon his death. (He'd probably derive some perverse pleasure from knowing a complete look at his correspondence requires visiting two separate museums in the same city.)*

In this previously unpublished letter Groucho indeed comes across as the wisecracking uncle Woody Allen described to Dick Cavett.

Dear Woody:

I am enclosing a letter from the Mellon National Bank and Trust Company and if you think I understood one word of it, you have more confidence in me than I have. The enclosed letter will probably require additional postage, but I think at your age it's important to know how people in the upper business brackets communicate with each other. After reading it to your friends, fortified with doses of LSD—who knows, you may emerge the hero of the evening. For God's sake don't return it because I have enough problems—not important ones, just little ones like getting older. Which reminds me . . . my brother Gummo, who is not known for his hilarious moments, told me the other day that when he was a young man he used to get laid every day and went to the doctor once a year. Now he said he gets laid once a year and goes to the doctor every day.

I've arrived at the age where I'm beginning to believe it's more fun to talk about sex than to have it. When I say "sex," I assume you know what I'm referring to. Man and woman. Which reminds me . . . I just saw "A Man and a Woman" with Anouk Aimee playing the lead. It may interest you to know—or it may not, depending on how you feel that day—when she came to America last spring, she said the only one in Hollywood she wanted to meet was Groucho. I was quite flattered. Unfortunately, she had her husband with her . . . a nice man whose face was completely covered with the kind of hair grizzly bears wear in Yosemite National Park. She was clean-shaven—but they're a lovely couple. I'm sure you've seen the picture. It starts off with an automobile race and I thought in the first few reels this was taking place in Indianapolis and that it would turn out in the end that Tony Curtis won the race. This wasn't easy because I learned in the last two reels that Tony wasn't in the picture. From there it blended into a story about two people in the sack crawling over each other. Watching this picture I learned many new positions, which they kept repeating over and over. I didn't clearly understand the picture, but despite that, it's in its eighth month out here—and so is my secretary. She is having a trial marriage with her boyfriend, who spends most of his time in a barroom selling insurance to the bartender.

I read somewhere that you were coming to Vegas. I don't get there too often, but I may come when you're there.

Now as to Bonnie Phillips, who you say claims to be a close friend of mine and Melinda's. She is a close friend of Melinda. The story as I heard it was that Melinda was trying to sell your wife a fur coat. When she left Beverly, she told me she was going to Israel to help the boys over there wipe out the dreaded Arabs. I later found out that she had become a furrier and is hawking cheap pelts to the comedians' wives in Manhattan. When Melinda left here she said she couldn't wait to get to Israel and pick some fruit for the Navy or the Army—I don't know which branch of the service she was concentrating on. Just recently I received word from the Histardut (that's the Israeli representative in New York) and a man named Mermelstein wrote me that Melinda had left Israel, obviously bored with the war, and had gone to parts unknown with a French citizen. This was the precise wording. I thought perhaps it might be DeGaulle, since he sticks his nose into everything. With that nose who couldn't! At any rate, I have no idea where she is and I haven't heard any word from her. Did Mrs. Allen buy the fur coat? I'd like to know because this might be your money Melinda is living on in La Belle, France.

Tell Dick Cavett I saw him on the Carson Show and he was very funny. In the future, I suggest, don't sign your letters "I remain obediently," for you know as well as I do that I've always been putty in your hands. Let me know when you get to Vegas or here or any place. I hope this letter doesn't make too much sense.

Regards,

Unpublished
July 28, 1967

A Letter from Groucho

A Broadway musical about the early lives of the Marx Brothers certainly seemed like a good idea in the spring of 1970, when Groucho's son Arthur and his partner Robert Fisher wrote Minnie's Boys. *But the show ran into trouble early and never recovered.*

The producers tinkered with Minnie's Boys *for an unusually long preview period in advance of the official opening. Groucho, making no secret of the show's problems, described his involvement in the show to Roger Ebert in a* New York Times *interview. "I'm the production consultant. That means they give me some money. I'm the guy who's supposed to holler if anything stinks. I'm keeping quiet. If anyone says I had anything to do with it I can deny it."*

As the opening of the show kept being postponed to allow more previews, audiences at New York's Imperial Theater began finding a letter from Groucho inserted into their Playbill.

Welcome to Philadelphia!

This is the town where our forefathers built a new nation. Today it's a place where producers take their new shows.

Imagine tonight you are Philadelphians seeing our show in its try-out period.

If it has a few rough spots, we feel you'll be willing to overlook them out of gratitude for not having to live in Philadelphia.

A LETTER FROM GROUCHO

Welcome to Philadelphia!

This is the town where our forefathers built a new nation. Today it's a place where producers take their new shows.

Imagine tonight you are Philadelphians seeing our show in its try-out period.

If it has a few rough spots, we feel you'll be willing to overlook them out of gratitude for not having to live in Philadelphia.

GROUCHO

P.S. If at the end of the performance you have complaints, just raise your hand and you'll be given permission to leave the room.

GROUCHO

P.S. If at the end of the performance you have complaints, just raise your hand and you'll be given permission to leave the room.

Minnie's Boys Playbill insert
March 1970

The Odyssey of the Goats

In the jargon of comedians, Groucho did not "work blue." In other words, he didn't believe there was any place for off-color language in a performance. As times changed and comedians like Lenny Bruce and George Carlin made careers out of language that old vaudevillians found shocking, Groucho was openly critical of the practice. But privately, Groucho could give any foul-mouthed comic a run for his money. Among friends at the Hillcrest Country Club, nothing was off-limits. A rare example of the private, slightly filthy Groucho found its way to the printed page as a result of a testimonial dinner honoring Hillcrest member Lou Halper.

Halper was something of a real estate investment mogul and he also owned a construction company. Along with Groucho, Harpo and Gummo Marx, Halper was one of the founders of the Tamarisk Country Club in Palm Springs, which had a member-ship very similar to that of Hillcrest. Among the other founders of Tamarisk were Jack Benny, George Burns and Danny Kaye. Lou Halper also built a house for Groucho in the Tamarisk Ran-cho community in Rancho Mirage and served with Harpo on the fundraising committee that endowed the new Mt. Sinai Hospital in Los Angeles in 1952.

The speech Groucho wrote and delivered at Hillcrest in Halper's honor survives—at least in print—as a result of Groucho sending a copy of his manuscript to his friend Max Gordon in New York. When compared to Groucho's salty 1973 language in The Marx

Bros. Scrapbook, *"The Odyssey of the Goats" is rather tame. The passage of time has made it even more so. But in 1956, this story was intended only for Groucho's close friends.*

What you are about to hear is true. Only the names have been changed to protect my money.

Although I have been a member of Hillcrest for many years, I know very few of the members intimately. On the rare occasions when I play golf with one of them, I am usually out of bounds—or on the fourth hole at Rancho. Over a period of twenty-five years I have only been in the card room twice. Once was to borrow a deck of marked cards for a poker game at my house, and once to get the phone number from one of the card players of a beautiful colored girl with very big tits who took in everything but washing.

Up to a few years ago I'd never met Lou Halper. Gummo was always talking to me about him and I knew it was inevitable that one day we would meet. I must say that this first meeting was a spectacular letdown. A tall, lumbering, hairy man, he looked a lot like a grizzly bear, and after a few minutes' conversation I realized he was just about as interesting. After this meting I tried to avoid him. But Gummo kept prodding me with golden tales of fortunes to be made. All I had to do was put myself in the hands of Lou Halper.

One day at lunch, after three Bloody Marys, they hooked me. It seems there was dairy up near Sacramento, whose cows gave so much milk that the surplus was donated to the street cleaning department to wash down the streets. Lou said, "You put twenty grand in this dairy and you'll never have to worry about your old age." What Lou didn't know was that I had been worrying about my old age for thirty years. When I hesitated, Gummo put on the pressure. Gummo said, "You put $20,000 in this dairy and in ten years you can tell everybody to kiss your ass." This seemed an awfully long time to wait for something I wasn't particularly crazy about, but anyway I went for the twenty thousand.

Two years went by. One day I ran into Lou at the club. I said, "Lou, do you remember that dairy up north?" I said, "Do you remember that twenty grand I tossed in there? Remember all that milk surplus they were giving the city of Sacramento to wash down the streets? It may interest you to know that, in two years, I have never had a statement nor a dividend." He said, "I'm sorry, Groucho, but the goats aren't f——." Over the years I have been a stockholder in many large corporations. I have frequently received annual statements explaining a company's inability to pay dividends. These reasons have ranged all the way from labor problems to increased costs of basic materials, and even management failure. But in all my years as a stockholder, no company has ever sent me a statement attributing its failure to earn money to the fact that their goats were impotent.

However, as you get older, your hearing—as well as your other faculties— deteriorates. So I said apologetically, "Lou, I don't hear very well. Would you mind repeating what you just said?" He replied, "It's very simple. The goats aren't f——."

"Lou," I said, "I'm sorry to hear that, but what has the sex life of a goat have to do with the twenty thousand dollars I invested in that dairy two years ago?" I had always suspected Halper of not being all there, so when he again answered, "The goats aren't f——," I saw that he had cracked wide open. Thinking of my money, I decided I had better play along with him. So I said, "OK, Lou, why aren't they f——?" He said, "Well, why ain't I f——?" I said, "I don't know, but the point is I don't have any money invested in your f——. If I wanted to invest money in f—— I would have put it in Greg Bautzer, or Harry Karl or even Swaps, certainly not in you." I said, "Have you ever discussed this sexual famine with your wife?" "No," he said, "I've discussed this with many a call girl, but never with my wife."

Thanks to Gummo, I suddenly realized I now had twenty thousand dollars invested—not in a flourishing dairy—but in the private sex life of Lou Halper. I said, "Lou, what about my twenty grand and all that surplus milk in Sacramento?" he said, "Groucho, you don't understand. We never made any money on our cows' milk. With the dairy in Sacramento we break even, and if you'll listen carefully I'll explain the whole thing to you. We have 3,000 goats in Arkansas. The milk that we get from these goats is sold to invalids and institutions. This is where we make our real profit. This year, for some strange reason, we are not getting any milk because the f—— goats aren't f——!" I said, "Lou, you mean that my twenty thousand dollars is gone?" He said, "Groucho, if I were a vulgar man I would say that you were up sh– creek." I said, "Is that in Arkansas too?" Luckily, he was scratching himself at the moment, and hadn't heard what I said. He said, "Look, Groucho, you're the only one who's complaining about your money. I'll tell you what to do. You go down to our farm in Arkansas and see if you can solve our problem." I said, "Why me?" To which he replied, "Well, you've been married three times so you must know something about f——." I said, "You're wrong, Lou. I don't know anything about f—— and that's why I've been married three times."

The next morning I packed my pajamas, toothbrush, a syringe and a suitcase of Spanish fly, and was off to Arkansas. The Spanish fly was a sensational success. In a week's time we not only had the goats f—— each other, but they were f—— anything they could get their horns on: dogs, turkeys, raccoons— and one of the goats was caught in Little Rock, f—— the Mayor's wife.

When I arrived back home I immediately called Halper and told him that the trip had worked out fine, that the goats were back to doing what comes naturally and, now then, what about some dividends on my twenty grand?

"Groucho," he said, "in your absence we got some bad news from the dairy up north." I said, "OK, what is it now?" He replied, "Groucho, you won't believe this, but now the cows up north have stopped f——." He said, "I suggest you get some more Spanish fly and see what you can do in Sacramento." "Lou," I said, "I'm sorry but there is no more Spanish fly. I bought up all there was in Los Angeles. I used most of it in Arkansas, and the little I have left I'm saving so that I can keep the home fires burning."

In closing, I would like to say a few words about a man called Gummo. For years Gummo has palmed himself off as one of the Marx Brothers, and has made a very good thing out of it. Actually, he is no more one of the Marx Brothers than Sammy Davis is one of the Andrews Sisters.

Gummo comes from a long line of Rumanian gypsies, and was deposited on our doorstep at the age of fifty. Ragged and hungry as he was, we took him in. And, in return, he's been taking us in ever since. Unlike Halper, he looks honest and straightforward, and his smile has considerably more oil in it than the wells he advised me to put money in. I recently learned, after a series of catastrophic investments, that he is the undercover man for Halper and his various shady ventures—and that he has grown rich fleecing his friends and relations.

So, gentlemen, watch out! If this half-assed Ponzi approaches you with one of his gilt-edged propositions, take to the hills and take your money with you. Or, in time, he'll do to you what Halper's goats did to me.

Hillcrest Country Club
Unpublished
November 25, 1956

Poem from *Animal Crackers*
(1928)

Did you ever sit and ponder as you walk along the strand,
That life's a bitter battle at the best;
And if you only knew it and would lend a helping hand,
Then every man can meet the final test.
The world is but a stage, my friend,
And life is but a game;
And how you play is all that matters in the end.
For whether a man is right or wrong,
A woman gets the blame;
And your mother is your dog's best friend.
Then up came mighty Casey and strode up to the bat,
And Sheridan was fifty miles away.
For it takes a heap of loving to make a home like that,
On the road where the flying fishes play.
So be a real-life Pagliacc' and laugh, clown, laugh.

GROUCHO MARX CHRONOLOGY

October 2, 1890   Julius Henry Marx born, New York City

circa 1901   leaves P.S. 86 after sixth grade, completing formal
                         education

July 1905   first job in show business with the Leroy Trio

February 2, 1906   first notice in *Variety* with review of singing act Lily
                         Seville and Master Marx

April 1906   joins Gus Edwards's Postal Telegraph Boys; the act
                         debuts at the Grand Street Theater, New York City

August 2, 1906   first performance of *The Man of Her Choice*, Colonial
                         Theater, Annapolis, Maryland—Groucho's first
                         dramatic role

June 24, 1907   debut performance of Ned Wayburn's Nightingales
                         (Groucho, Gummo and Mabel O'Donnell), Atlantic
                         City, New Jersey (they would soon be known as the
                         Three Nightingales)

June 1, 1908   Harpo becomes the fourth Nightingale, Henderson's
                         Restaurant and Music Hall, Coney Island, New York

late 1909/early 1910   Marx family moves to Chicago; the Four Nightingales
                         become the Six Mascots

fall 1910	first performances of "Fun in Hi Skule"
September 16, 1912	Chico joins the act for the first performance of *Mr. Green's Reception*, Orpheum Theater, Hammond, Indiana
May 15, 1914	the Marx Brothers get their nicknames from comic Art Fisher, Galesburg, Illinois
September 7, 1914	first performance of *Home Again*, Windsor Theater, Chicago, Illinois
February 22, 1915	the Marx Brothers appear at the Palace Theater, New York City for the first time performing *Home Again*
November 1918	Gummo leaves the act and joins the army; Zeppo replaces him
1919	Marx family moves back to New York
February 4, 1920	Groucho marries Ruth Johnson
July 21, 1921	Groucho and Ruth's first child, Arthur, born
1923	first published writings begin to appear in Franklin P. Adams's *New York World* column "The Conning Tower"
May 19, 1924	*I'll Say She Is* opens on Broadway
February 21, 1925	first magazine piece published in *Judge*
April 4, 1925	first *New Yorker* piece published
December 9, 1925	*The Cocoanuts* opens on Broadway

May 19, 1927	Groucho and Ruth's second child, Miriam, born
October 23, 1928	*Animal Crackers* opens on Broadway
May 23, 1929	filmed version of *The Cocoanuts* premieres in New York City
1929–30	numerous essays and articles published in the *New Yorker*, the *Saturday Evening Post*, the *New York Times*, *Collier's*, *College Humor* and other publications
September 13, 1929	mother Minnie Marx dies
early 1930	Groucho collaborates with Arthur Sheekman on sketches for Max Gordon's Broadway revue, *Three's a Crowd*
August 25, 1930	filmed version of *Animal Crackers* premieres in Chicago
September 1930	first installment of *Beds* appears in *College Humor*
November 1930	*Beds* published by Farrar & Rinehart
February 1931	the Marx Brothers move to California
September 19, 1931	*Monkey Business* released
1931–34	essays and articles published in *Redbook*, the *Saturday Evening Post*, *Variety*, the *New York Times*, *Liberty* and the *Hollywood Reporter*
August 10, 1932	*Horse Feathers* released
November 28, 1932	first broadcast of *Flywheel, Shyster and Flywheel* starring Groucho and Chico on NBC radio network

May 11, 1933   father Sam "Frenchy" Marx dies

November 22, 1933   *Duck Soup* released

March 4, 1934   first broadcast of *The Marx of Time* starring Groucho
                               and Chico on CBS radio network

March 30, 1934   Zeppo quits the team

October 6, 1934   the Marx Brothers sign a contract with MGM

November 1, 1935   *A Night at the Opera* released

December 1936   *The Kalmar and Ruby Songbook*, featuring an essay
                               by Groucho, published by Random House

March 27, 1937   *The King and the Chorus Girl*, with a screenplay by
                               Groucho and Norman Krasna, released

June 11, 1937   *A Day at the Races* released

1937   Groucho collaborates with Ken Englund on
                               unproduced screenplay, "Madcap Mary Mooney"

September 21, 1938   *Room Service* released

October 20, 1939   *At the Circus* released

1940–48   essays and articles published with great regularity
                               in *This Week*, *Variety*, *Liberty*, *Saturday Review*, the
                               Saturday Evening Post and the *Hollywood Reporter*

December 6, 1940   *Go West* released

April 1941   the Marx Brothers announce their breakup

June 20, 1941   *The Big Store* released

January 1942	*Many Happy Returns* published by Simon & Schuster
July 15, 1942	Groucho and Ruth divorce
March 27, 1943	Groucho's first broadcast as the star of *Pabst Blue Ribbon Town* on CBS radio network
July 21, 1945	Groucho marries Kay Gorcey
May 10, 1946	*A Night in Casablanca* released
August 14, 1946	Groucho and Kay's daughter Melinda born
May 30, 1947	*Copacabana* released
October 27, 1947	first broadcast of *You Bet Your Life* on ABC radio network
September 27, 1948	*Time for Elizabeth*, written by Norman Krasna and Groucho, opens on Broadway
April 1949	Groucho wins Peabody Award as radio's best entertainer
March 30, 1950	*Love Happy* released
May 12, 1950	Groucho and Kay divorce
July 17, 1950	Groucho's television debut on CBS's *Popsicle Parade of Stars*
October 5, 1950	first television broadcast of *You Bet Your Life* on NBC
December 20, 1950	*Mr. Music* released
January 23, 1951	Groucho wins Emmy Award as most outstanding television personality of 1950

December 24, 1951   *Double Dynamite* released

January 23, 1952   *A Girl in Every Port* released

October 1952   *Hooray for Captain Spaulding and Other Songs by
                     Harry Ruby and Bert Kalmar Sung by Groucho Marx*
                     LP released by Decca Records

July 17, 1954   Groucho marries Eden Hartford

July 26, 1957   *Will Success Spoil Rock Hunter?* released

October 8, 1957   *The Story of Mankind* released

March 1958   Groucho collaborates with Robert Dwan and
                     Hal Kanter on the unproduced television script
                     "Groucho on Laughter"

March 8, 1959   Groucho, Harpo and Chico give their final
                     performance together on the *GE Theater* in "The
                     Incredible Jewel Robbery" on CBS television
                     network (Groucho's appearance is an unbilled
                     walk-on)

September 1959   *Groucho and Me* published by Bernard Geis
                     Associates

September 21, 1961   final broadcast of *You Bet Your Life* on NBC

October 11, 1961   Chico dies

January 11, 1962   premiere of *Tell It to Groucho* on CBS television
                     network

October 1963   *Memoirs of a Mangy Lover* published by Bernard
                     Geis Associates

April 24, 1964   Groucho stars in the televised version of *Time for Elizabeth* on *Bob Hope Presents the Chrysler Theater* on NBC

September 28, 1964   Harpo dies

June 1965   premiere of *Groucho* (British version of *You Bet Your Life*) on BBC

October 1965   the Library of Congress requests the donation of Groucho's letters and personal papers

February 1967   *The Groucho Letters* published by Simon & Schuster

December 19, 1968   *Skidoo* released

December 4, 1969   Groucho and Eden divorce

fall 1971   *Why A Duck?*, a book of photos and dialogue from Marx Brothers films, published by Darien House with an introduction by Groucho

May 6, 1972   Groucho's one-man show at Carnegie Hall, New York City

October 1973   Richard J. Anobile's interviews with Groucho published as *The Marx Bros. Scrapbook* by Darien House

April 2, 1974   Groucho receives a special Academy Award

May 23, 1974   *Animal Crackers* rereleased after more than thirty years of legal difficulties prevented it from being shown

March 1976   *The Secret Word Is Groucho*, written in collaboration with Hector Arce, published by G. P. Putnam's Sons

April 1976	*Beds* finally gets a second printing after forty-six years; Groucho writes a new introduction for the edition published by Bobbs-Merrill
November 1976	*The Groucho Phile: An Illustrated Life* published by Bobbs-Merrill
January 16, 1977	the Four Marx Brothers are inducted into the Motion Picture Hall of Fame; Groucho and Zeppo appear at the ceremony at Hollywood's Wilshire Hyatt House hotel; it is Groucho's final public appearance
April 21, 1977	Gummo dies
August 19, 1977	Groucho dies
January 1979	Hector Arce's authorized biography, *Groucho*, published by Putnam
November 29, 1979	Zeppo dies

BIBLIOGRAPHY

Adams, Franklin P., ed. *The Conning Tower Book*. New York: Macy-Masius, 1926.

———. *The Second Conning Tower Book*. New York: Macy-Masius, 1927.

Adamson, Joe. *Groucho, Harpo, Chico and Sometimes Zeppo*. New York: Simon & Schuster, 1973.

Anobile, Richard J., ed. *Why a Duck?* Introduction by Groucho Marx. New York: Darien House, 1971.

Arce, Hector. *Groucho*. New York: G. P. Putnam's Sons, 1979.

Ashley, Sally. *FPA: The Life and Times of Franklin P. Adams*. New York: Beaufort Books, 1986.

Barson, Michael, ed. *Flywheel, Shyster and Flywheel: The Marx Brothers' Lost Radio Show*. New York: Pantheon Books, 1986.

Benchley, Nathaniel. *Robert Benchley: A Biography*. New York: McGraw Hill, 1955.

Benchley, Robert. *From Bed to Worse*. New York: Harper & Brothers, 1934.

———. *The Benchley Roundup*. New York: Harper & Brothers, 1954.

———. *Inside Benchley*. New York: Harper & Brothers, 1942.

Bernstein, Burton. *Thurber: A Biography*. New York: Dodd, Mead & Co., 1975.

Chandler, Charlotte. *Hello, I Must Be Going: Groucho and His Friends*. Garden City, NY: Doubleday & Company, Inc., 1978.

Crichton, Kyle. *The Marx Brothers*. Garden City, NY: Doubleday & Company, Inc., 1950.

Eyles, Allen. *The Complete Films of the Marx Brothers*. New York: Citadel Press, 1992.

———. *The Marx Brothers: Their World of Comedy*. South Brunswick and New York: A. S. Barnes and Co., Inc., 1966.

Ford, Corey. *The Time of Laughter*. Boston: Little, Brown & Company, 1967.

Gaines, James R. *Wit's End: Days and Nights of the Algonquin Round Table*. New York: Harcourt Brace Jovanovich, 1977.

Gale, Steven H. *S. J. Perelman: An Annotated Bibliography*. New York: Garland Publishing, Inc., 1985.

———. *S. J. Perelman: A Critical Study*. New York: Greenwood Press, 1987.

Gehring, Wes D. *The Marx Brothers: A Bio-Bibliography*. New York: Greenwood Press, 1987.

Goldstein, Malcolm. *George S. Kaufman: His Life, His Theater*. New York: Oxford University Press, 1979.

Hankel, Walter S., ed. *Whither, Whither, Or After Sex, What?*. New York: The Macaulay Company, 1930.

Herrmann, Dorothy. *S. J. Perelman: A Life*. New York: G. P. Putnam's Sons, 1986.

Kaufman, George S. *By George: A Kaufman Collection*. Edited by Donald Oliver. New York: St. Martin's Press, 1979.

Klingaman, William K. *1929: The Year of the Great Crash*. New York: Harper & Row, 1989.

Krasna, Norman and Groucho Marx. *Time for Elizabeth*. New York: Dramatists Play Service, Inc., 1949.

Lardner, Ring. *The Ring Lardner Reader*. Edited by Maxwell Geismar. New York: Charles Scribner's Sons, 1963.

Lister, Eric. *Don't Mention the Marx Brothers: Escapades with S. J. Perelman*. Sussex, England: The Book Guild Limited, 1985.

Marx, Arthur. *Life with Groucho*. New York: Simon & Schuster, 1954.

———. *Son of Groucho*. New York: David McKay Company, Inc., 1972.

Marx, Groucho. *Beds*. New York: Farrar & Rinehart, Inc., 1930.

———. *Beds*. Indianapolis: Bobbs-Merrill Company, Inc., 1976.

———. *Groucho and Me*. New York: Bernard Geis Associates, 1959.

———. *The Groucho Letters*. New York: Simon & Schuster, 1967.

———. *The Groucho Phile: An Illustrated Life*. Indianapolis: Bobbs-Merrill Company, Inc., 1976.

———. *Love, Groucho: Letters from Groucho Marx to His Daughter Miriam*. Edited by Miriam Marx Allen. Boston: Faber and Faber, 1992.

———. *Many Happy Returns*. New York: Simon & Schuster, 1942.

———. *Memoirs of a Mangy Lover*. New York: Bernard Geis Associates, 1963.

Marx, Groucho and Richard J. Anobile. *The Marx Bros. Scrapbook*. New York: Darien House, 1973.

Marx, Groucho with Hector Arce. *The Secret Word Is Groucho*. New York: G. P. Putnam's Sons, 1976.

Marx, Harpo and Rowland Barber. *Harpo Speaks*. New York: Bernard Geis Associates, 1961.

Marx, Maxine. *Growing Up with Chico*. Englewood Cliffs, NJ: Prentice-Hall, Inc., 1980.

Meredith, Scott. *George S. Kaufman and His Friends*. Garden City, NY: Double-day & Company, Inc., 1974.

Perelman, S. J. *Dawn Ginsbergh's Revenge*. New York: Horace Liveright, Inc., 1929.

———. *Don't Tread on Me: The Selected Letters of S. J. Perelman*. Edited by Prudence Crowther. New York: Viking, 1987.

———. *The Last Laugh*. New York: Simon & Schuster, 1981.

———. *The Most of S. J. Perelman*. New York: Simon & Schuster, 1958.

———. *That Old Gang of Mine: The Early and Essential S. J. Perelman*. Edited by Richard C. Marschall. New York: William Morrow and Company, 1984.

Teichman, Howard. *George S. Kaufman: An Intimate Portrait*. New York: Atheneum, 1972.

Thurber, James. *My Life and Hard Times*. New York: Harper & Brothers, 1933.

Thurber, James and E. B. White. *Is Sex Necessary?*. New York: Harper & Brothers, 1929.

Yardley, Jonathan. *Ring: A Biography of Ring Lardner*. New York: Random House, 1977.

ABOUT THE AUTHOR

BY GROUCHO MARX

While our khaki clad boys were slogging through the mud of Flanders and the market crashed to a new low, while airmen buzzed overhead, darting and flashing through the clouds, and call money zoomed to ten per cent, Groucho Marx was born in a little log cabin and the world heaved a sigh of relief. For here was not only a lover of children, but a man of destiny. A name that was soon to become a household word like plumbing, fruitcake and that good looking blonde neighbor that lived across the way. To go ahead with this is simply to mark time, and the less said about it the better.

College Humor
December 1930